BETWEEN POETRY AND POLITICS

Edited by Linda Hogan
and Barbara FitzGerald

Between Poetry and Politics:
ESSAYS IN HONOUR OF ENDA MCDONAGH

the columba press

First published in 2003 by
the columba press
55A Spruce Avenue, Stillorgan Industrial Park,
Blackrock, Co Dublin

Cover by Bill Bolger
Origination by The Columba Press
Printed in Ireland by ColourBooks Ltd, Dublin

ISBN 1 85607 415 3

Contents

Acknowledgments

Although only one editor's hand is evident in the text, this is a collaborative project in which Barbara FitzGerald played a major, though often invisible role. She has consistently underestimated her contribution. However, I am certain that this collection of essays would not have materialised without her assistance. Nor indeed would the collection have been possible without the support of all the contributors. I am especially grateful to Jane O'Malley who gave permission to use Tony O'Malley's *Sunday Morning Melancholia* on the cover of this collection. His extraordinary work has been a favourite of Enda's for many years and it wonderful to have the essays thus adorned. Thanks are also due to Rev Professor Ronan Drury who has been generous with his time and help. Slaine O'Hogain, Librarian, Hyo-Jung Kim, Mary Priestman, Christine Houlihan and Aideen Woods at the Irish School of Ecumenics, Trinity College Dublin, have provided invaluable help at different stages, as has Mary O'Malley who helped in the preparation of the bibliography. I am grateful also to Seán O Boyle and Brian Lynch at The Columba Press both of whom have been enthusiastic about this collection from the beginning.

Between Poetry and Politics:
Christian Theology in Dialogue

Linda Hogan

A onetime casual remark of Enda's that he did theology 'somewhere between poetry and politics' struck me at the time as an insightful comment on the nature of the creative and original corpus that constitutes Enda McDonagh's contribution to theology thus far. Spanning five decades his writing has challenged the traditional boundaries of the subject and placed moral theology in an ongoing conversation with politics, spirituality and the arts. Indeed he is fond of saying that he doesn't believe that such a discipline as moral theology actually exists. Instead he speaks variously of 'a theology or morality' or 'a theological ethics of society' as a more appropriate description of how 'moral theologians' ought to think of their work. Charles Curran's perceptive assessment of Enda's work draws attention to this refusal to be bound by the conventions of the discipline, present even in his very early writing, and to his determination to construct a theological voice that is influenced by the imaginative and literary possibilities of biblical texts, together with their political radicalism. His theology is thus biblically inspired, deeply ecumenical and politically provocative. Of course since the 1960s many moral theologians have conversed with politics, spirituality and the arts. However, although many moral theologians find their inspiration in either the arts or in politics, it is difficult to mention another theologian whose work is shaped so intensely by both. In this collection, artists, politicians and theologians come together to celebrate Enda's exceptional learning and wisdom, evident in his writing though also ever-present in his teaching as well as in his involvement with many causes, local and global.

Enda McDonagh was born in 1930 in Bekan, Co Mayo and was educated at St Jarlath's College, Tuam, St Patrick's College Maynooth and the Angelicum University, Rome. He took degrees in science, philosophy and theology. A doctorate in moral theology was followed by one from the faculty of canon law in the University of München on the subject of church-state relations in Ireland. He was ordained a priest in the Catholic Archdiocese of Tuam in 1955. Much of his academic career has been spent at St Patrick's College, Maynooth, where he is Professor (now Emeritus) of Moral Theology. Extended periods away from Maynooth have included time spent as Huiskings Professor of Moral Theology at the University of Notre Dame, Indiana and as a Visiting Professor at St John's University, New York. In the late 70s he also spent a period of time in Zimbabwe, then Rhodesia, analysing relations between church and politics during that period of transition, under the auspices of the Catholic Institute for International Relations. This resulted in the remarkable book *The Demands of Simple Justice*, published in the US as *Church and Politics: From Theology to a Case History of Zimbabwe* which remains one of the few theological analyses of political conflict in which the dialectical relationship between praxis and reflection is evident.

However, anyone with even a passing acquaintance with Enda will know that this apparent 'situatedness' in Maynooth belies an extraordinarily cosmopolitan life. Stanley Hauerwas captures it well when he describes Enda as a 'global presence that Catholicism, not capitalism, (has) made possible.' He remarks that Enda is a person who 'is at once so particularly Irish ... yet also able to identify with the struggle of the poor in Latin America, with the challenge of establishing social and political institutions in Zimbabwe, and dealing with the challenge of HIV/AIDS in Sub-Saharan Africa.'[1] Moreover, there is no tension between global and local in Enda's work. His theological concerns are in one way utterly local, as is evidenced by the 'Mayo Books of Theology' as well as by his longstanding involvement in Irish political and church life. This aspect of Enda's ethical concern for 'the local' is reflected here in Garret FitzGerald's essay on the changing nature of Irish marriage and family life during the last five decades. However, his nationally significant work on issues as diverse as medical ethics, constitutional law and the development of Irish university life, could equally be commented on. Yet Enda also possesses what

---

1. Stanley Hauerwas, 'Where Would I Be without Friends' in *Faith and Fortitude: In Conversation with the Theological Ethics of Stanley Hauerwas*, eds. Mark Thiessen Nation and Samuel Wells, Edinburgh: T & T Clark, 2000, 332.

Nicholas Lash calls 'a global imagination', witnessed by, among other things, his work with development agencies like CAFOD, Trócaire and CIIR. Former Irish President and United Nations High Commissioner for Human Rights, Mary Robinson pays tribute to this aspect of Enda's work in her essay 'Linking Ethical and Globalisation', as do Jon Fuller and James Keenan in their apposite contribution 'Church Politics and HIV Prevention: Why is the Condom Question So Significant and So Neuralgic?' Enda's ability to effortlessly reconcile the local and global, the particular and universal is as notable as it is rare. Moreover, it evidences Nicholas Lash's contention that the pursuit of a genuinely global imagination does not have to be in tension with the fact that 'we discern and utter and enact the truth in particular places, and at particular times', since as Lash rightly recognises 'the universal is not the antithesis of the particular, but its form and context.'[2]

The existence of such an extensive collection of published writings might tempt one to focus exclusively on these and yet, as many of the contributors to this collection suggest, Enda's lectures, seminars and media interviews have also made a lasting impression. It is his reconciling presence as much as his writings that have profoundly affected friends and strangers alike. In reflecting on the nature of Enda's unique presence, one is immediately struck by the manner in which his awareness of the ambivalence of human life is threaded through his work. Titles like *Salvation or Survival?*, *Between Chaos and New Creation* and *Faith in Fragments* mediate a sense of life's fragility and brokenness. Moreover, his attentiveness to spiritual and psychological frailty no less than material impoverishment means that his writings resonate deeply. And yet even amid this profound recognition of human pain and suffering, one can discern what George Steiner calls 'a wager on meaning'. However, this is no cheap grace, but something that is hard won. Redemption comes at a great cost, but come it does and often in and through the work of painters and poets. Thus Enda speaks of 'the cure of poetry', the creative/redemptive work of artists who through word and image articulate the possibility of presence, and thereby of hope. It is fitting therefore that this collection includes the work of three of Ireland's most significant modern artists; poet Seamus Heaney, sculptor Imogen Stuart and painter Tony O'Malley

2. Nicholas Lash, 'Conversation in Context', 58.

(RIP). Here we have but a glimpse of the ways in which word and image can be redeemed and through which

> a person is translated
> So far beyond it is impossible to consent
> To turn away to any other sight – [3]

Enda's theology is profoundly incarnational, attentive at every stage to the connections between divine and human creating. This sense that the theologian's task is to express, however inadequately, the majesty and mystery of God's creative work permeates his writing, transforming the philosophical and legal categories of traditional moral theology, particularly as it was practised in Catholicism. Writing in a similar vein, Gabriel Daly's essay in this collection makes a compelling case for an approach to theology in which the aesthetic, intellectual, spiritual and ethical are integrated. He commends the work of von Hügel who, according to Daly, when reflecting on the nature of religion 'knew what he was doing when he identified the three moments as institutional, intellectual and mystical and recognised them as synchronic rather than diachronic.'[4] Enda's characterisation of his own theology as located somewhere between poetry and politics and intimately engaged with both fits well with this rich understanding of religion à la von Hügel.

In his reflection on the work of the philosopher-theologian, James Mackey also suggests that at its best this work requires an interplay of intellectual, mystical and political/ethical sensibilities. In considering Enda's work one could note that it is the integration of these dimensions, and particularly the manner in which each informs, shapes and transforms the other, that gives his work its unique resonance. Thus, as Mackey implies, Peter Brown's characterisation of the philosopher-theologian as one who 'by renouncing political ambition, with its power, privilege and prestige, frees himself for the imaginative contemplation and the patient analysis that will best serve the wisdom that his culture carries to him' is particularly appropriate. This posture is described by Kevin Kelly as 'dis-engaging to re-engage' in his joyful essay 'It's Great to be Alive: Retirement and Human Flourishing.' Moreover, both Sean Freyne and Geraldine Smyth also comment on this concern to attend to both the contemplative and active dimensions of Christian existence as a hallmark

---

3. Seamus Heaney, 'The Light of Heaven', 13.

4. Gabriel Daly, 'Mysticism and Modernism', 31.

of Enda's work. Thus in 'Jesus, Prayer and Politics' Freyne discusses the significance of the dialectic between contemplation and action, prayer and politics, in the context of the biblical 'quest for the historical Jesus', while Geraldine Smyth picks up this aspect of Enda's work in her analysis of the field of ecumenical social ethics.

Though he has attended to many political and social issues over the years, it is perhaps the problem of political violence that has occupied Enda most. This is reflected both in his writing and also in his involvement with the cause of political reconciliation in Ireland, South Africa and Zimbabwe. It is signalled in this collection by the fact that three essays, those of Patrick Hannon, Stanley Hauerwas and Terence McCaughey are concerned with political violence and its aftermath. Patrick Hannon's 'Theology, War and Pacifism' provides a perceptive and comprehensive analysis of Enda's evolving position on the morality of violence, while Stanley Hauerwas discusses Enda and his most recent initiative, the 'Appeal to Abolish War', a proposal that is as compelling as it is ingenious. Continuing with this theme of political violence, Terence McCaughey contemplates the complex nature of reconciliation. Commenting on the diverse cultural constituents of conflict resolution, he suggests that there are many routes to relative peace and stability, involving different ways of dealing with the burden of memory. Here, continuing our theme of poetry and politics, the political and imaginative are shown to be intertwined, particularly in the ritualised attempts of the people of southern Mozambique to effect healing after conflict.

The coherence of this collection thus lies, not in the pursuit of a particular idea or the development of a theological theme, but rather in the rich texture of Enda's life and work. Certainly common themes do emerge, as friends pay tribute to Enda in ways they deem appropriate. The resulting volume is, not surprisingly, one of diversity of both form and content. The essays in this collection celebrate the work of an intellectual and visionary, whose work has consistently combined compassion with rigor and who, perhaps more than most, embodies the truth, expressed so eloquently in his tribute by Nicholas Lash that 'in the last resort, our best and truest speech is not 'monologue', our solitary utterance, but rather proslogue, address, response, to each other and to the holy mystery.'[5]

---

5. Nicholas Lash, 'Conversation in Context', 61.

The Light of Heaven

Dante, *Paradiso*, Canto XXXIII, lines 49-145

Seamus Heaney

With a smile Saint Bernard indicated
That I should raise my eyes; but already
Of my own accord I had anticipated

His wish, for my gaze was holding steady
And growing pure as it focused on that beam
Of the high Light which is *sui generis*

True. And thenceforth my vision was aswim
With sights beyond speech, which fails such witnessing
As memory fails when its contents overbrim.

Like somebody who sees things when he's dreaming
And after the dream has nothing to report
Except a recollection of the feeling,

So I live now, for the things I saw depart
And are almost gone, although a distilled sweetness
Still drops from them into my inner heart.

It is the same with snow the sun releases,
The same as when in wind, on swirled-up leaves,
The Sibyl's message eddies and disperses.

O Supreme Light, elevated so above
What mortal minds can rise to, restore to mine
Something of what You were when shown forth,

And empower my tongue so that I may illumine
The generations who are still to come
With a spark at least of Your pure serene,

Because, by returning to my memory some-
What, and being celebrated in these tercets,
Your overallness will be more brought home.

I believe – such was the sheerness of the light
I endured from the living ray – I would have been
Utterly lost if my eyes had been averted.

And it was on that account that I kept on
Looking directly into it, until
With the Infinite Worth my gaze made one.

O abounding grace, whereby I could still
Presume to look through the eternal light
So searchingly my absorption there was total!

In the depths of it I beheld infolded,
Bound by love into one single volume,
What is loose-leafed through the cosmos, far and wide:

Substances, accidents, and what connects them,
Diamond-bonded, fused so brilliantly
That compared with it my verse is a dim flame.

Everness of form I believe I saw,
Its knit and knot, because as I repeat this
I experience more and more onsets of joy.

Yet this very memory of it entails loss,
Oblivion greater than millennia have wrought
On the Argonauts and the Argo and their shadows

That astonished Neptune. And so my mind, all rapt,
Stood motionless and marvelled, concentrated,
Growing more eager the more it was absorbed.

In that light a person is translated
So far beyond it is impossible to consent
To turn away to any other sight –

Because the good, which is the will's intent,
Is all encompassed in it, and outside it
That which is perfect inside is much lessened

In perfection. But my language cannot
Equal what I remember: an infant's tongue
Bubbly with breast-milk would be more articulate.

Not because there was change within the one
Semblance apparent in the light I gazed on –
Which is ever simple, showing forth as shown –

But because in me my own altering vision
Was strengthened as it gazed, that same appearance
Seemed of itself to suffer alteration.

Within the incandescent deep subsistence
Of the Light on high, there appeared to me three circles
In three colours but of the one dimension

And one by the other as a rainbow by a rainbow
Seemed to be reflected, and the third seemed fire
Exhaled equally by those other two.

O how inadequate language is, how far
Short of my conception! Compared to what I witnessed,
My verse is weak, words barely register.

O Eternal Light who abide in your onliness,
Who know only Yourself and, self-known and knowing,
Love and smile on Your own radiance.

That circling – those rings born from this glowing,
Made manifest in You as reflected light –
When my eyes had watched it for a while, kept showing

Forth from within itself, where it shone bright
In its own colour, the Image of us; and for that reason
My look was entirely concentrated on it.

As the geometer, lost in contemplation
While he tries to square the circle, won't give up
Although bewildered and balked of his solution,

So I was lost in study of that sight:
I yearned to see how the Image had inscaped
The circle and is co-extensive with it.

But my own wings were not equal to the flight
Except that my mind was struck by a bright bolt
And in a flash was granted all it sought.

Here power upholding high imagining failed,
But as a balanced wheel revolves and whirrs
My will and my desire were now revolved

By the love which moves the sun and the other stars.

Mysticism and Modernism

Gabriel Daly OSA

The Belgian symbolist poet Maurice Maeterlinck claimed that a work of art or literature becomes obsolescent only in proportion to its anti-mysticism. It is the sort of remark that teases the mind. Maeterlinck is using the word 'mysticism' in an aesthetic context, which is a useful reminder of its manifold ambiguities. That mysticism can be given an aesthetic reference may irritate those for whom it represents the highest reaches of an austere spiritual life which is remote from the lives of ordinary people. Yet the fact that many of the mystics were poets raises a fascinating question about the connection between mysticism and art.

Of course there are dangers in giving mysticism an aesthetic reference. For one thing, it can make art critics intellectually lazy when they are trying to handle religion in a secularised age. Music critics, for example, often describe César Franck and Anton Bruckner as mystical composers. Although I think the description is perfectly defensible, I cannot help thinking that it is often employed simply because Bruckner and Franck were distinguished organists. The fact that the instrument one plays happens to be normally located half-way up a cathedral wall is not really a good enough reason for calling one a mystic.

Secular writers sometimes use the term 'mysticism' as a synonym for 'religion'. It sounds more sophisticated. Theologians have good reason to protest against such slack usage, not simply because of its imprecision, but for the more important reason that much religion is anti-mystical, not merely in Maeterlinck's sense but also in a stricter theological sense.

There is no single agreed definition of mysticism; but then there is no single agreed definition of religion either. Just as religion can be regarded as thoroughly undesirable by theologians like Karl Barth, there are also respectable *bona fide* reasons for distrusting and disliking the term mysticism. The not uncommon Protestant suspicion of mysticism may see it as a form of Greek or Gnostic religion which seeks to avoid the scandalous particularity of Christian faith. Everything of course turns on what one means by mysticism.

My principal concern here is to argue that mysticism needs to be treated dialectically, by which I mean that it has to be interpreted reciprocally in relation to other features of faith and life. I shall draw heavily on the work of Friedrich von Hügel, who took the view that mysticism is one, but only one, very important element in Christian life. Von Hügel had an inclusive view of mysticism and believed that it has a role to play in every Christian life.

The term 'mysticism' had its origin in early seventeenth century France.[1] There were of course many mystics in the preceding centuries, but their peculiar status in the Christian church was not dwelt upon nor was it analysed under the precise term 'mysticism'. Seventeenth century France was a theatre of religious debate: Jansenism, Gallicanism and Quietism were significant from a literary and political as well as religious standpoint. Quietism was a deliberate turn to mysticism away from the rigidities of some counter-reformation theology and spirituality.

Protestant pietism was establishing itself at much the same time and for much the same reason as Quietism. Schleiermacher's theology stems in part from pietism. The condemnation of Quietism ensured that there would be no Catholic Schleiermacher. The Modernists were to try to fill this gap at the turn of the nineteenth century. Quietism was a revolt against the self-conscious introspective methods of prayer which graded spiritual progress in terms of perfection and which placed mysticism in the refined upper reaches of union with God. This in effect removed mysticism from normal church life. You were not supposed to have spiritual aspirations above your station. Anti-quietism also tended to regard prayer not as an end in itself but as 'an instrument for acquiring the virtues'.[2]

Church authority has never really known how to handle mystics, who give the appearance of cutting out too many of the middle-men by going straight to the top, as it were, and who

---

1. B. Mc Ginn, *The Foundations of Mysticism*, London: SCM Press, 1991, 266-7.
2 R. A. Knox, *Enthusiasm: A Chapter in the History of Religion, with Special Reference to the XVII and XVIII Centuries*, Oxford: Oxford University Press, 1950, 248.

have traditionally been a source of anxiety to those responsible
for the maintenance of orthodoxy and church order. Quietism
had its origins in the teaching of the seventeenth century
Spanish priest Miguel de Molinos. It aimed at a totally selfless
love of God, such that one was not concerned with one's own
salvation. It rejected prayer of petition and structured meditation. In its extreme form Quietism seemed to exclude the need
for moral effort, since total submission to the will of God was
deemed to achieve everything necessary for salvation.

Quietism spread from Spain to France, where it had a following among the devout especially at court and where it was sponsored by the formidable and eccentric Madame Guyon. She defended herself against the attack made on her autobiography by
Bossuet with the remark: 'Since what I have written has not gone
through my head, it should not be judged by the head.' (Knox,
Enthusiasm, 332). By this alarming remark she simply meant that
discursive thinking was an activity which obstructed the action
of God. She won the support of François de la Mothe Fénelon,
archbishop of Cambrai. By the same token she incurred the en-
mity of Jacques Bénigne Bossuet, bishop of Meaux. Bossuet saw
mysticism as 'essentially a lamentable extravagance, a kind of
spiritual failing tempting the odder saints'.[3] Fénelon, on the
other hand, was a mystic and a friend of mystics (in seventeenth
century France mystics were practically unionised). He and
Bossuet engaged in a literary war which enriched French literature without achieving much else. The war was ostensibly over
Quietism but actually over the entire mystical tradition in the
church. Bossuet, the practised politician, got Rome to censure
Fénelon. The censure, when it came in 1699, was mild enough in
personal terms, but its effect on the church's mystical tradition
was devastating. Like most ecclesiastical condemnations it re-
sembled an act of carpet-bombing which obliterates an entire
neighbourhood in order to remove one suspect agent hiding in
an attic.

The condemnation of Quietism and of Fénelon produced a
widespread suspicion of mysticism and of the prayer of simple
regard. This 'rout of the mystics', as Henri Bremond, the great
friend of the Modernists, called it, created a spiritual vacuum
which was eventually filled by apparitions and all sorts of exter-

3. G. R. R. Treasure, *Seventeenth Century France*, London: Rivingtons,
1966, 453.

nal and sentimental devotions, often of highly questionable theological content and usually of appalling aesthetic taste in the repository art to which it gave rise. Bremond emphasised the connection between mystical interiority and a cultivated imagination. With the other modernists he protested against the divorce between reason and feeling which had resulted from the condemnation of Quietism. The destruction of true interiority favoured a desiccated scholastic theology on the one side and a sentimental and often superstitious devotionalism on the other. The Modernists in the late nineteenth and early twentieth centuries often used the term 'mysticism' as a serviceable antonym for scholasticism, with what they saw as its aridities and its rejection of experience as a significant religious phenomenon.

Henri Bremond and Alexander Dru have argued that the condemnation of Quietism and of Fénelon at the end of the seventeenth century resulted in the destruction of the mystical element in the Roman Catholic Church. 'Extrinsicism' (Maurice Blondel's word for reliance on externals such as miracles and preoccupation with authority), was having a twofold effect: It was making it impossible for the church to face the intellectual challenges of modernity, and it was destroying the interior heritage of the church's true spiritual tradition. Much of what passed for Catholic tradition in the nineteenth and twentieth centuries was in reality a recent creation brought about by an alliance between Roman authority and mandatory scholasticism, private devotion, puritanical morality, radical clericalism and an anti-mysticism which went back to the condemnation of Quietism and which owed more to Jansenism than to an authentic long-standing tradition. What Bremond called the 'rout of the mystics' was closely linked to what Paul Claudel called 'the tragedy of a starved imagination'.[4] As Claudel acutely observed, the crisis was not primarily one of intellect. Quite the contrary in fact. Intellect played a major role in neo-scholasticism, but its function was speculative and detached from experience. Modernism was in part a reaction against this situation.

The first challenge to externalism and the anti-mystical spirit came in 1893 with Maurice Blondel's *L'Action*, in which he laid down the principles of his 'method of immanence' and which

4. Alexander Dru in A.Drew and I. Trethowan, eds., *Maurice Blondel: The Letter on Apologetics and History and Dogma*, London: Harvill Press, 1964, 21.

undertook to examine the entire dynamic of human willing. It posed the question: Has life a meaning or not? This question became the core of Blondel's transcendental method.

Three years later Blondel wrote a long essay on apologetics which attacked the 'extrinsicism' of the neo-scholastic approach to Christianity. Extrinsicism in effect meant the total rejection of inner experience as a constitutive factor of Christian thought. The condemnation of modernism between 1907 and 1910 led to the expulsion of the very word 'experience' from the Roman Catholic theological vocabulary. Experience was deemed to be dangerously subjective: dogma was the only guarantee of orthodox truth. Blondel was never explicitly condemned, but because he was not a neo-thomist he found himself on the intellectual periphery of church life. He had, however, opened up a vein which was shortly to be mined by Friedrich von Hügel, who was already well disposed to appreciate its mystical possibilities.

Baron Friedrich von Hügel was born in Italy of an Austrian Catholic diplomat father and a Scottish Presbyterian mother from a military family. He had a cosmopolitan upbringing. His education was private and he was self-taught in the subjects in which he became an acknowledged expert. He was a keen student of science, philosophy, biblical criticism, history, and theology. (Charles Gore, bishop of Oxford, called von Hügel 'the most learned man living'.) He spoke and wrote the major languages of Europe —in an equally dense and obscure way, it must be said— and he corresponded with most of the major religious scholars, Protestant and Catholic, of his time. He practised a totally unself-conscious theological ecumenism that was unusual for the time.

He was drawn into the Modernist movement as much by temperament as by circumstances. In fact he became its communications centre. He brought new books to people's attention. He was known to his friends with affection and sometimes humour simply as 'the Baron'. He had a marvellous capacity for combining critical, even radical, scholarship with a seemingly simple faith; but he failed to realise that others did not always have a similar capacity. He nearly destroyed his daughter Gertrude's faith by discussing radical biblical and historical criticism with her, not realising the damaging effect he was having on her faith. Fortunately his new friend, Father George Tyrrell SJ, was able to play a major part in rescuing Gertrude from what nearly became a nervous breakdown. Tyrrell wrote to the Baron:

Things that your formed mind can easily swallow, without
any prejudice to simple faith, may really cause much uneasi-
ness in a mind less prepared. We must give minds time to
grow and feed them suitably to their age. Had I known twenty
years ago things that I know now I could not have borne with
them. If you want your daughter's company you must shorten
your steps and walk slowly, else she will lose her breath in
her desire to keep up with you.[5]

Tyrrell knew from painful personal experience the effect that
critical scholarship can have on a faith which comes upon it un-
prepared. Von Hügel kept him plied with all the latest works of
German theological and biblical scholarship. Tyrrell has left us a
moving description of the effect on him of some of the books
that von Hügel was plying him with. In a letter to Bremond he
describes saying midnight Mass for a community of nuns 'for
whom it was all so real', while he found himself 'loathing the
thin and windy manna of criticism and truth'.[6] Tyrrell was unable and unwilling to separate his theology from his prayer. He
could see the humorous side of von Hügel's ability to combine
his radical studies with a remarkably uncomplicated faith. 'The
Baron has just gone,' Tyrrell wrote to his friend Canon Lilley,
'Wonderful man! Nothing is true; but the sum total of nothings
is sublime!'[7] Von Hügel, on the other hand, had a technique in
prayer which enabled him to escape from the vexations of critical scholarship and to take refuge in the stillness of contemplation.

Is it not this, that minds belong, roughly speaking, to two
classes which may be called the mystical and positive, and
the scholastical and theoretical? The first of these would see
all truth as a centre of intense light losing itself gradually in
utter darkness; this centre would gradually extend, but the
borders would ever remain fringes. They could never become
clear-cut lines. Such a mind, when weary of border-work,
would sink back upon its centre, its home of peace and light,

---

5. M. D/ Petre, *Von Hügel and Tyrrell: The Story of a Friendship*, London,
1937, 17.

6. Cited in D. Schultenover, *George Tyrrell: In Search of Catholicism*,
Shepherdstown, 1981, 272.

7. A. R. Vidler, *A Variety of Catholic Modernists*, Cambridge: Cambridge
University Press, 1970, 117.

8. M. Ward, *The Wilfrid Wards and the Transition*, London, 1934, 301.

and thence it would gain fresh conviction and courage to again face the twilight and the dark. Force it to commit itself absolutely to any border distinction, or force it to shift its home or to restrain its roamings, and you have done your best to endanger its faith and to ruin its happiness.[8]

Not everyone would agree with, or be able to practise, this technique, yet it goes far towards combining what von Hügel described as the intellectual and mystical elements of religion. It suggests a practical application of negative or apophatic theology. No doubt Bossuet would have accused the Baron of Quietism, but it gives us a valuable clue to von Hügel's approach to mysticism. He gave spiritual guidance to several people, including his niece, Gwendolen, to whom he wrote, 'Religion is dim — in the religious temper there should be a great simplicity, and a certain contentment in dimness. It is a great gift of God to have this temper.'[9] One might call this 'prayer in soft focus'. It has aesthetic as well as theological implications. One thinks, for example, of the poet John Keats' idea of 'negative capability', a state of consciousness where one 'is capable of being in uncertainties, mysteries, doubts, without any irritable reaching after fact and reason'.

This notion of 'dimness', or 'vividness', or 'richness' is central in von Hügel's approach to mysticism. It is in the still centre of one's being that one experiences the sheer objective givenness of God. This approach reflects Pascal's God of Abraham, Isaac and Jesus Christ as contrasted with the God of the scholars. It can look like fideism or anti-intellectualism until one recalls that for von Hügel it is only one element in an overall Christian faith and life and it needs to be checked against two other elements which co-exist with it.

Von Hügel is indebted to two thinkers for the basis of the distinction he draws between the mystical and the intellectual in Christian experience. To the philosopher, Gottfried Leibniz, he owed the distinction between 'dim experience' and 'reflex knowledge'.[10] To John Henry Newman he owed the description of Christianity as initially an impression made on the imagination, which, when studied and discussed, yields doctrine. He

---

9. *Letters from Baron Friedrich von Hügel to a Niece. Edited with an introduction by Gwendolen Greene*, London: J. M. Dent & Sons, 1928, xvi.
10. F. von Hügel, 'Experience and Transcendence', *Dublin Review*, 138, 1906, 358.

also owed to Newman the famous distinction made in *The Grammar of Assent* between the real and the notional. The real is what von Hügel would call the mystical; and the notional he would call the intellectual. For neither Newman nor von Hügel is it ever a matter of choosing between the notional and the real, or between the mystical and the intellectual: both are necessary.

Many commentators believe that the presentation of mysticism as one element in Christian life is von Hügel's lasting contribution to the study of mysticism. It is contained mainly in his 1908 book, *The Mystical Element of Religion: as Studied in St Catherine of Genoa and her Friends.*[11] Here and elsewhere in his writings von Hügel makes very clear his rejection of 'exclusive mysticism', namely, the idea of mysticism as belonging exclusively to the upper reaches of the human ascent to God. There is, he says, no specifically distinct, purely mystical mode of apprehending reality. The mystic needs the concreteness of everyday life with its contingency and finitude. It is precisely our human sense of contingency and finitude (he calls it 'the sting of contingency') which triggers off mystical awareness. The mystical is, or ought to be, a dimension in the life of every religious person. Von Hügel once took Tyrrell to task for speaking of time as a preface or prelude to eternity. Eternity for von Hügel is present in time: '... eternity can and must begin here, if it is to continue, consummated, hereafter'. (Petre, *Von Hügel and Tyrrell*, 63.) For him religion is mystical by definition and must be complemented by other elements. J. J. Kelly puts it succinctly: for von Hügel 'Mysticism ... is only true when it is not everything in anyone but something in everyone.'[12] Von Hügel's mysticism is incarnational. Contemplation is not an escape from the scandalous particularity of Christian faith. He is therefore strong in his opposition to any kind of gnostic or neo-platonist elitism.

He sets the scene of the book in an opening chapter on the three chief historical forces of Western civilisation: Hellenism, Christianity and science. All three have contributed something necessary to human life. Von Hügel sees Greek philosophy and art as abstract, unified, and harmonious. Christianity is moral and religious and far more concrete than Hellenism. It is an-

---

11. Two volumes. Second edition, London 1926.
12. J. J. Kelly, *Baron Friedrich von Hügel Philosophy of Religion*, Leuven: Leuven University Press, 1983, 172.

chored in a person and it avoids the two extremes of pessimism
and optimism that one finds in Hellenism.

Finally science appears as the scourge of both Hellenism and
Christianity. 'They evidently cannot ignore it; it apparently can
ignore them.' (von Hügel, *Mystical Element*, I, 39) Science challenges metaphysics and religion with evidence and fact. It appears to take over and blot out metaphysics and religion. In
mathematics it is more abstract than Hellenism and in its rigorous empiricism it is more concrete than Christianity.

Science introduces 'the great concept of Law, of an iron
Necessity running through and expressing itself in all things,
one great Determinism ...' (ibid, 40). We have to remember that
von Hügel's paradigm of science was Newtonian and positivist.
This does not invalidate his contention that science, if properly
attended to, can have a purifying influence on religion. Today
he might agree that it also has a stimulating and beneficial effect
on, for example, the theology of creation. His recognition of the
autonomy of both science and religion is of continuing validity
and importance, though he does not work out a theology of
creation and nature. Religion, he remarks, has no place, and
should seek no place, in this world of science. On the contrary it
should welcome science as a purifying element in religious life,
an element which works against any gnostic temptation to escape from concrete reality into an ever more immaterial world.
Von Hügel's conclusion about all three forces is that they need
each other. Philosophy, religion and science are all necessary to
a rounded and complete human existence.

All this prepares the way for his famous triad, namely, the
three elements of religion: the institutional, the intellectual and
the mystical. He opens his argument with a piece of fairly homespun educational psychology which distinguishes three stages
in religious development: the child, the youth, and the adult.

The child lives in a world which it perceives as being simply
there. The child accepts what it finds and what it is taught as
simply true. At this stage, says von Hügel, 'the external, authoritative, historical, traditional, institutional side and function of
religion are everywhere evident'. 'Religion is here ... a fact and
thing.' (ibid, 51) Curiosity awakens. There are questions to be
asked and certainties to be challenged. Facts clamour for reasons
to support them. Reason and argument become important.
'Religion here becomes thought, system, a philosophy', (ibid, 52).

At this stage the emotional, volitional, ethical and spiritual powers develop and encounter the third side of religion – the experimental and mystical. 'Here religion is rather felt than seen or reasoned about, is loved and lived rather than analysed, is action and power, rather than either external fact or intellectual verification.' (ibid, 53)

Von Hügel emphasises that the three stages are never totally exclusive of the other two: there are traces of each in the other. Moreover, although they occur successively in the individual, one does not simply replace the other. Ideally they interact and correct each other. Thus ideally the institutional develops and matures under the influence of the intellectual and the mystical, and the same is true of the other two. Von Hügel's basic thesis is that each stage has both positive and negative features.

The positive characteristics of the institutional stage are those of strength and solidity. We might call them the conservative principle. The institutional supplies a structure for living. It constitutes the tradition within which we live. It tells the story of why we believe what we do believe. It gives us the means and the setting for worship. It emphasises the importance of authority. Sense and memory control its operations. In biblical terms it is Petrine.

The negative features of the institutional element are that it can become narrow, dry, and unrelated to the rest of life. Art and science will tend to be excluded. Religion will be assimilated to politics and economics and will be simply one thing alongside other things in life. Superstition and preoccupation with externals may dominate. Coercion may be resorted to. We thus get too great a preponderance of the 'Objective', of law and thing, as against conviction and person; of priest as against prophet; of the movement from without inwards, as against the movements from within outwards. (von Hügel, *Mystical Element*, II, 388)

The intellectual element enters when the believer, like the adolescent or young adult, feels the urge to question and challenge what he or she has hitherto accepted as simply given. The transition is both necessary and dangerous. It is necessary because without it the adult enters on life with the uncritical religion of the child. Uncritical religion leaves tradition uninteriorised and the speculative mind unfed. The intellectual element attempts to unify, analyse, and systematise the data of experience. In biblical terms it is the Pauline phase.

There are drawbacks as well as gains here too. The danger is that one can get lodged in this adolescent phase and remain a 'rationalistic fanatic' (ibid, 389), often vulnerable to agnosticism and indifference. The Baron's judgement on David Hume is interesting in this respect: 'He is the sort of person young people are taken in by ... he knows everything. He got to the bottom of everything by the time he was sixteen: he sees everything through clear glass windows.'

Von Hügel, who admired Immanuel Kant for his ethical teaching, regarded him as one of the worst enemies of mysticism. (One could hardly think of a more misguided approach than that implied by the title of Kant's book *Religion within the Limits of Reason Alone*.) As von Hügel saw it, this condemns religion to perpetual adolescence. The 'critical-speculative' element of religion is absolutely necessary; but it is also destructive, if left unchecked by the institutional and the mystical. He regarded the scholasticism of his own age as finally philistine.

The mystical element enters the scene as the mark of maturity and balance. This is the immediate and direct element of religion. It brings the intuitive, emotional, experiential, and volitional to complement and correct the institutional and the intellectual, both of which tend to resist the mystical. The institutional will find it to be subversive; the intellectual will think it sentimental and unstable. In biblical terms it is Johannine.

It is plain that von Hügel placed a very high estimate on the mystical element and lamented its absence in the church of his time. He is, however, quite clear-sighted about its dangers if unchecked by the other two. The mystic will be 'tempted to sweep aside both the external, as so much oppressive ballast; and the intellectual, as so much hair-splitting or rationalism. And if it succeeds ... fanaticism is in full sight.' (von Hügel, *Mystical Element*, I, 55) To cultivate the mystical at the expense of the other two elements is to fall into 'shifting subjectivity' which becomes a victim to the 'tyranny of mood and fancy' and finally descends into 'emotional fanaticism' (von Hügel, *Mystical Element*, II, 391.)

So then, in the balanced religious person the three elements exist in fruitful tension (or 'friction', as von Hügel liked to put it). This tension or friction is purifying: for the Christian it constitutes the cross and reflects the suffering of Christ. The mystic cannot with spiritual impunity opt out of the world of politics –

a point which is clearer to us today in the light of liberation theologies than it was in von Hügel's time. This is neatly summed up in Charles Davis' remark that 'mysticism without politics is false consciousness'.[13] Nor can the mystic rightfully evade his or her intellectual responsibilities. Von Hügel would have disagreed sharply with Dom David Knowles' remark, that a mystic 'who indulges in theological speculation is no mystic'.[14]

This point has some importance today when some at least of the contemporary interest in spirituality may be a flight from the intellectual asceticism of critical theology. Such a flight might be described as the quietism of today, with this difference: that today the retreat is less from ethical involvement than from intellectual responsibility. Instead of the physical asceticism often associated with the lives of the saints, von Hügel would recommend the asceticism, the 'costingness', as he liked to say, effacing the challenges which modernity places before faith. Keeping the three elements in a balanced relationship with each other is a difficult task: von Hügel had no hesitation in relating it to the theology of the cross. Tyrrell, whom von Hügel described as a mystic, practised it more intensely than the Baron did.

Von Hügel does not define mysticism but allows an understanding of it to emerge from his impressionistic treatment of it. The nearest he comes to a definition is in his article on St John's gospel for the 11th edition of the *Encyclopedia Britannica*. (XV, 455) Mysticism is 'the intuitive [impressionistic] and emotional apprehension of the most specifically religious of all truths, viz., the already full operative existence of eternal beauty, truth, goodness, of infinite Personality and Spirit, independently of our action.' In short, it is the all-embracing awareness of a being who is transcendent yet immanent and who is already present. The first appropriate response to this presence is adoration.

It is highly significant that George Steiner entitled his celebrated book *Real Presences*, for in it he stands up to the nihilism and intellectual terrorism of Derrida and the post-modernists with their insistence on the perpetual deferring of meaning and their refusal to allow that words refer to any reality outside of other words. Steiner in true Pascalian fashion sees the matter in terms of a wager. He describes his book as 'a wager on transcen-

---

13. C. Davis, *Theology and Political Society*, Cambridge: Cambridge University Press, 1980, 60.
14. D. Knowles, *What Is Mysticism?* London: Burns & Oates, 1967, 74.

dence'. 'It argues that there is in the art-act and its reception, that
there is in the experience of meaningful form, a presumption of
presence'.[15] Steiner establishes a strong link between mysticism
and art.

> Maturity of mind and of sensibility in the face of the aesthetic
> demands 'negative capability' (Keats). *It allows us to inhabit
> the tentative.* (Steiner, *Real Presences*, 176, emphasis added)

'The questions: "What is poetry, music, art?", "How can they
not be?", "How do they act upon us and how do we interpret
their action?", [these] are, ultimately, theological questions.'
(ibid, 227) 'What I affirm is the intuition that where God's presence is no longer a tenable supposition and where his absence is
no longer a felt, indeed overwhelming weight, certain dimensions of thought and creativity are no longer attainable.' (ibid,
229)

Steiner's contention that the deeper questions about art are
ultimately theological was implicitly recognised by some of the
Modernists. The pivotal notion is presence. Their understanding
of presence is bound up with their understanding of mysticism.
It is therefore significant that Bernard McGinn, one of the foremost contemporary scholars of mysticism, regards a heightened
consciousness of God's presence as more constitutive of mystical experience than is preoccupation with higher and closer degrees of union with God. He also prefers the term 'consciousness' to the term 'experience'. (McGinn, *The Foundations of
Mysticism*, xviii-xix). The paradigm of union lends itself to 'exclusive mysticism'; whereas the paradigm of presence favours
'inclusive mysticism', in which mysticism is seen as one element
in normal Christian faith and life.

It was from the poet Coventry Patmore that George Tyrrell
derived the idea and image of divine presence in created things.
In Patmore's way of seeing things, Tyrrell wrote, '... God is
placed, not alongside of creatures, but behind them, as the light
which shines through a crystal and lends it whatever it has of
lustre'. 'God is not loved apart from creatures, or beside them;
but through them and in them.'[16]

Tyrrell is happy to go along with this interpretation of divine

---

15. G. Steiner, *Real Presences: Is There Anything* in *What We Say?* London:
Faber, 1989, 214, emphasis added.
16. G. Tyrrell, *The Faith of the Millions*, Second series, London: Longman,
Green, 1901, 52.

presence as long as it is not seen as the only mode of approach between God and human beings. But von Hügel was impressed by it and utilised it in the first of two papers on 'Experience and Transcendence'. The Baron was no poet, but in this instance he created an image which many people find remains in their imagination. He is wrestling with the problem of sensing the presence of the Infinite. As a way of representing this presence he asks us to imagine 'a broad-stretching, mist-covered lake, only on occasion of the leaping of some fish upon its surface, and of the momentary splash accompanying the momentary glimpse of the shining silver'.[17] The important thing to note here is that von Hügel is not simply saying that we logically infer the existence of the lake from the flash and splash of the fish. His approach is much more direct and concrete: the flash and splash establish the presence of the lake, and he would call the impression of that presence 'vivid', 'rich', or 'dim'. It has no clarity or definition. This is why von Hügel associates the mystical element with intuition: it has the quality of vision, however dim and impressionistic. The focus is soft, but the presence is eminently real, in Steiner's sense. One reason why the image of the lake tends to remain in the imagination is that it is not simply an effective analogy, it could actually be a literal occasion for sensing the presence of God. Peter Berger has called such occasions 'signals of transcendence', because they seem to point beyond themselves. They may be mediated by nature, art or human love. If they derive from nature, they serve not merely as paths to heightened awareness of God but as reminders of our ecological responsibility to care for the environment. If Christian faith is to link into today's ecologically inspired sense of nature, it will have to seek a mystical approach which avoids pantheistic sentimentality while recognising the divine presence as the light which shines through all things, but is seen for what it is perhaps only occasionally in moments of heightened consciousness. Of course there is an abiding danger of aestheticism, and even of sentimentality and Kitsch. But if the mysticism is incarnational and rooted in tradition, the dark presence of innocent suffering will purify it. As the mystics have always known, presence implies the possibility of absence; and all the great mystics

17. J. W. Beatie, 'Von Hugel's 'Sense of the Infinite'' *The Heythrop Journal*, xvi, 2, April, 1975, 169.

have spoken and written about what John of the Cross described
as the 'Dark Night'.

Louis Dupré, the distinguished philosopher of religion, establishes a possible link between the mystical tradition and
today's alienated secular world. 'He argues that the mystical
sense of the Divine absence, such as the desert of Eckhart, provides a point of contact between classical Christian mysticism
and the wasteland of modern atheism'. (McGinn, *Foundations*,
325) Perhaps it is the mystical element of religion which has
most to say to an age which, without necessarily being atheistic,
has nevertheless lost confidence in the inherited structures of religious tradition. Perhaps this is a dark night through which the
Christian Church needs to pass if it is to renew itself in preparation for the future. This is particularly true of the Catholic
Church in Ireland. Enda McDonagh, in a thoughtful and deeply-
felt article in *The Furrow*, entitled 'The Winter Name of Church',
reflects on the need for the Catholic Church in Ireland to enter
willingly and in a penitential spirit into the institutional dark
night brought upon it by clerical paedophilia. This dark night
would extend far beyond the scandal of child sex abuse and
would become a wholesale enquiry into how the institutional
church has failed, and is failing, the people of God. Interestingly
Dr McDonagh places emphasis on the need for a thinking
church.

> It's the need for thought that is worrying. Irish Church energy
> is more available for any other activity. Without a serious
> commitment to scholarship and hard-headed intellectual
> analysis and debate, the church will remain captive to super-
> ficial diagnosis of its crisis and to shallow, quick-fix solutions
> … In any event a much more open and vigorous intellectual
> and theological life is a top priority for the church in
> Ireland.[18]

Discovering its mystical inheritance may be the church's best
way of resisting' the siren calls for strong leadership and for a return to authority-based simplicities which, as von Hügel pointed
out, are a mark of immature childhood. If an attempt is made to
jump from the institutional to the 'spiritual', bypassing the intellectual, we end up with what Enda McDonagh has described as
'shallow, quick-fix solutions'. Von Hügel knew what he was

---

18. E. McDonagh, 'The Winter Name of Church', *The Furrow*, January
1995, 12.

doing when he identified the three moments as institutional, intellectual and mystical and recognised them as synchronic rather than purely diachronic. Each is a strong word calling for robust analysis. The term,'mystical', however, when one is prepared to analyse it patiently and dialectically, is a notable improvement on 'spiritual' especially when the latter is employed as a fideistic alternative to 'theological'.

The Social Role of the Theologian from the Dawn of Western Civilisation to the Present Day

James P. Mackey

My first task is to trace as briefly as possible the origins in our Western civilisation of the discipline known as theology, and of the concomitant profession of theologian. As I approached this daunting task, I was reminded of the opening words of Walter Pater's famous piece on the Mona Lisa: 'she is older than the rocks amongst which she sits ...'

For, although not the oldest profession – however much it may sometimes resemble that in practice – theology is certainly much, much older than the Christian religion; and therefore older still and older than the rock upon which one particular church claims God raised the whole edifice of the same Christian religion, and in the shadow of which some in that particular church expect all true theology to remain. I refer of course to the Roman Catholic Church in which I was born and in which, by God's good grace, I fully intend to die.

Theology, then – and this is the first important matter that must be recognised and reconnoitred as honestly as one may – was already a long established discipline, fully formed and named, when Christianity arrived on the scene, in a Roman Empire the common language of which was still common or *koine* Greek and the mind and soul of which would be for long Greek educated. Theology in the West was fully fledged and flown, a good eight centuries old, when Christianity in a magnificent bid for the Greek educated mind and soul of that ancient empire, borrowed its method, and most of its central content. Christianity snared the most fully-fledged and high-flying theology the world had ever known, for future service and undivided loyalty to its own distinctive cause. Christianity made its own the best of that Greek theology for two purposes: first, as its *apologia* against its cultured despisers in that ancient world; and, second, in its missionary bid to convert the whole of that great empire, and any other lands which it and that empire might consequently manage to conquer.

In order to explain this large and – perhaps some may find it – surprising contention, namely, that Christianity when it was itself as yet but two centuries old, and as yet virtually without a theology, made an existing theology its own, rather than make up one of its own, and in order to explain how the major Christian innovators justified that move, I must say a little about the birth and growth to adulthood of pre-Christian theology.

First, then, the birth of theology in the West coincided with the birth of physics and philosophy amongst the Ionians of the sixth century BC – not in the sense that these three were triplets, but in the sense that they were names for one and the same baby: Physics-Philosophy-Theology; PPT, for short. Which probably explains why theology in all its forms to this day, has dominant philosophical genes in its make-up; why all philosophies, even those few and late modern Western ones which have turned critical of the gods, have demonstrable theological genes, however mutational their functions; and why, as we approach the present day, the major dialogue-partner of theology seems to have become the physical sciences in their broadest cosmological reaches.

Second, on the account of the matter given by those early Greeks themselves, the birth of the baby PPT came about or was, you might say, planned in the course of a critical move upon the prevailing *mythos*, the myths that hitherto had carried the tale of the development of the cosmos and of those persons, human and superhuman, involved with it. The critical move upon *mythos*, they gradually explain, was characterised by *logos*. Fine, but how to explain the seminal Greek term, *logos*, without sending everyone to sleep, or confirming the caricatures of reason and myth so widespread in contemporary culture, or both? *Logos* in Greek can be translated 'word' simply, but not denoting a single expletive. It is the root of these 'ology' suffixes in the names of the most varied disciplines: biology, sociology, theology; so it denotes an intelligent and intelligible expression, a formulation, a discourse about reality, or part of reality. *Mythos*, too though can be translated as 'word', but now words in the form of an account, a story of cosmic or historic significance.

So when the early progenitors of PPT made their critical move in the name of *logos*, they did not, at their best at least, take this to be a move to replace myth and its characteristic imagination with reason and its characteristic analysis: myths are a crucial part of the great Platonic dialogues, arguably the highest single achievement of Western PPT to this day. For the reason in question is investigative reason, envisaging, even envisioning reason, trying to see what a cosmos constantly in process *is*, that is to say, is becoming; and in the case of those cosmic agents that appear to have some freedom in the matter, what they *ought* to envision for this cosmic process which would be for the good of all. But this of course describes what imagination also does: trying to form images of what is and what simultaneously will and ought to be; which is why Wordsworth (or was it Coleridge?) called imagination 'reason in its most expansive mood'.

So the progenitors of PPT complained specifically that the imagination which produced the prevailing myths had cluttered the cosmos with imaginary beings and events, and many of them not all that exemplary; had indulged in the imaginary at the expense of the truly imaginative. Their corrective, for which they proffered the term *logos*, was a more analytical and critical reflection on reality, which would rid us of the more debilitating effects of the purely imaginary, and confine our reasoned and imaginative investigations to *ta onta* – the things that are.

A reasoned, imaginative investigation into the things that are, all the things that are, and only the things that are; resulting in a rational discourse, a *logos*, concerning these – that was the formula secured by the founding Western philosophers for the future of Western philosophy. But how could this philosophy come to be called physics, and then metaphysics and theology, simultaneously with being called philosophy? The answer to that question is contained in the answer to another one, namely, what was it about *ta onta*, the things that are, that these founding fathers wished to investigate? In their own words, it was the *physis ton onton*, the nature of things. *Physis*, nature, gives the term physics to the enterprise. But *physis* to a Greek, according to Aristotle, referred to a form of reality which contained in itself the source of its own movement (that is, its own change and development). So, investigating the nature of things, you are trying to envisage from what they reveal of themselves in action, the originating form of their continuous creativity, or what we nowadays call their evolution, and perhaps something of the fulfilment, end or goal to which this source of their life and movement directed them. Indeed from the very outset of such investigation there was an awareness of dealing, not with some haphazard collection of natures or dynamic forms of reality, but with a cosmos, a unified universe of interactive and interdependent forms, and that revelation of the inherently unified structure of reality, enabled the Greek use of the word *physis*, in the singular, for the whole – the great Irish philosopher-theologian of the Middle Ages, John Scotus Eriugena, entitled his comprehensive *magnum opus, Periphysion*. Now this perspective upon reality as a whole posed for the Greeks the deep and endlessly intriguing question: is the cosmos perhaps revealing some utterly original form, or perhaps paradoxically some unifying source working through all cosmic forms, but not itself just one form amongst others, something almost incomprehensible that gives the cosmos as a whole its origin and constantly creative movement towards fulfilment? To that source of coordinated cosmic movement, in so far as the founding fathers thought they glimpsed it, and variously described and named it, or declared it indescribable in purely human terms, they applied the adjective *theios*, divine, or the noun *theos*, god. And in this way their discourse concerning the *physis* of things, their physics, became without more ado, discourse concerning divinity, a *logos* concerning *theos*, theology.

Just two more points about this physics-theology from its formative centuries in the West, both of them from Heracleitus, though later taken up again by Stoic philosophy at the dawn of the Christian era; one to explain why this discipline was also called philosophy; the other to explain its attraction for early Christians in quest of a theology for their faith.

First, Heracleitus insisted that investigators of the *physis* of the things that are, are themselves forms of reality existing in inextricable interaction and interdependence with each other and all poor transient things; as he put it in his inimitable aphoristic style: we live each other's deaths, and we die each other's lives. And it is by doing this that we come to know reality in parts and as a whole, from deepest source to distant goal. Investigating, envisioning involves walking the ways of the world, and the result is more than just a form of knowledge that might remain purely detached and theoretical. Reflectively and responsibly participating in the great cosmic drama, knowing and painstakingly learning how to walk a way that is best for self and world, that is wisdom, *sophia*, and the investigations which comprise physics-theology are then simultaneously *philo sophia*, a love-driven quest for wisdom, philosophy.

Second, Heracleitus, and the Stoics long after him, used the term *logos*, not just for human reason and its consequent discourse concerning reality both created and divine. He used the term also for that source and central creative power that works in and through all the forms that thereby cohere interactively to continuously create cosmos – 'the force that through the green fuse drives the flower,' as Dylan Thomas described it. This creator of cosmos could be called *logos*, reason or word, because although itself beyond human powers of comprehension, it revealed its continuous creative presence in and through the dynamic forms of the cosmos that are rationally intelligible to us. It is therefore a *logos*-type power, of which T. S. Eliot wrote in 'Ash Wednesday':

If the lost word is lost, if the spent word is spent
If the unheard, unspoken
Word is unspoken, unheard;
Still is the unspoken word, the Word unheard,
The Word without a word, the Word within
The world and for the world;
And the light shone in darkness and
Against the Word the unstilled world still whirled
About the centre of the silent Word.

The Stoics also called this creative divine Word, again after Heracleitus's imagery, a *pur technicon*, a craftsmanlike fire, continuously consuming old life in the creation of the new, enabling 'all poor foolish things that live a day' to live each other's deaths and to die each other's lives, so that we might be able to see, to continue the quotation from Yeats, 'eternal Beauty wandering on her way'. A terrible beauty indeed, invoking awe and trembling, as it is revealed to us in all of this continuous creation, and expressed with least inadequacy in the most creative and imaginative of our rational discourse. (Incidentally, pre-Christian Greek PPT believed that this creator God was revealed, not just generally to all in that continuous cosmic creativity in which we all participate, but that it was also especially revealed at times through chosen individuals. Plato, for example, at the dawn of Christianity was already regarded by Platonists as a *theios aner*, a divine man, with a human mother but no human father, whose writings were commented on in much the same way as their scriptures were by Christians.)

Already one begins to see why this theology could be borrowed by Christians. Their motives for borrowing it are easy to describe. The apologetic motive: only if you equip your religion with as high a theology can you defend yourself against cultured despisers; and the missionary motive: you must speak the most developed religious language of your would-be converts if you are to succeed. But a little more in the line of justification is necessary for early Christian borrowing of so much of the central content of this powerful, pre-existing and still developing theology.

And this is the basic justification offered at the time. It is simple really: As can be seen from one of the first Christian apologists, Justin Martyr, these early Christian would-be theologians pointed to the opening of their fourth gospel, the gospel of John which reads: *En arche en ho logos*, In the beginning was the Word, the creative Word through whom everything that is, is created. And if it was not already obvious that this divine creator could be known to everyone at any and all times through that intelligible creative forming and structuring and empowering of all things, the prologue to the fourth gospel goes on to spell out that claim explicitly. Changing the metaphor from word to light, the prologue explicitly asserts that this creator of all thus enlightens everyone; enlightens, pulls back the veil of darkness, unveils, reveals himself to everyone.

This justification allowed those early Christians to claim that they were not ignorant, superstitious worshippers of an executed state criminal, but worshippers of the same creator God who revealed himself to Greeks and to all others. It allowed them, simultaneously, to claim that the Greeks could actually learn something more of this common revelation from them, the Christians – for, they claimed, this creator Word took human form in the life, death and destiny of their founder, Jesus of Nazareth, thus affirming the divine status of the latter. Further still, when Christians came to develop a theology of the relationship of this now incarnate creator Word to the kind of Father God that they, like Jews and Greeks also talked about, they said the Father created through this Word, and along this theological route they finally worked out of this originally Greek theology, a doctrine of a triune God; for which, by the way, by the third century AD, they could borrow the terms of a Neo-Platonist theology of divine trinity which these non-Christian Greeks had themselves developed.

Now such substantial borrowing on such justification had one inherent drawback about it and, sign is on, the Greek world was not convinced, much less converted straight away. For a Greek theologian might well say, and indeed in all sorts of ways did say as much: if you in borrowing so much allow that we already knew so much, why is it not you who are to convert to our religion, rather than we to yours? The Christian answer pointed to a claim that incarnation meant a special presence of the revealing, creative Word in their founder. When this did not quite wash – since Greeks made comparable claims for Plato, as did Philo the Jew, a contemporary of Paul, for Moses – the Christians then had the god-awful gall and general brass neck to declare that the Greeks were sinners and enslaved to the devil, as they were not, or anyway not so much! So, the great Augustine, in generous mood, is saying of the Platonists, 'change a few words or phrases, and they might be Christians'; but in another mood entirely, he is accusing them of sinful pride and a consequent blindness. But that is a long story, which cannot detain us longer here. What matters at the moment is that Christian theology to this day reveals its central and substantial borrowing from the Greeks, and not only in method but also in content.

II

So much for theology, then; and now for the profession of theologian in Western culture and history. But it would be well to keep two things in mind in this present transition between topics.

First, that even in Late Antiquity the theologian can be called simply the philosopher, without any latter day distinctions being intended. Although by Late Antiquity theologians had ceased to be called *physiologoi*, physicists, as would have been possible under the PPT project down to the days of Socrates and Plato, when physics, philosophy and theology were names for (reaches of) one and the same quest for wisdom.

Second, it would be well to keep in mind the sheer scope of the theology pursued by this profession. It involved the imaginative investigation into, the effort to envisage, the whole cosmic drama, the agents inanimate and living, human and divine, all mutually involved within it, and the manner in which all things might be well. So that the philosopher-theologian of late antiquity thereafter covered what would later be divided amongst such disciplines as cosmology, ethics, social and political theory, and so on. Only through the bi-focals of these two points can one catch a glimpse of the profession of theologian in antiquity and in subsequent centuries in the West.

The figure of the philosopher-theologian in that world of Late Antiquity was brought to my attention with unforgettable vividness in a paper by Peter Brown during my years in the Centre for Hermeneutical Studies at the University of California, Berkeley. The paper was entitled: 'The Philosopher (read: theologian) and Society in Late Antiquity.' In essence, in Brown's words, the philosopher-theologian internalised in his person the core of a culture. And he did so – and this is crucial – by a certain renunciation and withdrawal: specifically, a renunciation of, and withdrawal from political ambition and public life, with its power, privilege and prestige; thus freeing himself for the imaginative contemplation, the patient analysis and the most adequate and attractive critical expression, that would best serve the wisdom that his culture had carried to him.

Brown spent much time distinguishing this form of renunciation from that of the Christian monk, and indeed the distinction is necessary. The monk's is an essentially triune renunciation so as to cover all that we naturally reach for in order to support life and existence: material possessions, partner and family, and above all our own wills; so that by vowing poverty, chastity and obedience, in their inextricable unity and for this purpose, the monk (and of course the nun) might be living witnesses to the belief that God is source and support of all life and existence, here as well as hereafter. The difference between the two forms of renunciation, that of the monk and that of the philosopher-theologian, can be seen most clearly in terms of the Roman Catholic Church, in which the whole government, the whole hierarchy from priest to pope, is taken from the ranks of the celibate. It is precisely that kind of governmental status, with its power, privilege and prestige that, Brown was arguing, the philosopher-theologian is by vocation urged to renounce. And so, to express the matter in Roman Catholic terms, in terms of the mutually exclusive estates of clergy and laity, the theologian is by vocation, quintessentially a lay person.

It was good then that Ira Lapidus, Professor of History at Berkeley, on that evening in 1978, reminded Peter Brown that other religious cultures provide examples of the kind of renunciative, investigative, contemplative life characteristic of the

philosopher-theologian in Late Antiquity in the West. The med-
ieval Muslim philosophers, as much as the Sufi mystics with
their high philosophical teachings, belonged to Lapidus's own
culture and tradition. He used of them Max Weber's phrase,
'inner-worldly asceticism,' glossed by Brown's original phrase
about the theologian's 'contemplation in the service of worldly
action'; and he quoted one of them, Abu Sa'id, as follows: 'The
true saint goes in and out amongst the people and eats and
sleeps with them and buys and sells in the market and marries
and takes part in social intercourse, and never forgets God for a
single moment.'

But it was the comment on Brown's paper by the influential
sociologist, Robert Bellah, that best clarified and supported
Brown's case for the societal importance of those individuals
whose renunciative life of reflection enabled them to sum up in
their persons and work the core of a culture. 'A cultural tradition,' Bellah argued, 'is neither the simple expression of, nor easily embodied in any society. Indeed I think it can be argued that
the full insitutionalisation of any coherent cultural tradition is
strictly speaking impossible. The sociological realities of everyday life make it impossible for the average man fully to embody
the cultural values to which he is in an important sense committed. Therefore the exceptional man at the "core" is important to
maintain the continuity and lived reality of the tradition.' 'The
almost automatic response of a contemporary social scientist to
this situation,' Bellah then went on to observe, 'is to brand the
core culture and those who embody it "elitist"; 'which,' he
ended, 'is precisely to miss the point.' The point being that this
renunciative reflection on behalf of the whole society, and its expression in speech and writing, is in essence a necessary service
to the maintenance and development of the culture in question,
and hence a necessary service to the whole community which
carries and seeks to embody it.

Of course, there always was, as Brown himself so well described it, the paradox of an inevitable tension between the
renunciative ideal which made these men so important to that
society, and the forms of influence they thereby came to wield.
For the best of those whose best ambition it was to become leaders in public and political life, came to sit at the feet of these
philosopher-theologians, or sent their sons and would-be suc-
cessors to them to be educated; and often in that very process

drew these philosopher-theologians closer to the councils of state where power and privilege reside – and at times, it has to be said, without too much resistance from the latter. Hence the very integrity of the role of philosopher-theologian was some-times threatened by what might look like its most effective and spectacular form of success; while, simultaneously, the institu-tional office-holders might be tempted to see in some of these more spectacular forms of influence a challenge to their own particular kind of power. Yet despite this inevitable tension, and the tendency to which it gave rise to centralise and subsume one of these roles under the other one, even in that coincidence of church and state that we now call Christendom in the high mid-dle ages, the church maintained a clear distinction between the *cathedra magisterialis*, the chair of the teacher, the *magisterium*, the chair of the master, on the one hand, and the *cathedra episcopalis*, the bishop's chair, the seat of the officer of good order, on the other.

Finally that night in Berkeley, John Dillon, who has since re-turned to take the chair of Greek at Trinity College, Dublin, pointed up one result of the original identification of this role with the non-Christian philosopher-theologians, particularly at a time when an imperious Christianity was minded to oust their version of that great culture altogether. At that time, the remain-ing non-Christian exponents of this cultural function developed a sense of increasingly futile opposition; a conviction of preserv-ing old values and pieties in a world in which the 'new atheism' or 'the current madness', as they used to call Christianity, seemed destined to prevail. Their renunciation of worldly power and position then took the form of retreat to a secluded estate in the countryside, as to a hospice where the sole hope was death in peace and dignity. They thus spread the impres-sion, perhaps even to the Christian community, that the pivotal social role of the philosopher-theologian would die with them.

But of course, it did not die; as I have just hinted in reference to the Christian Church in the high middle ages. In fact, I have offered this brief and patchy sketch of an ancient and noble pro-fession precisely because such recollection on such formal occas-ions as this, is calculated to secure for such a profession renewal in the present and for the future. Yes, the role of philosopher-theologian did at times merge with that of the monk, and such a merger can be an enrichment of the vision of, say, the Christian way – although it can also result in a narrowing of the vision of what constitutes the best version of that same way, as when the false story is put about that celibacy constitutes a better Christian state than that of married folk. And yes, the role of philosopher-theologian did also at times merge with that of bishop. And once again, such a merger can bring enrichment from experience of collegial government of the whole church – although this too can also result in a narrowing of vision, because of the inherent conservatism of office. But when such mergers give way to an ethos which says that only the monk (or only that half- or one-third-monk known as the celibate) can be a theologian in the church, or only the bishop can be a true or 'authentic' teacher, then damage is done which could prove fatal to the profession itself, and which could virtually deprive church and society of a distinctive and irreplaceable embodiment of its constitutive truth.

So, in sum, the life-task of the philosopher-theologian consists in a loving reflection on the wisdom carried to him or her in the whole community, in its life and literature, its public liturgy, its developing structures and subsidiary social formations; using in this task the God-given gifts of intelligence and imagination; the critical power of being able to distinguish the better embodiments of wisdom from the worse; the visionary power to envisage, however dimly, what might be better still; or at least to envisage what changes become necessary in view of the natural and constant movements within the broader cultures which churches and religions share; and such clarity and cogency of expression as would make this life-work a true, core summation of the religious tradition for the culture of a particular time and place.

The ideal of the philosopher-theologian requires, as it did in the beginning, the renunciation of the power of office. The life of reflection entails this, as does the form of service in which the theological task is performed in and for the community. Correspondingly, the theologian is not primarily responsible to the hierarchy, the offices of good order in the church, although subject to the proper exercise of the authority of ecclesiastical government, as is any other role or vocation in the church. As the theologian's source of insight is the whole church, in all its varied life and literature, so the theologian's first responsibility is to the church as a whole, the testing ground as well as the

source of his or her service to the truth. Well, yes ... except that
formula too could be misread to mean that the theologian's task
is simply to provide the members of the church with a vision of
the truth by which they live, in a form of discourse which would
enable them to talk about it amongst themselves. To which the
obvious riposte must be, that theology is no more for the church
in this narrow sense, than the church itself is for itself. The
church exists for the world, and so it exists in its members in so
far as they are members of the whole race of God's people, and
of the whole universe of things that are all God's intimate gift
and continuous creation, and agents of God's universal revelation.

So, as we saw, from the beginning Christian theology had its
ears attuned to the voices of those philosopher-theologians from
other religious cultures who best responded to the divine revelatory light that shone for them in their particular history of time
and creation. And if Christian spokespersons have preferred to
harp on the benefits their theology and example could bring to
these other participative investigators of the great cosmic
drama, the long shadow of Christian history in this common
culture of the West, and latterly all over this planet, with its
presently undeniable litany of significant failures and, sometimes, of sheer inhumanity, should by now have wrung from us
the admission that some of these others might indeed have preserved some elements of vital wisdom better than we have done;
and that theology must address its task of providing a common
discourse and cooperation in the expectation that we shall learn
from other cultures as much perhaps as we can teach them by
word and example.

The theologian today who wishes to be responsible to the
whole church by helping the church to be responsive to the
whole world; the Christian theologian who seeks a vision of
Christianity as a religion open to the world, rather than a
Western religion imposed on the rest of the world; must be particularly open and attentive to the forms of inculturation of
Christianity now emerging in robust numbers around the
world. And that must involve respectful dialogue with all cultures and cultural options, and an openness to the wisest vision
of reality in its depths and heights which each of these cultures
and options both preserves and develops; not excluding the
ever-developing cultural options in the still-imperial West; and

not even the self-styled agnostic or atheistic versions of these; for these self-styled atheistic or agnostic humanisms do frequently forge and preserve high moral insights that somehow escape the canon lawyers; and it is the vocation of the theologian, as her role has developed in the Christian West, to work with all the wisdom that her widest culture has carried to her.

III

If that, or something very like it, is a true account of theology and the profession of theologian, as these have developed throughout the history of Western civilisation, a question might well arise concerning the place of theology and theologian in the modern, or indeed postmodern societies of the West.

Oddly enough, a set of distinctions already proposed by those pre-Christian Greeks who originally devised what they called, undifferentiatedly, physics, or the study of the *physis ton onton*, philosophy and theology, may still be of considerable help in answering that question today.

Already before Socrates and his immortaliser, Plato came on the scene, and with them the most influential theology in the whole history of the West (all Western philosophy, said Whitehead, is a series of footnotes to Plato), three different types of theology had been identified and named by the Greeks. These were, first, what they called *theologia mythicon*, and by that they denoted the theology contained in that discourse concerning the divine and the cosmos that is found in the myths of the Greeks and the barbarians, often corrupted by overdoses of the imaginary and the morally questionable, but found also in more acceptable form, for instance, in the cleaned up and organised version of Hesiod's *Theogony*.

Second, *theologia politicon*. Now this is an interesting one, for it suggests that there is a theology that is at least implicit in the claims to power made by mighty institutions like kingdoms, states and churches and in their practices of ruling and legislating for whole societies, if not indeed also explicit in their ideological or doctrinal proclamations. Third, *theologia physicon*. There's that word, *physis*, again, for this is the theology about which I have been talking throughout: the theology that is named after the imaginative investigation of the things that are, as ultimate sources, processes and prospects of the great cosmic moral drama are tantalisingly and gradually revealed, courtesy of both nature, in the Greek sense of *physis*, itself, and of those privileged individuals or groups who seem to their followers to have been especially favoured with revelations from that ultimate source that is otherwise always revealed to all.

All three types of theology, like the poor according to Jesus, we have always with us. Because the image, the symbol, their explosive tension when brought together in the metaphor, in poetry and story and, yes, in history, is the primordial heuristic device in our efforts to envisage our world, our myths will always stand to our philosophical inquiries in the stricter sense in the double relationship of that which illuminates and inspires, on the one hand and, on the other, needs at times to be subjected to constructive critical reflection. Examples of the mythic (in this determinedly non-pejorative sense of the word)? In the case of our quest for a moral universe, the Harry Potter stories, for instance. In the case of our intimations of an ultimate, immanent source worthy of the title, divine, much of modern science fiction. And of course in the case of Christian theology, pride of place goes to the stories of the founder found in the scriptures.

It is difficult to give any precise answer to the question of the place of this mythic philosophy in the modern world of the West. Since it is the work of the creative artist, and the spirit of creativity breathes where it will, we can hardly even say that its normal place should be in academia; merely that its ever-developing products must form a central part of the studies of any university; and not merely in departments of literature, fine art, philosophy or theology, or in arts faculties in general, but in faculties of science and social science that can scarcely make much progress unless they are reflectively, critically and constructively aware of the paradigms that have come to them in the overall wisdom carried by their culture.

The easiest instances from which to identify *theologia politicon*, the theology which is found in, and in the interests of the governmental structures of large societies, are in churches, and in the West in particular, Christian churches. But there are more political theologies on earth than there ever were, and in secular as well as ecclesiastical governments. I am not now referring simply to the Middle Ages and to a society named Christendom, in which church and state pretty well coincided for all practical purposes; or, in more recent times, to those Islamic countries which would be ruled purely by the shariah. And nor am I referring only to those modern nation states that make reference to God in their constitutions.

When you consider the fact that atheistic humanism in the English-speaking world is largely the product and the preserve of some philosophers, scientists and literati, and that the most practically successful form of atheistic humanism, Marxist communism in its various evolutions, substituted its own absolutes for a God declared either absent, dead or non-existent, you begin to realise that there are more political theologies than you had previously dreamt of – apart altogether from the less crucial fact that programmatic atheism is itself a theology. And, if only from these extreme examples, you may begin to notice a certain characteristic that governs all political theologies.

Those who feel it is their destiny to rule over others and to legislate for them in the larger social configurations of any age, naturally incline to think that the worldview which put them in this position, and which presents the moral vision and the view of human prospects that have served the society well enough to this point, that this worldview should be promulgated and preserved. To put the point at its mildest, all reigning political theologies are of their nature conservative, and quite frequently reactionary. Not from the ranks of their proponents can you normally expect that creatively imaginative investigation, that constructively critical reflection from which in actual fact all progress in human affairs, if not all advancement rather than regression in the great cosmic drama itself, devolves. Something of this perception also no doubt lay behind the insistence of the ancients that the physicist/philosopher/theologian should renounce the corridors of power. The place of political theology, incidentally, in the case of states, is with the ideologues who propose and promote the ideologies of communism, *laissez-faire* capitalism and so on; in the case of churches, it is in their seminaries.

Now the moment you move on from this point to consider the third form of theology, *theologia physicon*, you begin to sense already the intrinsic possibility of at least occasional antagonism between the exponents of this and exponents of the previous type of theology. Extreme instances of this antagonism do not occur that often, thank God, but when they do, they present powerful examples of its nature and its likelihood. Take the case of Socrates. He was executed by the government of Athens as one of the *physiologoi*, a practitioner of the third kind of theology which I have been trying to describe throughout this essay. He was executed because he criticised the gods of that mighty city state, because, that is to say, he undermined its political theology. He undermined the theology of those who preferred gods that were a little more favourable to Athenians in particular, gods that might well be favourable to those who joined Athens as subjects or friends, but gods that could with confidence be expected to be implacable to their enemies; gods that, compared to the god of which Socrates discoursed in his tentative, questioning way, had already conveyed to these good rulers of Athens in quite sufficient quantity and through various means, absolute truths about themselves and theirselves, and the moral and religious directives that would guarantee the prosperity of the Athenians in this life and the next; gods that would proffer them salvation from adversaries when needed. (This picture of a political theology is, I am sure, not unfamiliar to you from other traditions.)

Socrates swallowed the hemlock. He need not have done so; on Plato's account of the matter, he had enough powerful friends in Athens to have the sentence commuted or set aside, probably by bribery. But there are occasions when someone has to die, in order that the cause for which he or she lived, should not die. And Socrates, from Plato's account of his final hours in the *Phaedo*, seems to have sensed that his collision with the guardians of the political theology of the Athenian city-state was one of these occasions. In the event, the death of Socrates so inspired Plato that the cause of *theologia physicon* did live on, and over the next ten centuries arguably achieved the greatest measure of development recorded to this day. It lived on centrally in the Academy that Plato founded and that stood for a thousand years until, in what must rank as one of the great acts of vandalism in the history of the West, and despite the fact that Christianity had borrowed its method and most of its central substance, a Christian emperor, Theodosius, forcibly closed it down in the sixth century AD. But that thousand years was surely enough to secure the conclusion that the place for this third form of theology is still, to this day, in academia; where it can pursue its critical and creative service to the transmitted culture of any society, as Robert Bellah described that essential task.

For, with the destruction of the Academy this *theologia physicon*, this perennial quest for the moral and perhaps personal depths of reality, in response to all experienced revelations from its deepest source and constantly creative force; this attempt to envisage a way for humans to walk in and with the great cosmic drama for the betterment of all; by now thoroughly Christian-ised (or was it Christianity that was thoroughly Platonised?); this theology in that most expansive form, migrated to those mighty monastic institutions, many of them founded by those mighty Irish monks who led Europe out of the Dark Ages; the *Schottenkloster* as they came to be called on the continent (*Scoti* being the Latin word for Irish persons up to the twelfth century); and in turn it migrated from these centres of learning to Europe's first universities – Bologna, Paris, St Andrews, Oxford – so that it has remained a central part of the *universitas studio-rum* in all the great universities of the West to the present time.

Two points, then, to finish. First, I would not think so little of readers of this collection, or indeed of myself as a poor practi-tioner of this ancient and noble profession, as to leave any im-pression lying about to the effect that one has to argue for a place for theology in a university, much less that this is what I have been doing here. It is true that theology in the West in the mod-ern era has seen its natural continuity with physics and philoso-phy disrupted by various events, ranging from the sixteenth century Protestant attack upon reason, through T. H. Huxley's fabricated myth of natural warfare between religion and science, to the anti-religious philosophies such as Marxism and some of the more superficial brands of British Empiricism; and only in the university can theology re-attach to the roots it originally shared with the physical sciences and the rest of philosophy. But this does not mean that one needs to argue for a place for theology in a modern university. Quite to the contrary, in fact; if this essay argues anything about modern universities and theology, it ar-gues a responsibility on the part of any well-conceived university to include theology in its curriculum; for otherwise the university cannot fulfil its social role as a constructively critical think-tank covering all constitutive parts of a culture. I think that people who think that a case needs to be argued for allowing theology into a university are thinking, not of theology as it has devel-oped in academia in the West, but of seminary theology.

So, second and finally, neither would I like to leave behind the impression that any one of the three types of theology enum-erated above is bad in itself, or intrinsically inferior to either of the others. Seminary theology is by and large the political theology of a church as it is taught, text-book-like, to future preachers, ministers and leaders of that church. As such it is a good and necessary activity in any church; and its character as conservative is a good and necessary quality in its case. For it is the first duty of our establishments in church or state to conserve the wisdom that has been carried to us in our culture, safe so far from the ravages of time; and as a consequence to put to the test those who presume to take up the position of constructively critical reflection on the living, transmitted wisdom of the whole community. Even in cases where the establishment reaction to loyal and constructive criticism or to creative efforts to develop doctrine and praxis in altered cultural conditions proves to be truly reactionary or, worse still, to be mistaken in substance and unjust in its punitive effects upon an academic theologian; even then, although grave fault can be incurred in the form of misuse of hierarchical authority, all is not bad, and all need not be lost. For such experiences, and indeed the very threat of them, sharpen the theologians' sense of responsibility to the communities, those carriers of the wisdom to which we are entirely indebted; as they can prevent in us too much admiration for our own creativity, and a consequently cavalier attitude to change or demolition. There is nothing quite like an actual experience of powerlessness before an institutional establishment, to remind one of the powerlessness that one's vocational renunciation of the corridors of power entails; nothing reminds one more of the fact that the power lies in the truth one manages to sum up in one's person and work, and not to any degree to one's own person, or to the position one holds as a result of answering the vocation to theology.

Correspondingly, this third form of theology, like all the other disciplines, needs the support of the intellectual independence of the university; just as much as the establishment needs the loyal and constructive critique of its traditions at the range and depth at which the university alone can provide this. In Ireland up to very recently we had the potentially and mutually compromising conditions of one institution of university status providing for a full programme of the profession and research of Christian theology while at the same time functioning as the national seminary of the Roman Catholic Church: Maynooth. And indeed up to a mere couple of decades ago the chairs of theology and scripture at Trinity College, Dublin served as a virtual seminary for the Church of Ireland. It is greatly to the credit of these institutions that, despite the potentially compromising conditions, and indeed some actual instances of the use of hierarchical authority in the Roman Church to positively discriminate against the most constructively critical and creative of its emerging theologians, Ireland, relative to its size and population, did nevertheless produce a reasonable crop of practitioners of this ancient profession, who proved that they had the education, intelligence, imagination and courage to live up to its demands. Amongst these one would certainly number Enda McDonagh. And now with the gradual, if slow introduction of theology and religious studies into Irish third level institutions – together of course with the fact that Trinity's ancient school of Hebrew, Biblical and Theological studies, as it is currently called, has been for some time now a strongly developing department fully incorporated into the faculty of Arts – the flame that was kept alive must burn brighter and brighter into the future, to the benefit, one can only hope, not merely of all the Christian churches on this little island, but also of the other religions now increasingly sharing with us our small earthly space.

Conversation in Context

Nicholas Lash

Bekan, Sydney and Saint Anselm

The undertaker from Galway, having adjourned 'to a pub in downtown Ballyhaunis for a jar or two of grief therapy ... gleans the story of the Canon and brings it back to Galway with glosses. "This Canon, ye see, came down from Maynooth and was all about theology. Then he brought down these theologians to talk, but the people didn't turn up to hear them, d'ye see? They didn't want it. Why would they? Theology in Mayo?"'[1]

Things being the way they are, the undertaker had a point. And yet, as one of 'these theologians', I have the fondest memories of what we called 'the Bekan Council', presided over by 'this Canon,' J. G. McGarry, by then the parish priest of Ballyhaunis, and by Enda McDonagh's mother.

From the west of Ireland to the east of New South Wales and, to be more specific, to the Catholic Institute in Sydney. A few years ago, Cardinal Martini of Milan, staying with the Archbishop of Sydney, expressed a wish to visit the Institute. As they are being shown round the library, Cardinal Martini is delighted to see that the Institute subscribes to his favourite French journal of New Testament studies. 'What are your favourites?' he asks his host. 'Oh, in my job,' Cardinal Clancy is said to have replied, 'I don't get time to read books.' Or, as the undertaker might have said: 'They didn't want it. Why would they? Theology in Archbishop's House?'

I have been asked to reflect on the relationships between theology and the life of the church. The cardinal from Sydney and the undertaker from Galway speak (I suspect) for the vast majority of Catholics – bishops, priests and laypeople – in taking for

---

1. The story is told by Ned Crosby, 'Inferiority or Good News?', *Faith and the Hungry Grass. A Mayo Book of Theology,* edited Enda McDonagh, Dublin: The Columba Press, 1990, 114-121; 115-116.

granted that no relationships of general, direct and practical importance, exist.[2]

We might well ask who is to blame for this, wondering why bishops and priests show little interest in theology and whether it is true and, if so, why, that 'Lay people in general feel ignored by theologians and excluded from the world of theology'[3] but, for present purposes, I would prefer to try to break up a little of the ground of habits of imagination that we too easily take for granted, digging around the edges of what we take 'theology' and 'church' to mean. The best place to start, though this may well seem paradoxical, is with the relationship between them.

There is, of course, nothing we can say, or do, or suffer, that does not spring from, is not, in some measure, shaped by, the times and places and relationships that have made us who and what we are. Nevertheless, although it may take two to tango, there are some things that we can do more or less on our own. Thinking, or weeping, for example.

Setting down one's thoughts on paper is a kind of speaking and, in this sense, not all our speaking takes the form, directly and straightforwardly, of conversation. And so, Saint Anselm, more than nine hundred years ago, could name a little tract that he had written: 'monologue', or 'soliloquy'. And although much philosophy takes the form of conversation (usually as energetic and often acerbic disagreement) philosophers may, from time to time, soliloquise, write monologues.

Most of what we say or think, however, is said and thought, not only in context, but in company, as we react to circumstances and events, and respond to what others have already said and asked of us. Later in this essay I shall argue not only that the fundamental form of speech is conversation, and that

2. During the many years in which I sat on successive versions of the Theology Committee of the episcopal conference of England and Wales, the conference never sought our views on God or justice, on death or science or suffering. In the first five turbulent years after Vatican II, our opinion was sought three times: once to commission a statement on christology, once to ascertain our views on the appropriate age for confirmation, and once to ask whether there were theological objections to lay people receiving communion more than once a day (see Nicholas Lash, 'English Catholic Theology', *The Month*, October, 1975, 286-289).

3. Nuala Bourke, 'Lay Theology: The Search for a Living God', *Survival or Salvation. A Second Mayo Book of Theology*, edited Enda McDonagh, Dublin: The Columba Press, 1994, 141-148; 146.

serious speech is speech in which the speaker acknowledges responsibility for uttering, for giving voice to, some aspect of the world of which we are the 'speaking part', but also that the fundamental form of conversation is, in fact, contemplativity, attentive prayerfulness, recognition that all things come into being through the Word that God's own self is said to be.

Which is why, a year after writing the little tract that he had called *Monologion*, Saint Anselm wrote another, in which passages of prayer – of Anselm's conversation with the silent mystery of God – are seamlessly interwoven with passages of strenuous and demanding argument, as Anselm struggles, in this silence, for some understanding: 'Let me seek you in desiring you; let me desire you in seeking you.' In this tract, Anselm only speaks of God in speaking to him. Which is why he calls this tract *Proslogion*, address, 'an allocution'.[4]

The *Monologion*, we might say, is the work of a philosopher; the *Proslogion* of a theologian. Two hundred years later, Thomas Aquinas was to say that the subject-matter of what he called 'holy teaching' is the mystery of God and 'all things', *'omnia'*, absolutely everything, in its relationship to God, its origin and destiny.[5]

Geologists study rocks, historians what human beings said and did, astronomers the movement of the stars. The theologian, in contrast, has no particular piece of turf to call her own: she studies whatever it is that she has made her own particular interest in its relationship to God, its origin and destiny. And she can only do this well in the measure that her enquiry is rooted and grounded in contemplativity, in wondering relation to the mystery of God.

In a nutshell: the church is the community of those who know the fundamental forms of human speech to be conversation grounded in response to that one Word in whom all things come to be. And theology is the vastly varied forms of language in which this knowledge finds expression and through which it seeks some understanding.

---

4. *Saint Anselm's Proslogion*, translated with introduction and commentary by M. J. Charlesworth, Oxford: Clarendon Press, 1965, Chapter I, 114 ('Quarem te desiderando, desiderem quaerendo'), Prologue, 104 ('Quod ut aptius fieret, illud quidem *Monologion*, id est soliloquium, istud vero *Proslogion*, id est alloquium, nominavi').
5. See Thomas Aquinas, *Summa Theologiae*, Ia, q. 1, art. 7, c.

Globalisation and the Gathering of God

Modern Western culture has transformed the world far more dramatically, and irreversibly, than any previous episode in human history. In medicine and astronomy, in physics, in engineering and in economics, human beings have achieved breathtaking advances in their knowledge and control of the things and forces of which the world is made.

Increasing information and technical skill have not, of course, been matched by deepening wisdom or by growth in virtue. During the century just ended, we put our new-found power to use in slaughtering and enslaving million upon million of women, children, and men. And today, things are so organised by us as to enable a minority to live in luxury far beyond our needs while most of us are driven further and further into abject poverty, and our rape of natural resources threatens to tip into terminal imbalance the mechanisms which have, for billions of years, kept planet earth alive.[6]

During the eighteenth century, 'the Cartesian division of matter from mind, causes from reasons, and nature from humanity ... ceased to be of concern to natural philosophers alone ... [and] played a major role in social and political thought as well.'[7] The tragically ambivalent achievements of modernity have been driven by the bizarre conviction that something known as 'mind' or 'reason' is, or can make itself to be, the master of the world.

Ironically, of course, it did not dawn on those who constructed the worldview of modernity – devout Catholics such as Descartes, Lessius, and Mersenne – that their understanding of the kinds of things that human beings are, of the rest of the world, and of the relationships between them, was breaking quite new ground, at best in tension with, at worst quite contradictory to, the mainstream Christian and Jewish traditions on which they drew.[8] (An irony compounded, these days, by the

---

6. On that last point, see Kenneth J. Hsu, 'The Mortality of the Planet', *Is the World Ending?*, ed. Sean Freyne and Nicholas Lash, Concilium, 1988/4, 63-73.

7. Stephen Toulmin, *Cosmopolis. The Hidden Agenda of Modernity*, Chicago: University of Chicago Press, 1992, 107.

8. See Michael J. Buckley, *At the Origins of Modern Atheism*, New Haven: Yale University Press, 1987.

widespread and mistaken belief that something very like Cartesian dualism has been 'traditional' in Christianity[9]).

Briefly to illustrate: consider the 'soul', and the use made of the biblical injunction to 'Be fruitful and multiply, and fill the earth and *subdue* it.'[10] To sidle up to 'soul', let us begin with 'mind'. Are 'mind' and 'matter' best understood as two different things or entities? This is a question much discussed these days by scientists and philosophers. For what it is worth, my own view is that 'mind' is not well thought of as a 'thing'. This does not mean that I do not think that we have minds, can think and speak, make plans, and so on. It simply means that what it is to 'have a mind' is, I suggest, best understood (in the tradition going back to Aristotle) as a matter of having 'the capacity for behaviour of the complicated and symbolic kinds which constitute the linguistic, social, moral, economic, scientific, cultural, and other characteristic activities of human beings in society'.[11]

Think, then, of your mind, not as a 'thing' stuck somewhere in your head, but as your *ability* to do the kinds of things that human beings, distinctively and characteristically, do: they make plans, tell stories, dream dreams, and construct elaborate systems of organisation and behaviour. And then try to think in a similar way about the distinction between the 'body' and the 'soul'. In a similar way, but not identically. The distinction is similar because to speak of human beings as 'souls' is to speak of their capacity to do the kinds of things that human beings, distinctively and characteristically, do. However, talk of 'mind' stops there, whereas when we talk of ourselves as 'souls' (at least in Christian speech) we go further: we recognise our creatureliness, acknowledge that everything that we are and have is *gift*; that we are 'gift-things' given the capacity and duty to return the gift we are in praise and celebration.

If this was how we thought about our minds and souls, we would be less inclined to succumb to the illusion that we somehow stand outside and apart from the world of which we form a part, the world into whose webs of time and place we are, as all

9. See my remark about the philosopher John Searle in Nicholas Lash, 'Recovering Contingency', *Consciousness and Human Identity*, ed. John Cornwell, Oxford: Oxford University Press, 1998, 197-211; 199.

10. Genesis 1:28 (my stress).

11. Anthony Kenny, *The Metaphysics of Mind*, Oxford: Clarendon Press, 1989, 7.

things are, in everything we say and do and suffer, tightly woven. If this was how we thought about our minds and souls, we would be less inclined to read the biblical injunction to 'subdue the earth' as licence for exercise of power unchecked by solidarity with, and duty towards, the rest of the created world. The creator God of the book of Genesis is a king, who appoints a viceroy to rule as God would rule, expending infinite care on every creature; a king (to pick up the complementary metaphor from Chapter Two), who 'plants a garden', in which he places a gardener. Gardeners may tame the wilderness, but they do not pillage and destroy, understanding as they do their duties towards and interdependence with, the plants and animals they tend.

By now, the reader is entitled to some explanation as to why some elementary observations on what might be meant by 'church' should be approached from the vast and seemingly eccentric distance of a handful of polemical generalisations about the damage done by modern dualism. The answer would go something like this. The church is a people, an assembly of men and women. Therefore, we will not think sensibly about the church unless we think sensibly about the kinds of things that human beings are. Moreover, human beings are creatures, constituents of the world of which they form a part. Therefore, we will not think sensibly about human beings unless we think sensibly about the world which God creates.[12] It follows, I suggest, that, in order to think sensibly about the church, the best place to begin would be by saying something sensible about the world, and this apparently straightforward project has been made much more difficult by modernity's illusion that human beings, or at least their minds, do not form part of the natural world, part of the bodies that they are; that 'mind', or 'reason', or 'the soul', do not form part of nature, part of what (in fact) there is.[13]

Enda McDonagh, if I understand him, is thinking in a similar direction when he says: 'Without some basic trust in the earth

12. For those readers who prefer to have these things clothed in academic dignity, I am suggesting that our ecclesiology is shaped by whatever anthropology we simply take for granted, and that our anthropology, in turn, is shaped by whatever ontology we simply take for granted.
13. There are suggestive similarities between the way in which we often talk about 'nature' – as if it were something 'over there', outside us – and the way in which many people in England still talk about 'Europe'!

and its fruits, human life would be impossible ... Trust in the earth grounds human beings' trust in one another and ultimately their trust in God.'[14] Human beings – bodies, minds, and souls – form part of nature, part of what there is. Human beings are made to be the gardeners of the world. What gardeners do is cultivate, and 'culture' is the general term for all the ways in which we cultivate the world. And yet, too often, culture has, in modern times, 'been defined too narrowly' as if it referred exclusively to things like music, dance, or literature. In contrast, Donal Dorr reminds us, 'the old culture included agriculture, horticulture, and aquaculture'.[15]

Dissociate us – through misconstrual of 'mind', or 'soul', or 'culture' – from the earth-facts that we are, from the 'nature' of which we form a part, and we begin to wreak incalculable damage upon the bodies which we have forgotten that we are, and upon the earth of which we cease to see ourselves as being a part. Ethna Viney speaks with dramatic accuracy of Mayo's mountains when she says that 'Their salvation is necessary for our survival.'[16]

The founding fathers of modernity – Descartes and Galileo and their contemporaries – sought systematically to exclude the human mind from 'the subject-matter of science'.[17] This separation of consciousness from nature, of speech and thought from what we speak and think about, sustained the illusion that we can speak the truth from nowhere in particular, that 'reason' springs from no particular soil, knows no particular place or time.

Learning to put our minds back into our bodies is a matter of learning to put ourselves back into particular times and places, a matter of learning to acknowledge the interdependence of everyone and everything, including the interdependence between the things that human beings are and do and undergo and the operation of all the other forces and features which constitute the world.

All the talk these days of 'globalisation' is, perhaps, an incip-

14. Enda McDonagh, 'Shall We Hope?', *Survival or Salvation?*, 248-255; 252.
15. Donal Dorr, 'Exile and Return', *Faith and the Hungry Grass*, 66-81; 70.
16. Ethna Viney, 'Saving All Our Holy Mountains', *Survival or Salvation?*, 29-42; 30.
17. John Searle, *The Rediscovery of Mind*, London: MIT Press, 1992, 85.

ient recognition of this interdependence of everything. 'One
thing', however, 'which has thus far escaped globalisation is our
collective ability to act globally'.[18] In other words, the most urgent challenge that confronts the human race today is the requirement to imagine and construct a global *politics* which can
contain and counter the destructive violence unleashed by the
unchecked operation of a global market.[19] What shape such a
politics will take, we do not know. We have not been here before. It seems to me, however, that at least as important as the
construction of appropriate *institutions* will be the development
of what one might call a genuinely global *imagination*; a sense of
solidarity with the whole of humankind – past, present and future. In the development of such a global imagination, Christianity undoubtedly has a part to play – not merely because it has
been around for a long time and continues to shape the identity
of very many people, but also on account of its self-constituting
narrative, or what we usually call the doctrine of the church, to
which I shall turn directly in a moment.

Is there not, however, a tension between the demand that we
learn to develop a global imagination, that we learn to speak and
act in recognition of the interdependence of everything, and my
insistence that truth is only discerned and uttered and enacted
in particular places, and at particular times? No, because the
'universal' is not the antithesis of the 'particular', but its form
and context.

Thus, for example, Mary Robinson has said that local (and
hence particular) community is 'both a focus and a sign' of wider
(and, I would add, in principle, of universal) community.[20]
'Universality' that is not rooted in the richness of particulars is
illusory, and very dangerous, being itself no more than some in-
flated and disguised particularity. This is, perhaps, what
Padraig Flynn means when he says that: 'all truth is specific,
never general'.[21] Hence Enda McDonagh's insistence on the

18. Zygmunt Bauman, 'Whatever happened to compassion?', *The Moral
Universe*, edited by Tom Bentley and Daniel Stedman Jones, London:
Demos, 2001, 51-56; 53.
19. See Nicholas Boyle, *Who are we now? Christian Humanism and the
Global Market from Hegel to Heaney*, Edinburgh: T. & T. Clark, 1998.
20. See Mary Robinson, 'Preface', *Survival or Salvation?*, 7.
21. Padraig Flynn, 'Context and Continuum: Europe and Mayo',
Survival or Salvation?, 216-223; 219.

need for 'the localisation of theology ... as counter-balance to the rush to universalisation in commerce, of course, but also in politics and in culture'.[22]

Contemporary opposition to globalisation is grounded in the well-founded fear that, the way the world is at present constituted, innumerable fragile and vulnerable particulars – particular people, particular cultures, particular communities – are being flattened and obliterated by the steamrolling activity of what are, in fact, merely other and vastly more powerful particulars (economic and political) whose particularity is disguised by the illusions of necessity: 'You can't buck the market', as Margaret Thatcher once remarked.

The development of a genuinely global imagination, and of genuinely global institutions, require the recognition that: 'The social and political watchword ... is not dependence or independence but *interdependence*', and that 'interdependence is a reciprocal process involving mutual rights and obligations between the members' of the human race.[23] Which is where the doctrine of the Church comes in.

What do we mean by 'church'? The word itself may not seem particularly helpful: 'church', 'kirk', '*Kirche*', come from the late Greek word '*kuriakon*', 'the Lord's house'. Unless, however, we are well attuned to biblical imagery of the living 'temple', 'Lord's house' might mislead us into supposing that we were speaking of a building, rather than a people.

'*Ecclesia*' is more useful: the Latin transcription of a Greek word (with, in classical Greek, no religious uses or connotations) for an assembly of citizens. The Septuagint sensibly chose this word to render the Hebrew '*kahal*', which signified the assembly of God's chosen people.

'Church', then, is an assembly, a gathering, a people summoned, called together for some task, some common purpose. This people is, of course, the human race: called, *ex nihilo*, into common life, communion, in the life of God. It is, as *Lumen Gentium* puts it, the gathering, by God's reconciling grace, of all the just 'from Abel, the just one, to the last of the elect'; of which gathering, eschatological assembly, that which we usually call

---

22. McDonagh, 'Introduction: Between Westport and Asia Minor', *Faith and the Hungry Grass*, 7-13; 7.
23. Enda McDonagh, 'Shall We Hope?', 251 (my stress).

'the church' subsists as 'a kind of sacrament' or symbolic enact-
ment.[24]

More concretely, as article 26 of the Constitution puts it: 'This
church of Christ is truly present in all legitimate local [gather-
ings] of the faithful ... united with their pastors'.[25] Each celebration of the eucharist, each diocese, is not a fragment or small part
of some vast multinational corporation: it is the universal,
Catholic, 'global' church in its entire particular existence, in this
time and in this place.

But, of course, the universal church, God's gathering of humankind, will – in each particular place and time – be a community
of limited experience and resources; of only so much holiness,
and scholarship, and wisdom; a fragile group of sinful men and
women in continual need of strengthening and enrichment, of
education and correction, from all those – of every age and race
and culture – with whom it exists in communion. In other
words, the process of interdependence – of 'communion', solidarity, '*koinonia*' – is as fundamental to the identity and flourishing of Christianity as we have already seen it to be in social and
political affairs in general. (Nor is this, of course, in any way
surprising; it is merely an illustration of a principle I indicated
earlier: that we will not think sensibly about the church unless
we think sensibly about the kinds of things that human beings
are. Each and every account of what we mean by 'church' has
social and political presuppositions and implications.)

Article 4 of *Lumen Gentium* speaks, in imagery as ancient as
Ezechiel, of the church as the dwelling-place or temple of 'the
Spirit of life, a fountain of water springing up to life eternal'.[26]
This gathering into peace of humankind is what God does. It is
pure gift.

Historically, and sociologically, there is not, of course, the
slightest doubt that the entire 'symbol-system' that is
Christianity – this vast and ancient network of stories and associations, of images and rituals and enactments, confused, argu-

24. Dogmatic Constitution '*Lumen Gentium*', art 2 (quoting a homily of
Gregory the Great); see art 1.
25. *Lumen Gentium*, art 26. '*Congregationes*', in the Council's Latin, is
usually rendered 'congregations' but, in 'church-speak', we are sometimes in danger of forgetting that congregations are gatherings!
26. *Lumen Gentium*, art 4. Which brings us back to 'church' as 'Lord's
house'.

mentative, conflictual – is something that human beings have done, to both their glory and their shame.

Nevertheless, the truth of this acknowledgement is not undermined by the deeper recognition that, in the last resort, everything we are and have is gift; that (to invoke Saint Anselm) our best and truest speech is not 'monologue', our solitary utterance, but rather 'proslogue': address, response, to each other, and to the holy mystery whose world-making Word it is which moves us to respond. Hence my initial characterisation of the church as the community of those who know the fundamental forms of human speech to be conversation grounded in response to that one Word in whom all things come to be. Which brings us to theology.

The Possibility of Conversation

Or should do, if theology is, as I suggested earlier, the vastly varied forms of language in which such knowledge finds expression and through which it seeks some understanding. Yet ours, it seems, is a community in which almost everyone, from the undertaker to the cardinal, assumes theology not to be their business. This can only mean either that we have a strange view of theology, or that we have a rather curious attitude towards the gospel's truth. If it is true, then surely it is – interesting? And, if it is interesting, then is it not worth talking about, and thinking about, and making some attempt to understand? And what are the innumerable and endless exercises of our attempts to understand – from the questions of the child to the adult's cry of agony before the darkness of the world; from the meticulous explorations of the scholar to the poet's refreshment of narrative and imagery worn too smooth with casual use – what is all this vast and endless labour but the work of Catholic theology, the conversation of a community concerned to make its speech conformable with the music of God's eternal Word?

If these are not, for the vast majority of Catholics, the connotations of 'theology', then this may be, in part, because of the extent to which confession of the gospel's truth has become dissociated from the sense that Christian life consists in the unending labour of making this truth ours. It would, I think, be difficult to overestimate the challenge which the healing of such dissociation poses to the speech and practice, ritual and imagination of the church.

The one who 'suffered under Pontius Pilate' is said to be the 'utterance' of God, God's Word. Or, to be a little more exact, that man is said to be the appearance in our human history of the Word through whom all things come into being. Everything there is is grounded in God's utterance: *a fortiori*, it is that utterance which grounds the possibility of every human utterance, and hence of the possibility of common conversation between the fractured and disputatious peoples of the world; that utterance which underlies the possibility of fostering the global imagination which we so desperately need. This, at any rate, is the suggestion that I now want to unpack a little.

To talk of 'conversation' is to talk of language and (so deep-laid are the scars of dualism) this may mislead us into supposing that the recognition of our common humanity is something which first happens, as it were, 'inside our heads': that 'recognition' is a mental act. And yet, when strange tribes meet, it is each other's physical behaviour which they watch, to which they react. The recognition that the stranger is a fellow human being entails an element of mutual vulnerability, a requirement that a kind of trust be mutually offered – and accepted, or betrayed. (We might consider the history of the handshake as a parable of this.) In other words: underlying the conviction that global conversation may be possible is an openness to the sharing of a common human life which is, in turn, grounded in an acknowledgement of mutual vulnerability, a common trust.

Human beings are creation's 'speaking part'. We are the things that can, and must, articulate the drift and sense of things. 'Can', maybe, but how come 'must': where does a sense of obligation enter in? We are, as George Steiner put it, 'at liberty to say anything',[27] but whereas the frivolous nihilisms of post-modernity construe such liberty as licence (the tone is usually petulant: 'I can say what I want'), the liberty to say anything is better understood as the burden of our responsibility to attempt to speak the truth in an almost unbearably dark and complex, almost (it seems, at times) illegible, and hence unutterable, world.

Steiner is highly critical of the Wittgenstein of the *Tractatus* – a text which ends, notoriously: 'Whereof one cannot speak, thereon one must remain silent.' 'For the *Tractatus*, the truly

---

27. George Steiner, *Real Presences. Is There Anything* in *What We Say?* London: Faber and Faber, 1989, 53.

"human" being ... is he who keeps silent before the essential.'[28] Such insistence on keeping silent before the essential, now so pervasive in our society, may wear the masks of modesty or 'mysticism' to disguise our abdication of responsibility. We 'keep silent' before God, and truth, and justice. We 'hold our peace', and, in the silence, millions starve and die.

Many people still suppose that, with the God whose utterance grounds all human speech forgotten, and with silence kept about the things that really matter, we might settle for some modest, homespun humanism, some comfortable common sense. That is not, in fact, how things work out. Increasingly, in place of serious conversation, cacophony takes the form of a dangerous and unlovely combination of, on the one hand, strident and destructive *monologues* – the cultural, political, scientific and religious fundamentalisms which drown out courtesy and attentiveness on every side – and, on the other, what Steiner calls '*kitsch* ideologies'.[29]

To be human is to be able to speak, to say 'Yes' or 'No': to be able to *respond* to places, times, and people – and, perhaps, to God. Steiner handles, with impressive honesty, the difficulty (in our supposedly 'post-religious' culture) of giving intelligible expression to the recognition that the possibility of *speech* – of attending to and responding to each other – is grounded in the possibility of *prayer* – of attending to and responding to the silence of God's Word. He puts it this way: 'The embarrassment we feel in bearing witness to the poetic, to the entrance into our lives of the mystery of otherness in art and in music, is of a metaphysical-religious kind.' If that seems to be making rather heavy weather of it, do not forget that the 'witness' he is bearing is borne by one who would not, I think, easily classify himself as a believer. He goes on: 'What I need to state plainly here is both the prevailing convention of avoidance, and my personal incapacity, both intellectual and expressive, to overcome it adequately ... Yet the attempt at testimony must be made and the ridicule incurred. For what else are we talking about?'[30]

If, then, there is a sense in which the fundamental form of speech is prayer, response, our words' acknowledgement that all things come into being through the Word that is with God in

28. *Real Presences*, 103.
29. Ibid., 230.
30. Ibid., 178.

the beginning, the Word that God's own self is said to be, of what kind of prayer are we speaking? Of praise, for example, gratitude for all gifts given, or of petition, acknowledgement of need?

I remember, many years ago, having an animated debate about this with the late, great Herbert McCabe. I was arguing for praise, or gratitude, and Herbert for petition. Over the years, I have come to realise that the question was not well posed, the alternatives unreal. What is at issue is the creature's relation to the Creator, a relation which only human beings, the speaking part of things, can voice. That relation is one of radical contingency, of absolute dependence. Of ourselves we are, quite literally, nothing. This might suggest that the fundamental form of speech, of the 'voicing' of this relationship, should indeed (as McCabe insisted) be that of petition, because we are in need of absolutely everything. The creature is absolutely beholden to the Creator.

And yet, there is something wrong here. We do not need to *ask* for our existence. It is already given. It is as constituted creatures with an identity, a history, that we express, articulate, give voice to, our creaturely condition. If McCabe was not quite right, however, it does not follow that I had the better argument, and that it would be more accurate to say that the fundamental form of prayer is gratitude for what we have been given. Why not? Because the language of gratitude and praise does not, in itself, sufficiently express the continued absoluteness of contingency, of our dependence on the mystery of God. Moreover, neither answer, neither 'praise' nor 'petition', makes mention of the connection between our relationship to God and our relations with each other, and yet the latter are, of course, the expression of the former (as the twenty-fifth chapter of St Matthew's gospel spells out at some length).

The fundamental form of speech is prayer. What kind of prayer? We could do worse than call it 'contemplation', as defined by Rowan Williams: 'Contemplation,' he says, 'is a deeper appropriation of the vulnerability of the self in the midst of the language and transactions of the world.'[31] The notion of 'vulnerability' neatly combines recognition of contingency, of the creature's absolute dependence on the mystery of God, with the

---

31. Rowan Williams, 'Theological Integrity', *New Blackfriars* 72, 1991, 148.

point that I made earlier to the effect that the possibility of global conversation is grounded in openness to the sharing of a common human life which is, in turn, grounded in acknowledgement of mutual vulnerability, of common trust. To be human is to be able to speak. But to be able to speak is to be 'answerable', 'responsible', to and for each other and to the mystery of God.

Hospitality and Conversation: the Road to Emmaus

The darkness of the world is beyond all explanation. Which is why we speak about the 'mystery' of evil. We too often forget, however, that goodness is a mystery as well; that kindness, generosity, the 'giftness' of reality, is also beyond all explanation. 'Religious thought and practice make narrative images of the rendezvous of the human psyche with absolute otherness, with the strangeness of evil or the deeper strangeness of grace'.[32]

I like that: 'the deeper strangeness of grace'. The one example of such a 'rendezvous' which Steiner mentions is the meeting on the road to Emmaus. There is, I believe, an immensely important lesson to be learnt from the emphasis which all the gospels place upon the difficulty of recognising the risen Christ. What does God look like? The figure hanging on the crucifix. But to recognise this figure as the human face of God is to recognise the risen Christ.

As the disciples walked the 'seven miles' towards Emmaus, they were 'talking with each other about all these things that had happened'.[33] A lot of talking, but they did not know what to say (a familiar state of affairs, in theology and elsewhere). The stranger who joins them on the road does not change the facts. 'Jesus of Nazareth who was a prophet mighty in deed and word before God and all the people' (as they tell the stranger – a typical piece of Christian behaviour: telling God who he is!); Jesus of Nazareth remains, as they say, 'condemned to death and crucified'.[34]

What the stranger does, as he takes them back through the history of Israel, and the scriptures which they thought they knew so well, is to give them an entirely new sense of what has been going on. 'Were not our hearts burning within us?' they say later, as they gradually begin to see the point; begin, we might say, to speak a new language.

---

32. Steiner, *Real Presences*, 147.
33. Luke 24:13, 14.
34. Luke 24:19, 20.

At the end of the road, the context is one of hospitality: they invite the stranger in. He is the guest; they are his hosts. At least, this would have been so, in the old language. What they discover, when they are at table, is that it is they, in fact, who are the guests, recipients of hospitality; and that it is he who is the host.

And then, at last, 'they recognised him; and he vanished from their sight'.[35] That last phrase is, perhaps, misleading, because the one who 'vanished' was the kind of man you meet along the road: one in the figure of a human being bounded, as all human beings are, by mortality. What they 'recognised', as they began to see the point, was his new presence as the bread he broke, the life he shared, at this beginning of that new conversation which is, for all eternity, uninterruptible.

---

35. Luke 24:31.

Jesus, Prayer and Politics

Sean Freyne

One of Enda McDonagh's many talents is his gift for the pithy but challenging phrase, often expressive of a seeming paradox, which subsequently is illuminated through his penetrating reflections. One such essay of Enda's which deserves repeated reading is his 1979 article 'Prayer and Politics.'[1] This title suggested itself to me when I sought for an appropriate subject for this collection to honour his life and work. I have simply added Jesus to the title, as I propose to explore how the seeming paradox might apply in his case also, especially in view of current interest in the quest for the historical Jesus over the last 25 years.

In his essay, Enda seeks to explore the intrinsic connection between these two aspects of Christian existence, the contemplative and the active, each of which has given rise to different forms of Christian living over the centuries. Prayer is provocatively described as 'the liberation of God' insofar as the active recognition of God's self, which is the essence of prayer, 'allows, even enables God to be at home in God's own world.' (102) Once our recognition of God is informed by the Judeo-Christian story, our awareness of ourselves is also enlarged so that we perceive our identity as part of the global family, but within a particular historical setting. 'Prayer should impinge on our felt experience of ourselves,' he writes. 'Otherwise the deepest structure of our existence and identity will not enter into the conscious formation of that identity in a creative way.' And the phenomenon that is experienced is not an isolated 'God and me,' but rather 'God and us.' (107) Prayer, therefore, opens us up to political engagement, broadly understood, insofar as it reveals to us our true identity as part of the one family before God, and makes its welfare our immediate concern.

To pray for the kingdom of God is to pray for the realisation

---

1. Reprinted from *The Furrow* (1979) in Enda McDonagh, *The Making of Disciples*, Dublin: Gill and Macmillan, 1982, 99-111.

of the values of the kingdom now in the society where we live. Thus, politics, understood as our efforts to realise those kingdom values through our actions and our witness, leads us back to prayer. Social action gives rise to an awareness of the value of the other, especially those others who through circumstance, misfortune or systemic distortions have not been able to achieve their full potential as human beings. Being open to such people inspires us 'with awe before their mystery, humility and gratitude before their diverse talents and achievements'. We begin to feel more deeply about the puzzles and paradoxes of the world. Entering into their mystery and their pain extends us beyond our own concerns. Thus we are drawn into the 'transforming mystery' of the other, giving rise to attitudes of 'wonderment, awe, humility, thankfulness, forgiveness' – all characteristics of genuine prayer. (110) Thus, in the light of the doctrines of creation and incarnation the human other is a mediation of 'the ultimate other we call God,' who, as defined by the life, death and resurrection of Jesus of Nazareth, has been revealed to Christians as the God of love.

Throughout 'Prayer and Politics' the stress is on an incarnational theology in which Jesus' response to the Father is seen not just as paradigmatic for the Christian response to the God of love, but as enabling it. As befitted the theological climate of the time the pattern of the response rather than the detailed description of how it was achieved within the confines of Jesus' own history was what really mattered. In this particular article Enda was concerned with elucidating the relationship between prayer and politics for Christian discipleship today, in the light of Christ's total obedience to and acceptance by the Father. Developments since then suggest that the issue may also be profitably raised for Jesus himself with a view to fleshing out the details of Jesus' response more fully. Over the past two decades there has been an explosion of interest in the historical Jesus and many different and competing accounts of his life and ministry are currently on offer. From a christological perspective, one positive outcome of this trend is the challenge it poses for an understanding of the humanity of Jesus, expressed not in abstract terms but within the historical particularity of his own life situation. Starting from a consideration of what Karl Rahner once described as 'Jesus' human spiritual history,' the task is to conceptualise his relationship with God in such a way that his freedom to choose, his uncertainty and his struggle to understand God's will was not a given, but had to be worked out within the actual circumstances of his engagement with his own cultural context. As the author of the Epistle to the Hebrews so poignantly puts it: 'In the days of his flesh he offered up prayers and supplications with loud cries and tears to him who was able to save him from death, and he was heard because of his obedience.' (Heb 5:7) It should be noted that the author makes this very explicit reference to Jesus' spiritual struggle, despite the 'high' christology which he espouses throughout the letter.

What distinguishes this 'third' quest for Jesus from its nineteenth century predecessor, however, is the thoroughly secular context within which the debate is conducted, giving rise to a Jesus without Christianity, in some instances at least. The 'biographic' framework of the gospel narratives is jettisoned for a new narrative, which is the construct of modern concerns. In this late twentieth century account of Jesus, often presented in the guise of objective history, he appears either as a wisdom teacher espousing a Cynic-like detachment from political engagement, or alternatively, as a social revolutionary, who seeks to generate communities of resistance to Roman imperialism.[2] The impact of Jesus' spiritual life or his understanding of God on the shape and pattern of his ministry is rarely, if ever, discussed. Neither account, however, does justice to the gospels' portrait, and in what follows I propose to examine how the prayer of Jesus is presented in the gospels within the context of his actual ministry. Was it merely exemplary for Christian discipleship, or did the evangelists wish to suggest that it played a central role in the way in which his ministry evolved? A second step will be to suggest how insights from the gospel narratives might plausibly be suggested for the historical Jesus also.

Prayer and Politics in the Gospels
The fourth gospel presents an interesting point of departure for the investigation, despite the fact that it is generally accepted to be later than the synoptics. This gospel has been known as 'the spiritual gospel' since the patristic age, and for very obvious reasons. We may no longer find Clement of Alexandria's explan-

---

2. See Sean Freyne, 'The Quest for the Historical Jesus: Some Theological Reflections,' in *Texts, Contexts, Cultures. Essays on Biblical Themes*, Dublin: Veritas, 2002, 106-121.

ation of its difference from the other three altogether convincing, namely, that the evangelist decided to deal with Jesus' inner relationship with God, because he was aware of the synoptics' account of his public ministry. Today, various explanations, historical and sociological, are put forward to explain the Johannine christology, with its emphasis from the opening prologue on the unity between Jesus and the Father, as the *Logos* incarnate. This unity is expressed in functional rather than ontological terms, but the emphasis is clear and unambiguous: 'He who sees me sees the Father,' (Jn 10:30), and again, 'I and the Father are one (thing).' (Jn 14:9) Statements like these, or images such as light, life, water, bread, are to be found on almost every page, underlining the highly developed thinking of the author(s) about the divine origins and other-worldly character of the Jesus who is presented in this work. Indeed so successfully is this aim achieved that apparently a branch of the community to whom the gospel was addressed misunderstood its position to the point of denying the humanity of Jesus altogether. (1 Jn 1:1-4; 2:22; 4:2)

In the light of this it is surprising to find any reference to the prayer of Jesus in this gospel. His life is presented in such a light that the reader is repeatedly reminded that Jesus is in constant communion with the Father and this union of mind and will can be expressed in terms of his obeying the Father, doing the Father's will and allowing the Father to do his works through him. Prayer and politics in this account are identical, except that the Jesus of John's gospel is virtually apolitical in terms of an ongoing engagement with the social realities within the narrative world of the work. In this regard Rudolph Bultmann's remark that 'the Jesus of the Fourth Gospel reveals that he is the Revealer,' is highly pertinent. 'The world' is a generic term, referring to the theatre of Jesus' revelatory activity, inhabited for the most part by those who reject Jesus, characterised in the prologue as 'his own,' but who throughout the work are mostly named 'the Jews'. Jesus' actions are designated as 'his works' or 'his signs', both terms rich in theological significance. The pattern of the narrative episodes is such that the discussion quickly moves from the issue of human need (wine, food, bread etc) to another plane where the significance of the action for a proper recognition of Jesus as the Revealer becomes the sole point of the discussion. Likewise, very few of the sayings or longer discourses attributed to Jesus reflect real life situations similar to those attributed to him in the synoptic gospels.

Because of the dense character of the narrative it is all the more remarkable that the Jesus of the fourth gospel is represented as engaging at all in prayer. Twice he prays in a public way – at the tomb of Lazarus (11:41f) and at the entry to Jerusalem (12:27). On both occasions it is made clear that the prayer of Jesus in the first instance and the reply of the voice from heaven in the second are for the 'sake of the bystanders' and not because of any uncertainty or need on the part of Jesus himself. In both instances the prayer functions to remind the reader of the continued union between Father and Son, the confirmation of which is not required by Jesus personally. It is because of this controlling feature of the Johannine thought pattern that the concluding prayerful monologue of Jesus to the Father in chapter 17 is the highpoint of the account. On closer examination, this 'spiritual ascent to God' – to borrow C. H. Dodd's description of the chapter – is a summary of Johannine theology: the abiding union of the Father and the Son, despite the temporary separation while Jesus has been in the world; the union of the disciples with Jesus; their faithfulness to the word that Jesus has given them; the hostility of 'the world' and the ongoing dangers within which the community lives, as well as the hope for shared communion with God similar to that of Jesus.[3] His concern for his own is expressed in a prayer of petition that they would be saved from 'the evil one.' (17:15) There are echoes here of the Lord's Prayer of both Matthew and Luke, but whereas that prayer is concerned with the realisation of the kingdom and its values in terms of food for the hungry and the cancellation of debt within the on-going struggles of the world, the prayer of Jesus in John is concerned with the community's role in witnessing to the world after the pattern of Jesus, thereby continuing the 'crisis/judgement' of the world, which he initiated. Thus, while the Johannine Jesus may not be political in the obvious sense of the word, his revelatory role in manifesting the darkness of the world and its lack of love has the most profound 'political' implications. Faced with such tragedy of non-recognition of its true identity, politics in the normal sense of the term is irrelevant. Yet the aspiration for a community of believers living out their faith

3. Charles H. Dodd, *The Intepretation of the Fourth Gospel*, New York and Cambridge: Cambridge University Press, 1953, 417-23, especially 419.

as envisaged in this work would have been acknowledged as being deeply subversive. It is altogether probable that one strand of this faith is represented in the 'Johannine' writing, *The Revelation of John*, where Imperial Rome is viewed as Babylon the Great, whose imminent destruction can be celebrated (Rev 18).

If we move from the fourth gospel to the first in point of time, namely, Mark's, we abandon a setting of almost mystical union where prayer seems almost superfluous, to a much more messy world of cripples, demoniacs, hungry crowds and frightened disciples. Yet both works share a sense of hidden mystery surrounding the person of Jesus. In John's gospel this is communicated through the repeated misunderstandings, ironic twists and veiled manifestations that dot the narrative. Mark, on the other hand, creates his sense of mystery through various devices, such as the separation of his audiences into insiders and outsiders, sudden withdrawals of Jesus at crucial moments of apparent 'success' and repeated commands to people to remain silent about their insights, when such would seem to be impossible. Jesus' prayer seems to fit into this realistic, if strange world, climaxing, not in a prayer of union as in John, but in a cry of apparent despair: 'My God, my God, why hast thou forsaken me?' (Mk 15:34)

Apart from this cry on the cross, Jesus prays three times in the gospel, each at moments of breakdown in relationship between him and his disciples. The first occurs after a day of successful healings. Jesus left Caphernaum 'a long time before day' and went to a 'desert place' to pray, only to be 'hunted down (like a wild beast)' by Simon and those that were with him. They want him to return to the scene of his triumph of the previous day, thus affirming their honourable status as brokers of the healer figure, for whom all are searching. However, Jesus refuses to return and presses on to other towns and villages, focused not on the adulation of his admirers, but on the purpose of his coming. (Mk 1:29-39) The location of this first occasion of prayer, described as 'a desert place' recalls the 'desert' where, driven by the Spirit immediately after his baptism, Jesus had spent forty days considering the implications of the voice from heaven that had proclaimed him the messianic Son. (Mk 1:9-13)[4]

Unlike Matthew and Luke, Mark does not recount separate

---

4. Freyne, 'Mark's Urgent Message,' in *Texts, Contexts and Cultures*, 86-92.

temptations of Jesus, but it can be safely assumed that the reader is to understand Jesus' refusal to share the disciples' enthusiasm for the crowd as a rejection of the temptation to be a false messiah. These are categorised later by the Markan Jesus as those who 'deceive by signs and wonders even the elect' (Mk 13:20). As has rightly been stressed in a number of recent studies, Jesus' actions in expelling demons and healing the sick were political to the core in a Mediterranean culture, in that they removed the social stigma attached to certain classes of people who were regarded by the ruling aristocratic elites as social deviants. By restoring such people to the world of normal social relations, Jesus was providing an alternative vision of community, one that threatened those who established the norms for inclusion and exclusion in the first instance. It transpires a little later in Mark's narrative that Jesus regards his actions as an attack on Beelzebul's realm, further described in terms of the destruction of a kingdom and a house, already divided against itself, and so destined to collapse (Mk 3:22-32).

There may well be a subtle allusion here to the Herodian dynasty, Rome's representative in the Galilee of Jesus' day. In true apocalyptic fashion they are designated as representatives of the present evil age, whose demise is assured in and through the advent of God's kingdom, which Jesus is charged to proclaim and enact. But it is God's kingdom, and Jesus' silence in the desert and in his moment of 'escape' at Caphernaum ensured that his actions could never be divorced from the source of his power, namely, God's, not Beelzebul's, Spirit. Rather than adopting the 'easy' choice of a militant messianism, a ready option in Roman Palestine of the first century, Jesus chose another way, one that was symbolically more powerful and more pregnant than any act of terrorism against the occupying force. His politics were determined not by human motives of greed, resentment or self-service, but by an understanding of God's way of inclusive justice. Mark seems to be well aware of this connection between prayer and politics in Jesus' ministry. Was he equally conscious of its importance for his Christian readership of the late first century, whether these were in Nero's Rome where Christians were being scapegoated for the social ills of Imperial indulgence, or in Palestine, which was busily gearing itself for war against the might of Rome's advancing armies?

Mark strikes another note of messianic caution in chapter 6.

Here the temptation again comes from over-enthusiastic disciples. They shared Jesus' healing powers and were elated by their successes, only to show their elitist attitude by suggesting that Jesus send the crowd away hungry. They are anxious to show their status within the messianic community but Jesus, in an action reminiscent of Yahweh's concern for the physical needs of the wandering Israel in the desert, feeds the crowd first and then dismisses the disciples, forcibly, it would seem, before departing again to a mountain alone to pray (Mk 6:30-46). This cluster of scenes – feeding in the desert and crossing of the sea – inevitably evokes for the attentive reader Israel's experience of liberation from Egypt. It is noteworthy that according to the Jewish historian, Josephus, a return to the desert was one option taken by sign prophets, deeply disaffected by Rome's imperial presence in the land in the first century AD. In that light the feeding miracle and its setting has all the symptoms of a possible messianic uprising, something that John's gospel makes explicit, with its statement in the parallel scene that the crowd wanted 'to take Jesus by force and make him king,' causing him to flee alone to the mountain (Jn 6:14f). It would seem that when it came to messianic uprisings of a popular kind, even Jesus' own disciples could not be trusted. Again, we must suppose that Mark wants us to understand Jesus' prayer as his way of confirming for himself that there was a way other than that of popular uprising by which to realise the messianic dream, no matter how attractive that option was for many in Roman Palestine of the first century, including, it would seem, those who found Jesus an inspiring figure in other respects. Jesus was not eschewing political engagement. Rather, he was operating with a different image of the messianic hope to that of the populace at large. It is significant that among some recently discovered fragments of messianic texts from Qumran several refer to the messianic age as one of peace and an end to war, echoing Isaiah's great prophecies (Is 9:2-7; 11:1-9), and thereby offering an alternative to the more usual image of the messiah as a militaristic figure who would rid Israel of her enemies.

The third account of Jesus' prayer in Mark, that in the garden of Gethsemane (Mk 14:32-42), also offers the possibility of a reading in an alternative messianic key. The symbolic group of the Twelve have been Jesus' constant companions in the days of feverish excitement in Jerusalem, sharing something of the atmosphere of the city, its buildings and its throngs of people in a state of high messianic expectation on the occasion of the great feasts. But Jesus will have none of it. After the Passover supper he takes Peter, James and John with him to the garden – the three among the group of the Twelve who had been given special names in the Markan list (Mk 3:16f). Mark paints a picture of Jesus as sorrowful and conscious of the challenge he was now facing, the cup that the Father had given him to drink and which he wanted to be rid of. His prayer was one of petition that he might be able to carry through the lonely and difficult messianic role he felt called on to fulfil, which now, it would appear, was about to end in failure. He expects the companionship and support of the specially named three leaders of the group, but they were oblivious to their role, once again showing their all-too human attitudes, sleeping when they should have been watching with Jesus. As in the episode in chapter 1, the leader is addressed as Simon, not Peter, the new name he had received to indicate his new role, a role he had singularly failed to live up to throughout the narrative (Mk 8:33; 14:50). Jesus' final prayer on the cross – My God, my God, why have you forsaken me? – which preceded the loud cry accompanying his final gasp, was for Mark, deeply ironic. For the evangelist, God had rewarded, not abandoned, Jesus, and his messianic movement was now again being asked to opt for the more difficult way of a peaceful kingdom, when faced by the might of Rome. Jesus' prayer had not been in vain because Mark's narrative ensures that the memory of his alternative politics of God's, not Rome's kingdom, could continue to function after his death.[5]

Both Matthew and Luke share a common source, an early collection of sayings of Jesus, which contains the 'Our Father', the prayer which Jesus gave to his disciples. Presently we shall examine in more detail Luke's presentation of our theme of prayer and politics, since of all the evangelists, his is the most developed treatment in both aspects of Jesus' career. By contrast Matthew is sometimes regarded as having 'spiritualised' the more radical social demands of the gospel, as for example, in his rendition of the beatitudes in the introduction to the Sermon on the Mount. 'Blessed are the poor' becomes 'Blessed are the poor in spirit,' and 'Blessed are those who hunger' is rendered as

5. Richard A. Horsley, *Hearing the Whole Story. The Politics of Plot in Mark's Gospel*, Louisville, London, Leiden: Westminster, John Knox Press, 2001.

'Blessed are those who hunger and thirst for righteousness' (Mt 5:3-10). However, this impression ignores what Matthew means by 'righteousness'. Throughout his work this concept is developed in an ethical, rather than a theological manner as in Paul, to refer to the new way of discipleship of Jesus. In this respect the evangelist's rendering of the 'Our Father' is particularly significant in terms of the present discussion. Jesus' prayer and that of his disciples is for the coming of the kingdom, but in the first part of the prayer Matthew adds a petition in line with his ethical concerns: 'Thy will be done.' Furthermore, in the second half of the prayer Matthew's use of the terms *opheilema*, which literally means 'debt', (as distinct from Luke's *hamartia*, meaning 'sin') in conjunction with *aphienai*/release' has a clear echo of the Jubilee programme of Leviticus 25, which deals with economic-debt release.[6] Thus, at the very centre of the prayer of Jesus as rendered by Matthew, social, and by implication, political concerns are emphasised, together with the desire for union with God, which is expressed in the longing for the realisation of the kingdom. A similar pattern can be discerned in the great 'community discourse' of Matthew chapter 18 where the ideals of forgiveness, reconciliation and care for 'the little ones' – all ethical norms enjoined in the Sermon – are underpinned by reference to the community's life of prayer, following the example of Jesus: 'Wherever two or three are gathered in my name, there am I in the midst of them.' (Mt 18:20)

As already indicated, it is in Luke's gospel that we meet the most developed account of the connection between prayer and political concerns in the life of Jesus. Luke's second volume, *Acts of the Apostles*, shows just how aware he is of the larger political arena within which the Jesus-movement must operate. It is a fine line between writing an apology for the movement which presents it as no threat to Roman imperial order and at the same time re-presents the radically subversive nature of Jesus' ministry *vis-à-vis* that order in the context of the movement's growing attractiveness for the upwardly mobile inhabitants of the Greco-Roman cities.[7] This was Luke's task, as he saw it, and it is conducted with style and imagination in his two-volume opus.

6. Michael H. Crosby, *House of Disciples. Church, Economics and Justice in Matthew*, Maryknoll, New York: Orbis Books, 1988, 188-91.
7. Jerome H. Neyrey, ed. *The Social World of Luke-Acts. Models for Interpretation*, Peabody, Mass: Hendrickson Publishers, 1991.

The beginning of the gospel story is set in the context of both Palestinian and imperial politics: the census that brought Jesus' parents from Galilee to Bethlehem and the political synchronisation that marks the beginning of the public ministry (Lk 1:5; 2: 1; 3:1). The story ends with Paul in Rome, having appealed his case to the imperial court, and yet actively engaged in meeting with the Christian community in the city (Acts 28). Rome and its world of domination is one constant horizon within the Lukan optic. At the same time, Jerusalem, the holy city, is also central to Luke's presentation. Not that Jerusalem is always friendly and welcoming. Indeed it is impossible for a prophet to die outside Jerusalem, since it has had a history of killing those who were sent to it (Lk 13:33-35). Above all Jerusalem is the religious centre, and Luke chooses to begin the story of Jesus at the hour of sacrifice in the temple with the appearance of an angel to Zechariah, the father of John the Baptist, as the people waited outside praying. The first volume closes on a similar note with the disciples at prayer in the temple as Jesus had departed from them into heaven (Lk 1:8-12; 24:53). Politics and prayer, Jerusalem and Rome, are inextricably intertwined in the Lukan story of Jesus.

These two horizons which frame the whole story are fully exploited by Luke in his presentation of Jesus' ministry also. Whereas Mark is sparing in his depictions of Jesus at prayer, Luke seldom misses the opportunity to emphasise this aspect of his career. Alone of the evangelists, Luke emphasises the importance of prayer for Jesus at the pivotal moments of his career: at his baptism when the heavens opened (Lk 3:21), when he is about to encounter the scribes for the first time (Lk 5:16), when he enquires from his disciples as to their views about his identity (Lk 9:18), when he ascended the mountain of transfiguration (Lk 9:29), and when he taught his disciples the Our Father (Lk 11:1). In all these instances prayer is not an escape for Jesus but provides the context and impetus for the deeper understanding of and engagement with the mission with which he has been entrusted. In particular, the baptism and transfiguration scenes are pivotal and pregnant with deeper meaning in terms of Jesus' prophetic ministry 'to the poor, the crippled, the blind and the lame' (Lk 14:21), that is, the marginalised in terms of both the Jewish religious cultic system and the dishonourable outsiders on the scale of the Roman honour/shame culture.

At the baptism the heavens are opened as Jesus is at prayer and the Spirit descends on him, even as a heavenly voice confirms him as the beloved son, with whom God is well pleased (Lk 3:21-22). This scene has been rightly understood as a confirmation of the messiah for his mission to all Israel. Luke merely alludes to the actual baptism, concentrating instead on the heavenly communication. This is described subsequently as his 'anointing' for his messianic mission (Lk 4:18; cf Acts 4:27), when, in the synagogue at Nazareth, Jesus claims that the Spirit of the Lord has anointed him to preach good news to the poor, liberation for captives, sight for the blind, and the acceptable (Jubilee) year of the Lord (Lk 4:14-18). In between the baptism and this programmatic statement of his prophetic ministry Jesus is led by the Spirit to the desert to encounter Satan who offers him an alternative role to that of the prophetic messenger of God. However, he rejects any idea of a messiahship based on power and prestige in favour of one that is at the service of those in need. Thus, Luke clearly establishes for his readers that Jesus' public ministry is from the start under the guiding influence of the Spirit of God. His prayer life is his point of contact with the power that directs and shapes his ministry, enabling him to resist the blandishments of power and privilege. Jesus has clearly triumphed in this first phase of his struggle with the powers of evil and he can proceed unfettered to a ministry of consoling and healing. Satan, we are told, only leaves him 'until an opportune time' (Lk 4:13). The ministry will bring its future temptations also, and Luke will not miss the opportunity then to remind us of the real source of Jesus' power to resist.

The transfiguration scene at the mid-point of the narrative constitutes a second pivotal moment in this drama of a ministry that challenges the value-systems of both Jerusalem and Rome. Following a moment of prayer, Jesus poses the question of his true identity to the disciples and his messiahship is acknowledged, however insecurely, by Peter, (Lk 9:18-20). However, Jesus immediately indicates the path of suffering and rejection that this would involve for him and for the disciples. Once again there is need for communing with the divine before this new phase of 'turning his face to go to Jerusalem' can be undertaken (Lk 9:51).

Luke's version of the transfiguration story itself has several distinctive features (Lk 9:28-36). It is while Jesus is at prayer that

the appearance of his face was transfigured and his clothes became dazzling white; his conversation with Moses and Elijah
concerns the exodos that he is about to accomplish at Jerusalem,
and at the conclusion of the scene the bewildered disciples too
are covered by the cloud from whence the heavenly voice comes
confirming Jesus' role as pointer for their own lives in obtaining
the status of God beloved children. In Richard Kearney's words
this is 'a saturated event' in which 'Jesus comes into his own,
being "othered" as Christ.'[8] His person transforms into the *persona* latent in his self, 'the very distinctive otherness of his finite
being, his in-finity.'

In his highly suggestive reading, Kearney adopts the approach of a phenomenologist-hermeneut, seeking to retrieve the
story's meaning rather than dealing with all the exegetical and
historical questions that the account gives rise to. He notes in
particular how the disciples' fearful and confused reactions to
the experience differ from those of Moses and Elijah, who 'appear in glory.' The former want to hold to this moment of presence, whereas the latter, who have already in the biblical narrative themselves resisted the temptation to idolatry, challenging
imperial powers in the process, can speak freely with Jesus of his
'going out' which must take place in Jerusalem. At stake in this
dense narrative are contrasting notions of Jesus' messianic status
and its implications for his politics of the kingdom. The disciples,
like Satan in the temptation story, are interested in co-opting the
Jesus of glory, turning him into a cult object, whereas Jesus himself and his two prophetic forerunners acknowledge that messiahship implies a process of becoming his true *persona*. This occurs in and through his struggle to realise the values of God's
kingdom rather than acceptance of the values of either Rome or
Jerusalem, a struggle that can symbolically be described as his
exodus. In Kearney's words, the presence of the two biblical fig-
ures 'is a reminder that the transfigured Christ is a *way*, not a ter-
minus, an *eikon*, not a fundamentalist fact, a *figure* of the end, not
the end itself.' If the disciples are to learn this truth, they must
obey the words spoken to them in the cloud: 'listen to him.'

8. Richard Kearney, *The God Who May Be. A Hermeneutic of Religion*,
Bloomington Ind: Indiana University Press, 2002, 39-52, especially 40-
44. See also Barbara E. Reid, 'Prayer and the Face of the Transfigured
Jesus,' in James H. Charlesworth ed., *The Lord's Prayer and Other Prayer
Texts from the Greco-Roman Era*, Valley Forge, Pa.: Trinity Press
International, 1994, 39-53.

During the final scenes in Jerusalem, this emphasis on the prayer of Jesus intensifies as his concern is expressed for the disciples, faced with the great trial of witnessing to the gospel in the world after Jesus' departure. The 'opportune time' for Satan's return, alluded to at the end of the temptation story, has arrived at last and the disciples are in danger of succumbing. At the last supper Jesus informs Peter that he has prayed for him so that he might 'confirm the brethren' whom Satan had sought to sift like wheat (Lk 22:31). This information is part of his farewell speech to the Twelve in which he praises them for having persevered with him in his trials (*peirasmoi*), while promising a future participation at the messianic banquet in his kingdom because of their faithfulness (Lk 22:28-30). However, when Peter suggests that he has armed himself with a sword he is rebuked, since he clearly has misunderstood the nature of the struggle for kingdom values that Jesus has been engaged in. His challenge is not engagement in a violent revolution but rather the living out of an alternative value system to that of imperial Rome and its allies such as the Jerusalem aristocratic elite.

The scene in the garden, which is focused on Jesus' own agony in both Matthew and Mark, becomes for Luke the occasion to admonish the disciples three times to pray earnestly 'so that they would not enter temptation' (Lk 22:39-46). Once again Luke has used the same quasi-technical term *peirasmos* for the tribulations facing the disciples, a clear echo of the 'Our Father' prayer which he had taught them and which, by association, we are lead to believe, was his own prayer also (Lk 11:1- 4). In addition to the social concerns already indicated, this prayer also has a highly apocalyptic colouring. The trial in question is the final struggle between the forces of good and evil which, according to various apocalyptic scenarios, would usher in the new age. Even though Luke, unlike Mark, does not anticipate the end of this drama soon, the apocalyptic *schema* of history is retained in order to underpin the mission of the church and the life of discipleship in Luke's own day. The vocation of the church is to continue Jesus' mission in the world 'until the times of the gentiles are fulfilled' (Lk 21:24), and that means that it must continue the prayer and politics of Jesus 'gathering in their homes for the breaking of bread and prayer' (Acts 2:46) and 'turning the world upside down' (Acts 17:7) by their radical and inclusive lifestyle which constituted a 'values revolution' as far as the elite of Roman society was concerned.

The Prayer of Jesus and his Politics

Reference has already been made to the fact that the recent discussion of the historical Jesus has focused on his public activity, with little or no attention to what would be regarded as his inner life. This emphasis has to do with the search for criteria of authenticity, which can be defended in the court of secular history. The question of Jesus' inner life, especially his prayer life, was in an earlier generation bound up with the question of his 'messianic consciousness' that is, the levels of Jesus' self-awareness when viewed from the perspective of later christological faith. Karl Rahner's remark already alluded to, showed how difficult it was for even progressive theologians to take the humanity of Jesus in full seriousness. If, following the fourth gospel, one attributes to the historical Jesus the consciousness of the eternal *Logos* (as in fact Rahner does) then it is a very short step to the scholastic debates about Jesus' threefold knowledge – experiential knowledge, prophetic knowledge and beatific knowledge. Clearly such a *schema* leaves little room for Rahner's 'human spiritual history' in any meaningful sense, which should not be denied to a truly human Jesus.

It is not difficult to point to the problems with such an approach from today's standpoint. In particular, it seems difficult to imagine how one could attribute to Jesus prayer in the sense of 'turning the mind and heart to God' on the supposition that he already enjoyed the beatific vision in his human state. Inevitably, there has been a reaction, and even the question of Jesus' messianic consciousness is now only rarely discussed in the current crop of books about the historical Jesus. It is only with the publication of the Messianic fragments from Qumran in recent times that scholars have felt free to reopen the issue as an historical question. It is now recognised that to ask the question of Jesus' possible awareness of his messianic status should not be dismissed in the name of critical scholarship in view of the fact that it is possible to reconstruct a number of different types of messiah in the late second temple period, and point to several individuals who seem to have appropriated one or other of these during the first century AD. There would seem to be no plausible historical reason for not at least allowing for Jesus also to have thought of himself in that role in some distinctive fashion. The issue then becomes, not whether Jesus might have thought of himself in messianic categories, but rather what specific understanding of the messianic profile might he have appropriated or displayed and how was this 'received' by various strands of Judean society at the time.[9]

As the preceding survey has demonstrated, all the gospels in their different ways relate Jesus' prayer to the acknowledgement of his messianic status both by himself and by others. In Mark it seemed to be directly concerned with the failure of the disciples in particular to understand a deeper dimension to his person and ministry. Luke's emphasis is on the exemplary character of Jesus' prayer for his community as it comes to terms with its role of continuing Jesus' prophetic ministry of 'good news for the poor', thereby challenging Roman imperial values, just as he had done long ago in Galilee and Jerusalem. Matthew includes the prayer of Jesus for the coming kingdom in his great synthesis of Jesus' moral instruction, the Sermon on the Mount, which constitutes the messianic charter for the true Israel. Indeed many of the instructions of the Sermon itself, as well as others in the five discourses that dot the narrative flow of this gospel, can be seen as commentary on the 'Our Father'.[10] This pivotal location of the prayer of Jesus has the double effect of insisting that the ethical life of the community is grounded in the realisation that it is God's kingdom that is anticipated and lived, while at the same time ensuring that the moral concerns of the community's daily existence are not lost in some other-worldly contemplation. The fourth gospel, despite its emphasis on Jesus' divine status from the start, still does not hesitate to present Jesus at prayer at the poignant moments of the narrative, most especially as his impending 'departure' from 'his own' comes closer. Again the emphasis is on the manner in which the community will function in a hostile world in the absence of Jesus, and the prayer is one of petition for their unity, replicating the unity of Jesus and the Father in which they have been privileged to share and to which they are now being asked to witness in the unbelieving world.

If early Christian imagination placed such importance on the prayer of Jesus as an integral part of his public life, it is surely plausible to suggest that they did so because this was a well-remembered feature of his career. Indeed the prayer of Jesus made

9. Sean Freyne, 'A Galilean Messiah?' *Studia Theologica*, 55, 2001, 198-218.
10. Mark Kiley, 'The Lord's Prayer and Matthean Theology,' in Charlesworth ed., *The Lord's Prayer*, 15 –27.

such an impression that already at an early stage of the community's life a version of that prayer in its original Aramaic form had already been passed on to Christian groups in Asia Minor (Gal 4:6) and Rome (Rom 8:15). One does not need to follow the claims of uniqueness which Joachim Jeremias made for the *Abba* formula on the lips of Jesus, to recognise its importance for his own self-understanding.[11] If one is looking for the distinctive voice of Jesus' prayer it is important to see the address, *Abba*, not standing alone in splendid isolation as a sentimental term of endearment or as an expression of special closeness with God.

Rather it should be understood as the introduction to his particular version of the *Qiddush ha-Shem* prayer from his Jewish upbringing which we have inherited as the 'Our Father'. Such a comparative approach underlines Jesus' grounding in the spiritual longing of Israel, yet also highlights the particular concerns which he brings to his prayer, originating in the concrete experiences of his ministry. In particular the tension between the eschatological urgency of his millennial dream and the social needs for daily subsistence are clearly reflected. It is this latter aspect – the combination of social concerns with the wish for eschatological fulfilment – that distinguishes Jesus' prayer from its Jewish antecedents and allows us to see how integrally prayer and politics were combined in his life.

For Jesus the experience of a divine calling finds a particular expression at the baptism and in the subsequent period in the desert under the guidance of the Spirit. It was this encounter, so the evangelists would have us understand, that transformed him from the apocalyptic prophet of imminent judgement, following his teacher John the Baptist, to the one who would proclaim and enact a different understanding of God's kingly rule. This was to involve an on-going struggle with his Jewish followers to appreciate the newness of his vision, disabusing them of some of their preconceived notions of both the messiah's role and the nature of God's rule. Jesus' confidence in his own experience must have been shaken and challenged by their repeated failure to understand the purpose he had set himself and their efforts to have him adopt a different role. In this light his *Abba* prayer may not have differed greatly from that of others like Elijah and Jeremiah within his own tradition, who had been

---

11. Joachim Jeremias, *New Testament Theology. The Proclamation of Jesus*, English translation, London: SCM Press, 1971, 61-68 and 178-203.

called by God to speak the unpopular or unfamiliar message, and who had communed with their God in the hope of being relieved of their difficult burden.

This relationship between his prayer and his healing ministry is dramatically illustrated in the Beelzebul controversy, of which there are two independent versions (Mk 3:22-32; QMt 12:22-30 = QLk 11:14-22). This episode has all the hallmarks of originating with the historical Jesus, with his Jerusalemite opponents trying to discredit the 'mighty deeds' of this provincial 'holy man' by attributing them to Satan rather than to God's Spirit. Jesus' reply is to appeal to the Spirit with which he has been endowed as the true source of his power and inspiration. It is this Spirit that makes him 'the stronger one' to whom John the Baptist had earlier referred (Mk 1:7), a metaphor that Jesus himself draws on to explain his actions: he is the one who can enter 'the strong man's house' because he can 'bind' the strong man, and therefore plunder his goods (Mk 3:27). As already mentioned, Jesus' deeds were not just individual cures but highly political acts of including those whom Roman aristocratic values and priestly religious taboos had excluded to the margins of life. His confidence to continue on such a collision course stemmed from his consciousness of being endowed with the Spirit of God, not the spirit of this evil age. When challenged, it was to the inner confidence in the divine call and the divine assistance that he appealed as legitimation for his actions. It was to the same well-springs that he would return when faced with the impending failure of his project in the garden and on the cross. To paraphrase again the words of the author of the Epistle to the Hebrews, 'his loud cries and tears,' of which these two incidents are just examples of an-ongoing process in his life, 'the days of his flesh,' were heard because of his trust in, and respect for the God whom he believed had called him to this difficult and dangerous mission (Heb 5:5-10).

'To raise one heart to God is to be open to his coming, not only in oneself, but in all others.' Enda McDonagh's insightful meditation from a Christian perspective on the links between prayer and politics was intended to bridge the often yawning gap between piety as practised by many people of goodwill and their apparent lack of concern for 'justice, peace and the integrity of creation.' It has also provided an important starting point for a consideration of how one might begin to consider this relation-

ship in Jesus' own personal life, following the lead of the evangelists, an aspect that has been notably absent from so much
recent discussion of the historical Jesus. Enda's own words provide an eloquent conclusion to such a discussion also, when he
writes: 'This dependence on human response for God's emergence as God of love in human history may be traced through all
the covenant relationships with humankind. It naturally found
its critical and normative form in Jesus Christ. Here God took on
fully the human condition. In the life and death of the man Jesus
God was admitted in the fullest way to the very centrepiece of
his own creation. God was finally and fully at home in his
world.'[12]

---

12. 'Prayer and Politics,' 101 and 103.

Sustaining Connections:
The Field of Ecumenical Social Ethics

Geraldine Smyth OP

'Only Connect'

At the end of EM Forster's novel, *A Passage to India* set in colonial India in the early twentieth century, we encounter Dr Aziz and Captain Fielding who have managed despite injustice and ethnic snobberies to sustain a friendship that tested their courage to an extreme. They come together for a morning ride following a long period of cultural rift, tentatively hoping to re-establish connection. The final scene recalls what they actually achieved in that inter-cultural friendship, but in the end it seems but provisional and ambivalent. This is gestured in their two horses finally swerving apart taking them on their different paths. It was as if the whole physical, religious and social geography rose up against them, whispering in a million voices, 'No, not yet ... No, not there.' But, that they had managed for a while to resist such forces, that they had co-inhabited for a while a strange space, touches the moral imagination and inspires the hope that by such failed attempts are closed worlds prised open to disclose a glimpse of another possibility.[1]

Roots and Directions

Whatever the constraints of the title, and notwithstanding the attempts of those who would throw an ugly ditch between ethics (claimed as a science) and theology (deemed a soft discipline and at worst, church-regulated dogma), I will hold – since the context of the discussion here is Christian – for a necessary, and necessarily critical, connection between theology and ethics.

While rightly insisting that ethics are not derivative from nor subordinate to theology, Enda McDonagh asserts, '[like] person and community, they belong together and exercise mutual influence'.[2] In this context he adopts a fourfold moral structure – of

---

1. E. M. Forster, *A Passage to India*, Harmondsworth: Penguin, 1979, 316.
2. See Enda McDonagh, *The Gracing of Society*, Dublin: Gill & Macmillan, 1989, 52-63.

truth, justice, freedom and peace – as at once, 'social virtues' and 'kingdom values', the former with a philosophical provenance reaching back to Plato and Aristotle, and the latter, shaped by the biblical-theological reality of the reign of God, inaugurated by the presence and power in history of Jesus Christ.[3] This correlation is not without its demands. Enda McDonagh acknowledges some of the distinctive challenges involved, including the in-eradicable social nature of the human person, and the 'persistent difficulty of distinguishing the many overlapping, intertwining and sometimes conflicting societies to which people belong … religious, cultural, economic, political, ethnic, familial …'[4] But whatever the difficulties as theologians of society or as Christian ethicists – struggle we must with this complexity if our ethics are to be truthful, ecumenical and social.

We shall have more to say later on the need for adequate ways of mapping the nature and complexity of these mutual interactions. But, it can be noted with satisfaction that McDonagh – with his preferred term of designation – a 'theological ethics of society', can be adduced in the case for sustaining strong rather than weak connections between ethics and theology, with his emphasis on 'the social nature of humanity, salvation and grace, and finally of God', as the only setting 'proper for Christians to discuss the issues usually treated in social ethics.'[5]

Writing from a Reformed and equally ecumenical perspective, Duncan Forrester, has traced the emergence of the discipline of ecumenical social ethics from Christian ethics and Christian practical theology (itself a distinct discipline in the late eighteenth century, which combined – according to Schleiermacher – 'scientific spirit' and 'ecclesial interest'). Insisting with Karl Barth that all theology is practical, Forrester points to liberation theology as one of its most radical expressions of relevance and rigour, and claims that it has broadened the range of the subject 'beyond the narrowly ecclesial' to encompass the whole field of practice, proposing and pioneering ways of relating theology, social analysis and practice in mutually fruitful ways, without falling into 'either the trap of idealism or the barrenness of materialism.'[6] We cannot but agree with Forrester that if ecclesial

3. Idem., 59.
4. Idem., 51.
5. Idem., 49.
6. Duncan B. Forrester, *Truthful Action: Explorations in Practical Theology*, Edinburgh: T&T Clark, 2000, 31.

interest is abandoned, Christian ethics is likely to lose its
grounding within a particular community of faith in the real
world and therewith, one might add, its living connection with a
tradition that includes prophetic memory and liturgical imagination. But, conversely, if its scientific spirit weakens, Christian
ethical discourse easily degenerates into an in-house code without claim to public truth or significance,[7] thereby rendering itself less capable of the kind of interdisciplinary analysis and exchange that is increasingly required in a world in which the poor
and hungry are so conveniently shuffled from view. If it loses its
critical edge, theology will drift back towards dogmatic slum-
ber. However, if Christian ethics contents itself with a precari-
ous or snug seat at the table of public policy, it is difficult to see
where it can find its sustaining roots and guiding vision.[8] Thus,
it is necessary to seek for a sustaining connection. On another
front, an analogous debate is being waged in terms of argued
preferences for a Christian communitarian approach rooted in
the particularities of the biblical narrative and an inner constructive hermeneutic, or for a Christian liberal-universalist approach
capable of finding some middle ground and mutually critical
correlations with other disciplines and belief systems. Linking
back to Schleiermacher, with more recent articulations from
Paul Tillich and David Tracy, ethics in this tradition are characterised by possibilities of mediation, dialogue and critical accountability. Of this, more later.

The Emergence of Ecumenical Social Ethics
Turning Points and New Departures
Having examined some of the broader challenges and deeper
presuppositions in the correlation between theology and ethics,
in what follows, the World Council of Churches will be the reference point in highlighting some historical, thematic and
methodological developments in ecumenical social ethics. The
field of ecumenical social ethics has expanded throughout the
twentieth century, influencing the dynamic and focus of the ecumenical movement through the disruption of two world wars,

---

7. Forrester, op. cit., 43.
8. Following McIntyre here Forrester concludes that as morality and theology become evacuated of concerns with truth, they too will become
matters for private allegiance, ironically forfeiting academic credibility,
Forrester, op. cit., 50.

decades of Cold War deterrence and the radical redefining of international relations after 1989. From its beginnings, the ecumenical movement interpreted the commitment to unity as intrinsically related to the search for freedom, peace, social justice, and more recently, to the integrity of creation. Ecclesiology and ethics were seen to be connected, primarily through a one-way imperative of mission.

Thus could Ernst Lange describe 'the ecumenical movement [as] itself the advance of Christendom from a no longer tenable position – that of parochialism – into the wider horizons of the inhabited earth, the inescapable context of the human development of mankind [sic]'.[9] Visser't Hooft, one of the veteran founders of the WCC argued for this nexus of ecclesiology and ethics with his negative claim that 'Church members who deny their responsibility for the needy in any part of the world are as guilty of heresy as those who deny this or that article of faith.'[10]

This has been the case increasingly since theology's turn to society in the 1960s, which was the context for an international WCC Conference on Church and Society in Geneva, 1966.[11] The impact of liberation theology was already at work: debates were heated, and the conference was to prove a turning point. It was followed by decades of contestation on the method by which the WCC should do theology and ethics in a structurally divided church and world. At its first meeting of the Ecumenical Society of Third World Theologians (EATWOT), in Dar Es Salaam, 1976, this methodological concern was explicitly linked to issues of power, and in their message, theologians declared 'an epistemological break' with an academic theology divorced from action. Insisting that theology is not neutral, the association challenged theologians to be self-critical in relation to their conditioning by the dominant value system. They argued that theology's first act ought to be commitment and 'critical reflection on praxis', con-

---

9. Quoted in *The Ecumenical Movement: An Anthology of Key Texts and Voices*, Geneva: WCC, 1987, 6.

10. Ulrich Duchrow and Gerhard Liedke, *Shalom: Biblical Perspectives on Creation, Justice, Peace*, Geneva: WCC, 1987, 38.

11. See World Conference on Church and Society, July 12-26 1996, *Christians in the Technical and Social Revolutions of Our Time: Official Report*, Geneva: WCC, 1967.

tending that henceforth theology must be done alongside the victims – those on the underside of history.[12]

Following the Fifth General Assembly of the WCC in Nairobi in 1975, by which time the churches of the South had come to make a stronger impact on ecumenical concerns, Philip Potter, the West Indian General Secretary of the World Council of Churches, denounced the abject failure of trickle-down development and of neo-colonial dependency theories, calling for the liberation of the church from its imprisonment in Western social and cultural forms:

> The whole burden of the ecumenical movement is to co-operate with God in making the *oikoumene* an *oikos*, a home, a family of men and women, of young and old, of varied gifts, cultures, possibilities, where openness, trust, love and justice reign.[13]

Taken together these statements outline an ecumenical vision that is ethically responsible, culturally diverse and ecclesiologically inclusive. It must be admitted, however, that in the subsequent two decades, as ecumenical social ethics more fully evolved as a proper disciplinary field, the protagonists of the ecumenical movement became engaged in a debate about how best to integrate the spheres of ethics and ecclesiology. Between the WCC General Assemblies of Vancouver (1983) and Canberra (1991) the working focus was that of the 'Conciliar Process (Covenant) for Justice, Peace and the Integrity of Creation.'

This culminated in a World Convocation at Seoul in 1989, when the full scale of the problem came into view. Despite the claim at Vancouver that all the ethical challenges constituted one struggle for life, which required from the churches a unified response, what characterised Seoul was the failure to find an integrating theology and ethical vision. A closer look at this Seoul Convocation yields findings relevant to the analysis in hand.[14]

---

12. See Theo Witvliet, *A Place in the Sun: Liberation Theology in the Third World*, London: SCM, 1985, 27, 33ff.

13. Philip Potter, 'One Obedience to the Whole Gospel', *Ecumenical Review*, Vol 29, No 4, 1977, 38.

14. *Seoul Final Document: Justice, Peace and the Integrity of Creation*, Document No 19, Geneva: WCC, 1990.

*World Convocation on Justice, Peace and the Integrity of Creation,
Seoul, 1989*

Responses to the Seoul Convocation vary from disappointed to
scathing. I shall argue that it was a significant learning experience and turning-point for ecumenical social ethics. The best
level of agreement that could be reached came in the form of Ten
Affirmations on a range of ethical issues. There were too many
foci, and too many protagonists, all striving desperately to make
their specific interests the primary focus – human rights, land reform, debt relief, gender equality, empowerment of youth, the
integrity of creation, etcetera. The difficulty can be seen as a crisis
of limits. This was dramatised in the failure to find a suitable
framework – large enough to encompass the range of ethical and
ecclesiological concerns and methods, yet without loss of common vision and commitment. It was an impossible task.[15] In the
end, no consensus could be arrived at on a Final Message; just
Ten Affirmations, four formal covenants, and a multiplicity of
specific covenants between diverse churches and groups.

To some insiders, social ethics in the WCC was in disarray,
and a group of 'Friends' gathered for a series of meetings to
mount their critique: that the WCC's theology and ethical analysis
was insufficiently rigorous, was reliant on shock-tactics, issued
unfocused rallying calls on too many issues, and had developed
over-reaching liberationist models. These were deemed to have
contributed to the Roman Catholic Church's shyness of structured collaboration.[16]

One may partially concur with the diagnosis. I would argue,
however, that the deeper problem was linked to the confusion

---

15. With more than 800 participants representing churches from every
continent, including an official Catholic presence, even the plan to focus
on developing three inclusive covenants corresponding to the three
overarching themes of economic justice, peace and the integrity of creation – could not be adhered to. The anti-racism protagonists were
strong enough to achieve a fourth covenant on that topic. See my *A Way
of Transformation: A Theological Evaluation of the Conciliar Process of
Mutual Commitment (Covenant) to Justice, Peace and the Integrity of
Creation, World Council of Churches, 1983-1991*, Berne: Peter Lang, 1995,
especially Chapter 4.

16. Paul Abrecht (previous and long-time Director of Church and
Society) and Ronald Preston were among the critics who were known
as the Vancouver Group. See, Ronald H. Preston, *Confusions in Christian
Social Ethics: Problems for Geneva and Rome*, London: SCM, 1994, 167-178.

besetting social ethics in general, including methodological con-
troversies over the precise nexus of praxis and theory and conflicting perceptions over the degree of influence of liberal or liberationist ideologies. Within the WCC these two approaches
had run side by side at least since 1970. The older Church and
Society Unit's 'ecumenical social realism' emphasised individual freedom and social responsibility, and operated with predominantly Western lay experts advising on ecumenical
processes, usually within a church-state framework, on specific
centrally decided issues. There was also the parallel structure of
the Commission on the Churches' Participation in Development
(CCPD) which focussed on the Just, Participatory and Sustainable Society programmes (JPSS), which reflected different thematic priorities and methodological approaches, was less cent-
ralised and more interested in the churches' involvement with social movements and civil society than with state-centred politics.

The 'Friends' group, chafing under the dominant liberationist influence of CCPD in the WCC warned of the danger of
collapsing theology and ethics into politics. We shall comment
further on the subsequent attempts at reconciling these approaches within the WCC. But one point should be underlined
here: For all the apparent differences in approach, in point of
fact, each position drew their guiding biblical metaphors,
christological images and ecclesiological models from the political sphere. Whether related to Exodus, Covenant, the Kingship
of Christ or the Kingdom of God, the respective ethical visions
were politically derived, within the tradition of God's saving
acts in history, rather than arising from the creation-wisdom
tradition of *shalom* and blessing that might shape an ethics of
abundant life. I shall argue later that a sustained dialectic of
(various) politically-based ethical approaches with an ethics of
abundant life, is demanded, instead of forcing a choice between
liberal or liberation approaches in theology and ethics.[17]

Staging Conflict
Standing back, one can argue that the best role for the WCC (or

---

17. See Geraldine Smyth, in cooperation with Jesse Mugambe and Peter
Scherle, *Liberating Communion*, Unit III, Justice, Peace, Creation,
Geneva: WCC, in which these movements are described in terms of a
dominant current (Church and Society), a cross current (CCPD) and a
sustaining undercurrent (Theology of Life/Ethics of Abundant Life).

any worldwide ecumenical body) is that of intermediary; that the WCC does well to assume responsibility for 'staging the conflict' already there in terms of the clashes of interest and diverging ethical methodologies. As at Seoul, the energy and focus were not to be found in the plenary meetings or in the production of agreed statements. Besides the four formal covenants, the spontaneous, even chaotic emergence of small-scale mutual covenants between churches or quasi-ecclesial groups witnessed to a vitality and desire for interrelationship. There was an energy too, arising from shared faith convictions and solidarity. The Ten Affirmations also gave substance to people's suffering and struggles, and suggested an integrative framework.[18] One 800 strong, week-long convocation could not harness these energies. But the need for this was glaringly obvious.

The WCC did in fact read the signs, did pick up the threads to form the basis of a more integrating model. In two important strategic decisions following Canberra, the WCC would take on the role of intermediary and catalyst by facilitating a process of local-global alliances. This 'Theology of Life' process was structured around the Seoul Affirmations. Thus, for example, churches in India and Germany would co-operate on the affirmation that God's option is for the poor; churches in Brazil and Australia, on the affirmation on the equal dignity of women and men, created in the image of God, and so forth. Joint study and exchange, team visits and shared learning opportunities would be sustained by WCC resources, but with the essential agency coming from the joined-up case-studies. The various twinned groups would gather later for a common meeting in Nairobi in 1997. This *Sokoni* (traditional African marketplace) affirmed a vision and praxis that was thoroughly local, yet was an expression of catholicity and held out the prospect of unity.[19]

18. This would be structured via the WCC's, *Theology of Life* Programme and in a number of sustained study processes which were intentionally based on systematic collaboration between Faith and Order (Unit I), and Justice, Peace, Creation (Unit 3). See below.

19. See Special Feature Issues of *Echoes*, October 1996, on *Theology of Life*, Geneva: 1996; on *Sokoni*, January 1997; also, Report of Concluding Consultation on 'Theology of Life' Project, Union Theological Seminary, NY, *Working on Theology of Life*, Unit III, Geneva.

Staging Peace

Reading the *Sokoni* accounts one can acknowledge the WCC's ecumenical role not merely in staging conflict, but also in 'staging peace', by creating a space for fostering a 'worldwide communion of particular local embodiments of acted-out, shared, obedience to the gospel'.[20] Such global gatherings *rooted in preparatory local-to-local interaction* symbolically create a theatre wherein energies for an alternative transcending ethical-ecclesiological vision can be expressed and shared. In such ecumenical spaces people come in their diversity, break the bread of their lives and of the Word, united in story and song, lamenting, praising, sharing pain and thanksgiving. In sharing faith, prayer and liturgy, they ritualise the root memories that sustain them and the hopes that inspire them in their pilgrim journey.[21]

The second strategic decision related to a mandate to the two bodies linked into the WCC, the Faith and Order Commission, and the Justice, Peace, Creation Unit. These bodies were to collaborate strategically and in an in-depth way.[22] As in every

---

20. See Konrad Raiser, *For a Culture of Life: Transforming Globalization and Violence*, Geneva: WCC, Risk Books, 2002, 145-146. Interestingly, Raiser draws heavily in this short book on Robert Schreiter's *The New Catholicity: Theology Between the Local and the Global*, Maryknoll: Orbis, 1997.

21. This was repeated at the Eighth WCC Assembly at Harare, 1998, through the *Padare* (Shona word for 'Market-place') an open space where any interested group had the freedom to set up stall or activity. As days wore on one experienced the vibrant sense of the disparate groups coming to share their multifarious cultural and spiritual struggles, dreams, projects and gifts, thereby transforming the public space into a global *ekklesia*.

22. One of these was addressed to the Overcoming of Violence, which so far has combined theoretical approaches via conferences and also support for practical initiatives such as the 'Peace to the Cities' Campaign, whereby a constructive ecumenical peace initiative has been supported in seven cities: Rio, Boston, Belfast, Colombo, Durban, Kingston and Suva (Fiji) with networking and solidarity links being facilitated. Another has been a joint study process on Ethnic Identity, National Identity and the Unity of the Church. These were given heightened visibility and support at the Eighth Assembly of the WCC in Harare 1998, which also made the decision to initiate the Decade to Overcome Violence (which came into effect in 2001); see also, *Overcoming Violence: WCC Statements and Actions 1994-2000*, ed. Eskidjian and Estabrook, Geneva: WCC, 2000.

decade of the twentieth century, protagonists in the ecumenical movement have had to make a conscious effort to sustain a self-critical interaction between visions of church unity and social responsibility amid unrelenting violence, injustice and ecological degradation. Yet, there is within the ecumenical movement a returning conviction of the significance of its founding purpose, together with a conviction of the need to imagine itself along the double helix of ecclesial and ethical transformation.[23]

Two Contesting Approaches
There is no doubt that there is a need for wider dialogue with people of other beliefs. But this should not detract from the urgency of ecumenical engagement between churches, recognising that Christian unity is both gift and task, open to the grave ethical challenges of our day. It is now necessary to look more closely at the two well-established approaches to doing Christian ethics. Following this general assessment, it will remain to be seen if a kind of double vision can be maintained, in the interests of keeping the ecumenical way open to different ethical perspectives. With this in mind reference will be made to some current reflections on ethics and ecclesiology in the WCC which suggest that these seemingly divergent approaches can be interconnected towards an ecumenical social ethics that is both effective and expressive of the Christian way within in the public domain.

Following the publication of Alisdair MacIntyre's *After Virtue*, there has been a re-assertion of the communitarian vision so keenly observed by de Tocqueville, against the tide of the prevailing individualism and in the face of what McIntyre described as procedural, managerial and therapeutic society.[24] Stanley Hauerwas' presentation of this approach is found in *The Peaceable Kingdom*. Clearly, Hauerwas has no desire to see the Christian community circle its wagons and shut out the world. However, he does argue that morality is bound to a particular tradition, and for Christians, the inspired narratives of belonging are formative and normative. Christian morality has no meaning outside the story-formed community. Thus, Christian

---

23. Konrad Raiser, *Ecumenism in Transition: Paradigm Shift in the Ecumenical Movement?* Geneva: WCC, 1991.
24. Alisdair MacIntyre: *After Virtue: A Study in Moral Theory*, Indiana: University of Notre Dame Press, 1981.

ethics is addressed to the church and only indirectly to the world, through the witness of lives rather than through pretences to a universally appealing moral discourse.

By contrast, the Christian liberal position seeks to transcend the particularity of any one tradition. A plurality of particular worldviews may be endorsed, but not as a universalisable moral theory. Thus there is an imperative towards common foundations. Hence the importance of openness to other views, and the supposition that dialogue with other traditions is fruitful in promoting a sense of the common good. This position has a concern for the common good and resists the fideistic route that would set reason to one side or argue in apologetic terms from *a priori* beliefs deriving directly from biblical revelation, confessional dogma or church *magisterium*. Christian liberals are wont to remind communitarians that the human rights tradition arising from Kantian universalism, has been at least as responsible as the gospel-formed lives of Christians in effecting protections of individual conscience or legal enactments against slavery or child labour. Yet such arguments from whichever side are radically disrupted by the memory of the *Shoah*. We do ethics, like theology, with our backs to Auschwitz.

Christian communitarians must guard against sectarian fundamentalisms with absolute norms derived without any hermeneutical move from biblical texts, and against claims bound to unreconstructed confessional identities. And Christian liberals must recognise that rational appeals to thin theories of moral autonomy, dis-embedded from a particular community's suffering or hopes, do not sustain moral vision and energy, and can be morally impoverishing.[25] Each approach needs to be put into dialogue and mutual accountability with the other.

---

25. See Robert Gascoigne, *The Public Forum and Christian Ethics*, Cambridge: Cambridge University Press, 2001, 16-24. The author rightly argues for a reconciling of autonomy and community as a key aspect of the contribution of Christian ethics to public life, insisting that as a Christian one can hold a liberal pluralist approach to morality without resort either to universalist abstraction or particularist reduction. Provided one's view of revelation does not wilfully cling to a now theologically discredited propositionalism, there is still scope for avowing traditions of meaning and value as enriching and sustaining of rational-liberal claims.

From 'Either-Or to Both-And': Reconciling Signs in Ethical Discourse
No doubt it is fruitful for Christians and churches to be able to
call upon or engage both of these ethical approaches in different
measure and in different contexts.[26] Clearly critical judgment
and sensitive discernment is called for, as is the capacity to cross
the grain of one's own preferred model together with a willingness to scan the horizon for the signs of the times. Thus Mary
Robinson's indefatigable advocacy for human rights and ethical
globalisation, as President of Ireland or UN High Commissioner
was matched by her awareness of the need for a dream that inspires. Hence her constant affirmation of small community
groups working in marginal spaces of civil society for human
well-being and social co-operation. We need a paradigm that can
relate rights to needs, that can sustain solidarity, and keep hope
alive even as the campaigns for civil and religious liberties are
being waged.

One can almost agree with Hauerwas on the narrative basis
of all moral reasoning and yet, one must put a question in both
directions: first, can secular moral enquiry exist cut loose from
religious narrative?; and second, by what complex means does
religious narrative underwrite moral reasoning? Habermas asserts the possibility of an ideal speech situation wherein inter-
locutors' speech claims can be submitted to a process of scrutiny
and emancipation from morally blinding presuppositions, and
from cultural or religious biases and interests. But even in an
ideal speech situation, the inherent problem of how to arrive at
agreed critera by which conflicting ethical claims and positions
can be adjudicated remains.

The work of Seyla Benhabib is *à propos* here in that she insists
on the need to speak not simply of some 'generalised other', but
of a 'particularised other'. Within the paradigm of a communic-
ative (as distinct from a communal) ethic, she argues for the
need to recognise the particularised other, but without relin-
quishing a universal horizon. She calls for an

---

26. See James Gustafson's typology of modes of ethical discourse
(Narrative, Prophetic, Philosophical and Policy), proffered to the WCC
with respective identifying features and genre-aptness to particular
ethical challenges and communication purposes. This emerged from
his having been invited to examine the documentation of the Church
and Society sub-unit of the WCC over a number of years: 'An Analysis
of Church and Society Ethical Writings', *Ecumenical Review*, Vol 40, No
2, April 1988, 267-279.

interactive universalism [which] regards difference as a starting point for reflection and action. In this sense, 'universality'
is a regulative ideal that does not deny our embodied and
embedded identity, but aims at ... encouraging political
transformations that can yield a point of view acceptable to
all [through] the struggle of concrete, embodied selves, striving for autonomy.[27]
Thus discourse is seen to be narratively shaped through embodied experiences of suffering. But universalism is achieved
through interaction. Thus she recognises 'the dignity of the generalised other through an acknowledgement of the moral identity
of the particularised other' (164). Through actual communication and embodied experiences of grief, anger and struggle an
alternative can be found to what went before. Here, what is required is to see life from the point of view of another's experience. This 'reversibility of perspectives' creating an 'enlarged
mentality' becomes the basis of agreement for action and
change.[28]

In his appeal to the symbolic imagination pointing to integrating possibilities, the poet prayed, 'God guard me from those
thoughts men think/In the mind alone;/ He that sings a lasting
song/Thinks in a marrow bone.'[29] Thus, the opposite of a true
proposition is a false proposition, but the opposite of one pro-

27. Seyla Benhabib, *Situating the Self*, Cambridge: Polity Press, 1992, 153.
While calling for a redefinition of moral theory in gender terms,
Benhabib is not seeking either a moral or political theory consonant
with the standpoint of the concrete other (e.g. female), but rather to 'develop a universalistic moral theory, that defines the 'moral point of
view' in light of the reversibility of perspectives and an 'enlarged mentality.' 164.
28. Linda Hogan in her *From Women's Experience to Feminist Theology*,
Sheffield: Sheffield Academic Press, 1995 strikes a similar dialectic note.
She cautions those who make experience and praxis their primary theological categories, on the need to appreciate 'the truly revolutionary
character of these primary resources, since they place difference and
conceptual instability at the core of our theorising' (119). Arguing that
the commitment to such 'conceptual instability' as an analytic category,
without either opening the door to relativism nor avoiding common
bonds, is to 'adopt a risk-filled and thoroughly honest stance in relation
the universalising potential in our theology' (177).
29. W. B. Yeats, 'A Prayer for Old Age', *Collected Poems of W. B. Yeats*,
London: Macmillan, 1969, 326.

found truth may be another profound truth. Our epistemology must be grounded in the double vision of intelligent reason and symbolic imagination.

Bringing Different Approaches Together in an Ecumenical Social Ethics
The keystone of the argument in this essay is the need for social ethics to be ecumenical. This changes everything: our perception of ourselves and of our churches, our relationships with other religions and ideologies, and the way we approach ethical issues. Diverse confessional preferences open up a spectrum of ethical traditions that can be mutually fruitful rather than antagonistic: Eastern Orthodox, Reformed, Historic Peace Churches, to mention but three, can each with their respective hermeneutical keys for understanding the relationship of church and society ('liturgy after the liturgy', '*Status Confessionis*', 'Covenant', 'Witness') contribute to a unifying vision. Within the Roman Catholic Church even the characteristic natural law tradition admits dynamic interpretations which can be thoroughly grounded in creation, salvation, sanctification, and eschatology.[30]

But in this time of 'liquid modernity', the churches must risk new forms of interactive engagement with the world in all its instability and identity fragmentation. Such a process will change the churches' self-understanding and public engagement, will change too the social form of the church and ways of thinking and acting. Being ecumenical is precisely not about discovering the single grand unifying plan. In developing a social ethic, the whole world is our theatre, and it is an arena of competing ethical needs, clashing interests and different interpretations and ways of action. Within an ecumenical vision these conflicts should be recognised, not suppressed. Rather ecumenical bodies such as the WCC can help dramatise the conflict and provoke debate. This they do by bringing the actors together, by enabling processes of conversation and by facilitating exchanges between local contexts. In this they will take a quasi-political approach, alert to the complexity of competing rights; challenging sys-

---

30. See for example, Charles E. Curran, *The Catholic Moral Tradition Today: a Synthesis*, Washington: Georgetown University Press, 1999, 33, in which the author outlines the Catholic perspective in moral theology, proposing 'a horizon involving the fivefold Christian mysteries of creation, sin, incarnation, redemption and resurrection destiny as the stance for moral theology, the church and the individual Christian'.

temic abuses of power; taking sides with the poor against oppressive structures and advocating for legal redress on a range
of social and economic issues.

But in this theatre, the WCC and ecumenically oriented
churches or groups can call into play another kind of action arising from their own spiritual life and practice. This ethics of
abundant life provides a countervailing ethical approach, rooted
in faith and in celebration of the living, life-giving memory and
imagination of the Christian story. It knows how to create spaces
too where the faithful can gather and celebrate their creative and
saving visions, participate in symbolic rituals of resistance or
healing, and join in creation's groaning or praising. It must be
remembered however that these life-affirming visions are incor-
rigibly plural. There are gifts of abundant life to be shared – for
example in regard to a theological, ethical and liturgical understanding of creation. Yet however plural, when Christians gather
in *Sokoni*-type shared ecumenical spaces, the ecumenical imperative is one of respectful openness, mutual learning and shared
participation in the pluriform riches of the Christian story
whether mediated through the great Orthodox tradition of *doxa*
or from the ancient 'Songlines' of indigenous peoples.[31]

Both of these approaches – a politically-based ethic and an
ethic of abundant life are open to ecumenical expression and
have ecclesiological significance. Both are necessary for the
church's moral being and well-being. In a recent ecumenical
study on ecclesiology and ethics, ethical reflections are expressed in ecclesiological language, thus attesting to the need for
common ethical engagement by the church, within and across
its own boundaries. The sense of community 'though not ecclesial, may have implications for the way in which we understand
church in so far as such communities embody prophetic signs of
the reign of God, and bring not only the world, but also the
churches closer to God's mysterious purpose in the world.'[32]

---

31. See Myra Blyth, 'Praise, Prayer and Praxis: Connections Between
Liturgy and the Decade to Overcome Violence', *Ecumenical Review*, Vol
53, No 2, 206-215.

32. See Tom Best and Martin Robra, eds., *Costly Commitment, Faith and
Order-Justice Peace, Creation*, Geneva: WCC, 1995, pars 32-42, par 42
(also found in idem, *Ecclesiology and Ethics*, Geneva: WCC, 1997, pp 32-
36). The text here is in response to the challenge issued in the Final
Report of the Fifth World Conference on Faith and Order, Santiago de
Compostela, August 1993, on the real, but imperfect *koinonia* between

Ethical struggle and engagement is, as we have claimed above, implicit in the church's mission to the world, but also truly part of the *esse* and not just the *bene esse* of the church's life. If we understand the word 'ecumenical' both in terms of the church's mission to the world and of the churches' claims on one another, the logic is that there is an inherently ecclesial dimension to ecumenical witness 'across the lines of confession and tradition, and, through their common service, of 'being Christ for the other' (Martin Luther) in that place.' Must it not also be said that 'if the churches are not engaging these ethical issues *together*, then *none of them individually is being church*?'[33]

In a time when they are dedicating energy to renew their internal vision and practice as moral communities of formation, focused on their own story-forming identity, churches must also beware of the irony that they are so doing in the very time when they are losing their power of public moral influence and there are also signs in certain quarters of a self-absorbed preoccupation with 're-confessionalising' church identity. Remembering, renewing and passing on the gifts we have been given is part of who we are as communities of believers. And this is happening at a time when there seems to be no end to the possibilities of pluralism but where the test of being open to certain 'Others', can stretch too far our particular version of liberal pluralism.[34]

Christian churches, in their embodying of the NT practices of the apostolic community. See, *On the Way to Fuller Koinonia: Official Report of the Fifth World Conference on Faith and Order*, Geneva: WCC, 1994, pars 25-32.

33. Ibid., par 17. It should be particularly noted that although the Roman Catholic Church is not a member of the World Council of Churches, it is a member of the Faith and Order Commission in the World Council of Churches.

34. See *Ecclesiology and Ethics: Ecumenical Ethical Engagement and Moral Formation and the Nature of the Church*, ed. Thomas F Best and Martin Robra, Geneva: WCC, 1997. This relatively successful attempt to hold together this double focus in a dialectical way is the work of the joint Faith and Order and Unit III study procession in the 1990s (in which the Roman Catholic Church has been structurally involved through its Faith and Order delegates). While these models were acknowledged previously, this was perhaps the first self-critical debate on ecumenical social ethics. Ideas of the church as moral community and a neo-Aristotelian emphasis on self-conscious moral formation and commit-

Towards a Field Theory of Ecumenical Social Ethics
Under the influence of ecological insights and in a bid to find alternative visions of globalisation, ethicists and theologians of
society are increasingly thinking and speaking in spatial categories
to symbolise life in terms of an ethos and ethics of peace, security,
solidarity and community, lived within an ecology of the Holy
Spirit the sustainer of creation.[35]

Lewis Mudge, reflecting on the Eighth General Assembly of
the WCC, Harare, 1998 on the human impact of globalisation in
both the economic and communications spheres, speaks of the
discourse as including 'tactics and strategies of resistance', but
also of the assembly (and church) as a 'space for reconciliation'[36]
within the global sphere. He appeals to Schreiter's metaphor of
global theological flows and adds another – discourse about
democracy and civil society – to the existing liberationist, feminist, ecological and human rights ones. These he suggests exem-
plify 'a multitude of distinct cultural expressions ... without
sharing common theoretical structures', and manifest a species
of universality different from that of Enlightenment rationality.
Thus even churches and ecumenical bodies hold open a spiritual
and moral space for Christians of different cultures and traditions to gather and celebrate their community rituals in all their
revelatory power ('household of faith'). They also have a role in
creating spaces of 'moral hospitality' where dialogue with those
of other cultures, disciplines and religions can take place
through conceptual and symbolic exchange, informed by the
narratives and practice that 'stand behind them'[37] ('household

---

ment are reasserted (the metaphor of the Church as 'household', for example); yet there is also an internal struggle for a more robust engagement by the ecumenical church with the raw edge of poverty, economic
exploitation and the reduction of many to the status of non-persons.

35. This is reflected in the creation-pneumatological themes of the WCC
Seventh Assembly, Canberra, 1991; *Come Holy Spirit – Renew the Whole
of Your Creation*. See also, Jürgen Moltmann, *The Spirit of Life: a Universal
Affirmation*, trans Margaret Kohl, London: SCM, 1992.

36. Lewis S. Mudge, *Re-Thinking the Beloved Community: Ecclesiology,
Hermeneutics, Social Theory*, Lanham, Maryland: University Press of
America Inc, and Geneva: WCC, 2001, 260-261.

37. Lewis S. Mudge, op. cit., 264ff. These recurring spatial metaphors
suggest that the idea of a 'Field Theory for ecumenical social ethics' is a
metaphor with enormous potential whereby communications occur beyond the normal bounds of different disciplines and cultures.

of life'). Thus Konrad Raiser proposes that the *oikoumene* be construed as 'an 'energy field' of mutual resonance and recognition generated by the Holy Spirit'[38]

This 'field theory' was actually specifically referred to in ecumenical social ethics as far back as the Geneva Church and Society Conference, 1966. It is worth retrieving, for it holds the potential for re-imagining ecumenical social ethics by giving due scope to these three constitutive terms that comprise a field of disciplines, and in which, as we have seen, problems of incommunicability and moral incommensurability are rife. Thus, Geneva spoke of society as moving forward

> by means of the interaction of a vast number of decisions by both the humble and the mighty. Ethical ideals and great political religious symbols sometimes act not unlike a magnetic field on molecules of iron, exercising a certain drag and directional pull on each of the innumerable decisions, introducing a bias – towards good or ill – in the total result. These ideals and symbols can also have a direct influence on some important collective decisions. This creation of an ethical field is perhaps the most important task of the church.[39]

As if harking back to this Jürgen Moltmann, after the Canberra Assembly, spoke of energy, form and space as 'formative metaphors' connected to the life of the Holy Spirit. Thus,

> the divine Spirit is experienced as the Lord who sets free, and the free space in which there is no more cramping … and the people who have this experience know that they are kept safe and set free in the broad space of the spirit in which they can breathe deeply and unfurl their potentialities.[40]

One embodiment of this ethical field (in which one can imagine the Holy Spirit 'renewing the face of the earth') appeared through the Jubilee 2000 Campaign. Thus, the biblical structure of the Jubilee (Lev 25; Is 61; Lk 4), was given new meaning and effect in relation to the campaign to have the debts of the poorest countries cancelled, influencing governments and international

---

38. Konrad Raiser, *For a Culture of Life: Transforming Globalization and Violence*, Geneva: WCC, 2002, 155.
39. *The Church in the Technical and Social Revolutions of Our Time*, op. cit., par 60.
40. Jürgen Moltmann, *The Spirit of Life: a Universal Affirmation*, op. cit., 277.

financial bodies in an unprecedented way.[41] The significant thing in terms of an ethical field theory is that this revelatory symbol-structure was rendered ethically effective in a totally innovative way when harnessed to a secular moral imagination and economic strategy. 'Let me not to the marriage of true minds admit impediments' exclaimed Shakespeare. And Paul urging on his friends a shared way of seeing and thinking, sought them to be 'transformed by the renewal of [their] mind...' (Rom 12:2). These give intimations of faith, hope and love at work if we imagine ecumenical social ethics as a field of interactive life, vibrant with the sustaining power of the Spirit of all creation. A field theory of ecumenical social ethics is a symbol-structure which still has much to yield.[42]

As a renewed vision of the ecumenical comes into view, it calls for expression through action and confident relationships. But it needs to be modest and always on the way, ever on the alert to its own excluding pre-suppositions and ready to listen to alternative views. Visions stand in need of correction from those who stand outside or in sites of struggle, whether by choice or powerlessness. On the pilgrim journey towards a lived and living ecumenical social ethic, the churches will find that the gifts bestowed in risk or compassion are graces at once secure and insecure, and are known only as penultimate, experienced as here, now and as not yet. As with Forster's protagonists, Fielding and Aziz, our best ethical discoveries are provisional, born in liminal spaces where many voices echo, 'No, not yet ... No, not there', yet offering glimpses of an impossible moral possibility: 'Maybe now, perhaps there' ... Only connect.

---

41. See, *Real World Outlook: the Legacy of Globalization: Debt and Deflation*, ed., Ann Pettifor, Palgrave, London: Macmillan, 2003.

42. Margaret J. Wheatley, in *Leadership and the New Science: Discovering Order in Chaotic World*, San Francisco: Berrett-Koehler Publishers, says that fields can be conceived in different ways (gravitational, electromagnetic, quantum). Whereas in the Newtonian world space contained independent particles, the quantum field is conceived in terms of an 'implicate order' (Bohm's term) revealing hidden connections beneath the apparently discrete or dissonant events. In the quantum world 'space' is filled with invisible fields and non-material influences that can be observed only in their interactive effects. Fields carry messages and influences, and in our symbolic understanding – vision, values, concepts, culture, ethos and ethics.

The Church, Society, and Family in Ireland

Garret FitzGerald

Asked to contribute to a Festschrift in honour of Enda McDonagh, my instinct has been to write something related to an aspect of Irish family life, seen in the context of the church and society in Ireland. For he has for long been a part of our family, and I know of other families also – not just officiating as a priest at christenings, weddings and funerals, but sharing as a warm human being in day-to-day family life. This is, of course, just one aspect of a much-loved and multi-faceted man, whose many different aspects will, no doubt, ensure that this will be a very wide-ranging volume indeed.

I start with the fact that tensions between the individual and society lie at the root of the human condition. For the human being derives from a particularly social species of mammal, the ape, but by virtue of the development of a self-conscious intelligence has become a highly individualistic species.

The reconciliation of these two conflicting aspects of humanity poses a permanent ethical problem. On the one hand, the individual human being expects and is entitled to the respect due to a self-conscious being; on the other hand, individual human beings have to find a way of controlling their individualism to a sufficient degree to be able to live together in amity.

It has always seemed to me that a particular strength of the Christian Church has been the balance it has struck between the individual and society. The individual, seen as made in the image of God, is accorded huge respect, but the need for a social ethic to optimise relations between these individuals has been given equal recognition.

Of course Christianity derived from Judaism, to which much of the credit for this harmonisation of the individual and the social must be given. But building on this inheritance, Christianity produced a philosophically sophisticated ethical structure that in the broadest sense has stood the test of two millennia.

True, there have from time to time been aberrations. Some at least of the strictures of the Christian moral code as it has reached us after such a long period of time reflect *ad hoc* responses to specific past situations. Examples of this include the Council of Trent's over-reaction to the problem of clandestine marriages, which it declared to be invalid rather than illicit, or the continuing claim by the Roman Catholic Church, inspired by over-enthusiastic missionary zeal, to have the power to dissolve marriages with or between non-Christians where this might facilitate conversions to Christianity. And, more generally, a church with a celibate clergy clearly went over the top on the subject of some aspects of sexual behaviour.

But, overall, the balance maintained by Christianity between the individual and the social was well-judged – and in terms of optimising the human condition in society its ethic compares favourably with the extremes of both socialism and economic as well as social liberalism, as these developed in the nineteenth and twentieth centuries. Both of these 'isms' were challenged at different times and in different ways by the Roman Catholic Church in particular.

From the vantage point of the start of the third millennium, we can now view in perspective the events of those two centuries. Looking back in this way it seems to me that, however intemperate, and even at times apocalyptic, may occasionally have been some of the Catholic Church's criticisms of these two 'isms', the time and energy that it devoted to them reflected accurately the relative scale of the long-term threat that each posed to a balanced social order.

Only for a relatively short period in the mid-twentieth century did the church allow itself to become concerned primarily with extreme socialism which, for all the moral attraction of its appeal to justice and equity, ensured by its dismissal of the market system its own eventual failure.

From the start, the church's instincts were right in identifying the extremes of liberalism, in both their economic and social manifestations, as posing by far the most enduring threat to an ordered and just society. Economic liberalism's threat to the social order derives from its insidious appeal to human self-interest, often at the expense of social solidarity, while for its part extreme social liberalism appeals to human impatience at restraints on individual behaviour required for the good of society.

Both forms of liberalism involve much more powerful self-interested motivations than the concern for justice and equity that lies behind socialism, and the relative proportions of time and effort that the Catholic Church devoted in the nineteenth and twentieth centuries to what it identified as two rival secular heresies was well-judged. For a few decades in the mid-twentieth century it did focus its criticisms principally upon extreme socialism, but for most of the nineteenth and the remainder of the twentieth century it directed its strictures primarily at the threats emanating from extreme liberalism.

The fact that the Catholic Church seems to have judged wisely the relative magnitude of what it saw as two rival threats to a balanced social order does not, of course, mean that its specific critiques of either socialism or liberalism were always well-judged. In the nineteenth century, and especially during the papacy of Pius IX after his early shift to the right, it went totally overboard, even going as far as to denounce democracy – although that curious throw-back to attitudes close to those of the *ancien regime* was firmly and quickly corrected by his successor Leo XIII.

The radical changes in society that have taken place since the end of the nineteenth century have posed an exceptional challenge to human beings in society, and to societal norms we have inherited from the past. Some of these norms are firmly founded in human nature itself, others may derive from the way people can best live together in a particular culture, e.g. in a tribal extended family culture effectively independent from and unaffected by the kind of organised state system to which we are accustomed.

The Roman Catholic Church has sometimes been tempted to over-generalise from its experience of the particular culture within which it developed in the Middle East/Europe area – proclaiming norms that may be historically or geographically specific to this area as applicable to human nature itself and thus to be part of a natural law. But, by and large, its ethical norms are well-rooted in the character of the human condition itself.

Perhaps a more serious weakness has been a tendency to over-claim a unique capacity for sociological insights, by proclaiming in the same breath that certain social ethical principles represent a natural morality, deducible by pure reason, but that, at the same time, these can be subject to accurate specification only by the authority of the Catholic Church. Even committed members of the church may have difficulty with this claim.

However, in one important respect the church's reasoning seems markedly superior to that of many who challenge it. This is its clear understanding and wise insistence upon the extent to which the behaviour of individuals can be influenced for the worse, or better, by how other people are seen to behave. This view challenges a prevalent liberal proposition that only the direct and immediate negative impact of aberrant behaviour upon another individual has any moral significance.

This self-serving proposition, which is widely used today to excuse individual amoral behaviour, might perhaps be described as an ethical 'fallacy of the heap', the assertion that, in relation to cause and effect in human behaviour, only a large and highly visible change in a causal factor can have a significant consequence.

(Some half-century ago I disproved this proposition in relation to human reactions to small changes in air fares. In 1953, as an Aer Lingus official I experimented with a one-year extension of cheap mid-week cross-channel fares to Monday as well as Tuesday, Wednesday and Thursday. This experiment demonstrated that for every reduction of one shilling in these fares, two percent of people changed their day of travel – a shilling in 1953 being worth about €1.35 today. This experiment enabled me to convince my bosses that a low air fare policy would prove profitable – a proposition that, unhappily for it, Aer Lingus forgot during the subsequent quarter of a century!)

Where it seems to me that the Roman Catholic Church in particular has recently lost much of its former power to influence social behaviour has been in its overuse of authority rather than reason in promulgating its views on social morality. It had always been shy of pointing to the rational basis of so much of its moral teaching – perhaps because it feared that this might expose occasional irrational elements that had been allowed to creep into its teaching in response to particular challenges it had faced at various points in the past.

There can be no doubt about the significance of the 1960s worldwide, although the form that its impact on society took varied from country to country. In the United States, and in much of Europe, it involved an actual sexual revolution. In Ireland its immediate impact was, perhaps, less drastic, but an

inter-action between the global liberal mood and the debates of
the Second Vatican Council made many Irish people for the first
time think seriously and for themselves about the moral teachings of their religion.

Amongst many thinking Catholics the early impact of this
process was positive. The Catholic Church, instead of being pas-
sively accepted as part of the national wallpaper, so to speak,
came to be seen in a new and generally more challenging light.
For the first time a genuine interest in theology emerged
amongst sections of the laity. The concept of the church as the
people of God, rather than just the episcopacy and clergy,
gripped the imagination of many Catholics.

But into this new situation was thrown in mid-1968 the
bombshell of *Humanae Vitae*. For many married people, this created, at least for a period, agonising problems of conscience.
They were torn between traditional, instinctive loyalty to church
teaching and what they saw as their marital responsibilities. For
some the strain on their adherence to their church proved too
great. Others, often aided by sympathetic confessors, many of
whom found the theology of this document unconvincing, survived this test and, despite their rejection of this particular
teaching, remained practising Catholics.

In this connection it is worth remarking that the problem
with this document did not lie with its basic insight into the potential impact of widespread availability of contraceptives upon
extra-marital sexual behaviour – an insight that has been fully
justified by events – but rather in the conclusions it drew from
this insight with regard to the use of such methods by couples
seeking to regulate the spacing of their families.

On the one hand, given the Catholic Church's earlier acceptance of the use of women's ovulatory cycle for this purpose, its
objection to other means being employed towards the end of
spacing and limiting pregnancies could not be justified on
grounds of intent. At the same time, whilst there was a difference between the ease and effectiveness of these two methods,
this was a matter of degree that could not, rationally or theologically, carry the weight of permitting one and flatly rejecting the
other for family planning purposes.

Moreover, at quite another level, *Humane Vitae* can be argued
to have taken inadequate account of the change that had by then
taken place in the global population situation. Insofar as the

church's earlier negative approach to family size limitation may have been influenced by the appropriateness at the time it was written of the biblical injunction to 'increase and multiply', by 1968 there was clearly a strong ecological case for reversing this injunction by seeking instead to slow down population growth in order to avoid overcrowding the planet. That would appear to have been more in line with what the church describes as a 'natural law', designed to optimise the conditions for human existence.

As had been the case with some other earlier aspects of its teaching on sexual matters, the Catholic Church's disciplinary insistence on clerical celibacy – designed in an earlier period both to secure the undivided attention of clergy to their duties and to prevent the alienation of church property by their families – deprived it of the insights that a married clergy (and above all a married episcopacy!) might have had into issues of this kind.

The impact of all this upon hitherto unthinking acceptance of the church's authority, already under question as a result of the changed mood of the 1960s and perhaps also as a result of the well-reported debates in the Council, proved quite profound. Thereafter, to an ever-increasing extent, many Irish Catholics began to do their own theology, so to speak, testing the Catholic Church's teaching against their own rational morality. In many, probably most, cases, the test was passed – for, except where some aberration had distorted the church's teaching at some point in the past, Christian morality was of course firmly based on natural morality – viz. the ordering of social relationships in a manner conducive to the optimisation of the human condition.

But authority had lost its power to compel. Indeed to some degree 'authority' had become a bad word – as 'authoritarian' had already become, at least from the period of fascism earlier in the century.

Given the manner in which over the centuries the church had identified, in many cases correctly, the kind of criteria for behaviour that would secure optimal relationships between individuals in society, a visionary and prophetic church might perhaps have chosen to grasp this opportunity to demonstrate the extent to which its inspiration in the past had in fact led it to develop a wise balance between individualism and social needs – wiser than that of various discredited rationalist attempts in the nineteenth and twentieth centuries. Such a demonstration of the value of its insights and of their broad compatibility with natural reason might have strengthened its moral authority and reduced its increasingly counter-productive dependence on deploying its hierarchical authority, with a view to attracting rather than seeking to compel adherence to its views.

Instead, the central authorities of the church preferred to command the absolute allegiance of its clergy to its teaching on the contraception issue by intensifying disciplinary measures *vis-à-vis* theologians whose views it disapproved of, and by appointing as bishops only members of the clergy who agreed in all respects with the views of Rome on this matter.

Over the past thirty-five years these authoritarian measures proved hugely counter-productive. In order to avoid censure by higher authority, perhaps even loss of their clerical status and thus of their livelihood, very many of the clergy have been forced to dissimulate their views on an issue which, to say the least, was not central to the faith. This has, of course, hugely weakened the moral authority that they exercise as individuals, which derives from their giving witness to the truth as they see and believe it.

This uncomfortable situation, continuing over several decades, left the laity ill-prepared for the revelation in the 1990s of an unresolved back-log of clerical child abuse cases in at least the English-speaking world. These crimes had been carefully hidden from view by church authorities more concerned about institutional 'scandal' than about the protection of children – which for many of the laity is the most crucial moral issue of all, and one to which, unhappily, many bishops, perhaps trapped by their celibacy, proved disastrously insensitive.

The fact that decades of past abuse came to light and were investigated and prosecuted within a relatively short period of time has given an exaggerated, indeed false, impression of the scale of this problem and this, together with the insensitive attitude of the church authorities to the clerical paedophile problem, shattered the confidence of many lay people in their church.

Meanwhile, the younger generation of Irish society had for long been protected by both church and state from changes in mores in the world outside Ireland. With the advent of television this dangerously over-protective screen disappeared almost overnight and, within the short space of thirty years, Irish society faced changes that elsewhere in the developed world had taken place over a whole century.

To give but one example, between the mid-1960s and the end of the century the proportion of births outside marriage rose from 1.5% to 33%. Of course the former figure may have under-stated the scale of extra-marital intercourse in the pre-contraception 1960s, when some non-marital pregnancies were converted into marital births through shotgun marriages and a small num-ber were also aborted in Britain. But the current 30% non-marital birth proportion equally under-states the extent to which today's first pregnancies are extra-marital for, when account is taken of the fact that three out every eight first non-marital births are now aborted in Britain, it emerges that over half of all first pregnancies in our state are now non-marital.

In the even shorter period of twenty years since 1980 the pro-portion of women married by the age of 25 has fallen from 53% to 8%. And whereas in 1980 over two-thirds of first marital births were to women under 27, only one-sixth of first marital births are now to women in that age group.

Today only a small minority of non-marital births today are to teenagers: one-sixth, as against two-fifths in 1981. By contrast, the proportion of non-marital births to women aged 25 and over is rising towards half of the total. Many of these non-marital births now are to couples in a stable non-marital relationship: one-sixth of couples with children under 5 are co-habiting rather than married.

How has all this impacted upon Irish family life? To date little has been written about the effect of these huge, and extraordi-narily rapid, changes in mores upon our society, and in particular upon inter-generational family relationships. So, for the mom-ent, pending overdue sociological research in this area, for an impression of this aspect of Irish family life we must depend upon anecdotal evidence.

What can, I think, be said is that in contrast to the starkly neg-ative and defensive character of the church's reaction to these changes in Irish social mores, Irish parents and grandparents seem generally to have chosen to protect the integrity of their family relationships by accepting co-habitation by their child-ren, even where this continues after the birth of a child. They tend to keep to themselves any qualms they may have about this practice.

I believe that there has always been a marked difference between the approaches of urban working-class families and that of other social groups to non-marital pregnancies. In contrast to middle class urban, and almost all rural families, urban working-class families, at any rate in the larger conurbations, have long tended to incorporate into the nuclear family the non-marital child of a daughter living at home, treating it as if it were a late-arriving sibling.

We know all too well what happened in the past in many other families, however. A birth would be handled with secrecy, the child adopted, often outside Ireland, and its mother sometimes even incarcerated thereafter in a convent asylum.

Although today there certainly remain girls who greatly fear parental disapproval, parental attitudes seem now to have generally changed. I suspect that today an abortion in Britain is more often the choice of a mother unwilling to become a single parent rather than a choice determined by fear of parental disapproval of single motherhood.

In general it seems to me that most parents have a more relaxed relationship with their children than formerly and, however much they may privately regret their children's different approach to sexual matters, they seem to forbear from overt criticism or disapproval of co-habitation. It may even be that the sense of family solidarity has been strengthened rather that weakened by the need of the parents to accommodate to a rapidly evolving society.

There is also clear evidence that this more relaxed parental approach is reciprocated by their children. Precisely because so many Irish parents, and grandparents, have adapted successfully to a rapidly changing social situation, many young people in Ireland today have more open, and thus often stronger, relationships with their parents and grandparents. Just as they benefit from tolerance on the part of the older generation, so also, I observe, do they respect that generation's uncensorious commitment to their traditional views on these matters.

In the absence of research into these issues, some concrete evidence of the continuing strength of Irish family relationships can be found in the quite disparate approaches of Irish and English students to the choice of third-level institutions to attend. In England there has traditionally been a positive preference amongst third-level students for a university distant from their home – although for economic reasons the proportion of English students choosing a university near their homes is estimated to have doubled in the past few years. English school-leavers appear to have seen their entrance to third-level education as an opportunity to get away from their families. And there is anecdotal evidence that, in many English families, parents and children have lost contact at that point.

By contrast in our state, students have always shown a marked preference for a university or Institute of Technology near their home, unless of course, they intended to pursue a course not locally available. This partly reflects the fact that, in contrast to Britain, standards in Irish universities are fairly uniform: there is no strong academic reason to choose one rather than another and a dominant consideration for a majority of third-level students appears to be the nearness of their chosen third-level institution to their homes. And where students' homes are too remote from their third-level institutions to permit daily commuting, they very often return home each weekend. Thus, in contrast to England, third-level education in the Irish State has not sundered the relationship between the generations.

The situation in Northern Ireland is somewhat different, for Protestants in particular. For obvious reasons there has been always a greater tendency by Protestant than Catholic third-level students in the North to see themselves as part of a wider United Kingdom educational system. In recent times this factor, combined with the stronger educational motivation of Catholics, has led both of the Northern Ireland universities to have a majority of Roman Catholic students, which seems to have further accelerated the flow of Protestant third-level students to Britain. The fact that there are only two universities in Northern Ireland may also have encouraged this outward flow to Britain which, even amongst Catholic students, is many times greater than in the case of the Republic.

But a higher proportion of Catholic than Protestant students seem to return to Northern Ireland and, of course, in both parts of the island, (in marked contrast to what was the case in the nineteenth century and the first half of the twentieth, when emigration in most cases involved a final breach with home), many young emigrants, whether or not they have been third-level students, now take advantage of much cheaper travel to return frequently to their homes in Ireland.

Despite the gap in social attitudes that has sprung up between the generations in the past thirty years, the strength of Irish family ties has been well-maintained. This aspect of Irish society is little recognised and is, I believe, greatly underestimated by commentators on the Irish scene. It is an important stabilising factor in a rapidly changing society, and is something that should be cherished and built upon.

It should be recognised that it is precisely because the older generation has not sought to impose on its teenage and adult children the minutiae of the moral code in which they were raised in earlier decades that Irish family life has survived the immense strains of this recent period of ultra-rapid social change.

Of course, in all this we must distinguish between the hedonism of sexual promiscuity, on the one hand, and what seems, on the other, to be an altered approach by a new generation to family formation, involving in the case of very many young people what are, in effect, trial marriages in the form of a period of cohabitation before commitment through a marriage ceremony to a permanent relationship.

It is clear that for whatever reason many young people today are hesitant about entering into a life-long commitment to a partner and, insofar as they are willing to contemplate this possibility, feel it unwise to do so without a preliminary experimental relationship.

The sources of their hesitation about a commitment for life are unclear, especially as these doubts seem to be shared by many young people who are themselves products of successful marriages as well as by those less fortunate in their upbringing. The longer span of human life under modern conditions does not seem, as has sometimes been suggested, an adequate explanation, because the lengthening of young people's expectation of life has evolved over a longer period than that within which this decline in commitment has taken place.

The traditional argument against trial unions have behind them the experience of many centuries. But we live in a different world today. And the decision of many young people to approach a life commitment to a partner by this different route cannot reasonably be described as irresponsible. Indeed, as they see it, they are acting more responsibly than those who make a life commitment without first testing their compatibility by means of a prior period of cohabitation.

Although my own experiences and instincts have favoured entering early into the kind of permanent commitment that we sanctify as marriage, I have to accept that early marriages often carry a risk of breakdown because of lack of maturity on the part of one or both partners. I am forced to recognise that the recent practice of postponing a permanent commitment and the initiation of the procreation of offspring until the late 20s or early 30s may have a good deal to say for it, even if earlier child-bearing is more attuned to female biology.

The latest data on marriage breakdown, from the 2002 Census, does actually suggest that marriage postponement in the 1980s and 1990s may have had a favourable impact on marriage breakdown – for the proportion of early marriages breaking down is lower now than formerly, although this may be because some at least of the early marriages in the 1970s may have been shotgun affairs.

Of course, the fact that parents and grandparents have been wise in not challenging this generational shift in the sexual mores of their progeny is not of itself an argument for the church to modify its teaching on the subject. Nevertheless, it is certain that, in the long run, the interest of church and society lies in maximising the number of stable unions within which children are brought up in happy surroundings, and perhaps the church should not be too dogmatic about how best to secure such an outcome under modern conditions – for which past experience may not provide an infallible guide.

Theology, War and Pacifism

Patrick Hannon

For war is evil. If war is ever justified, it is still evil.
– Denys Turner

War looms in the Gulf again as this is written, and by the time of publication the uncertainties of these days will probably have been resolved. It would not be useful to become mired in the detail of the proposal to make war on Iraq, yet it would be artificial to attempt a reflection on the subject-matter of the chapter without some reference to that proposal and to the debate now surrounding it. For the debate has raised and pressed all the questions which must be faced if the problem of warfare today is to be addressed

At the heart of the present debate is the question whether it is immoral or not to go to war on Iraq. This on one view is the question of the applicability of the doctrine of the just war. Is there just cause? Is there a right intention? Is there legitimate authority? Is there due proportion between the end sought and the means which will be used in furtherance of that end? Are we at the point of last resort, the point at which it can truly be said that there is no alternative to war now? What, realistically, are the prospects for a successful outcome? What indeed will be reckoned in all the circumstances to be a successful outcome?

And what then if war is declared: what, for example, of non-combatant immunity, one of the most ancient and enduring of the conditions of just war theory, and one which modern experience has caused to be brought, as it were, under a microscope? For on the one hand there is weaponry now available which allows for the possibility of more exact targeting, even if this 'smart' weaponry is not always smartly employed, owing to human or computer error. But on the other hand there are also now available 'weapons of mass destruction' which, if used, are of their nature and necessarily in flagrant violation of the condition of non-combatant immunity. And it is well known that even conventional weaponry is sometimes used in a way which makes impossible the observance of the principle that the innocent may not directly be killed, as when bombs are dropped from a height which simply precludes discrimination.

These and other questions arise when the proposal to go to war on Iraq is discussed in terms of just war doctrine. But of course there is also debate about whether it can be moral to go to war at all. This is sometimes canvassed in terms of a thorough-going pacifism which holds it to be immoral to inflict violent harm or death upon another in any circumstances. Sometimes a pacifist stand is taken out of a conviction that, whatever of the past, it is impossible in modern times to keep within the restraints called for by just war principles. The existence of weapons of mass destruction, biological and chemical, and nuclear, and the danger, proximate or eventual, of their being used, precludes conformity with the principle of proportionality in such a way as to preclude entitlement to resort to war (*jus ad bellum*) as well as any realistic prospect of non-combatant immunity (*jus in bello*).

A thorough-going pacifism is sometimes argued from an avowedly Christian standpoint; that is, it is maintained that only total non-violence is compatible with the teaching of Jesus, and with the ethos and conduct of the early Christian Church. In this view the just war doctrine is a betrayal of the Christian imperative not to meet evil with evil, and of Christian witness to the evil of violence and the possibility of non-violent resolution of conflict. A less radical version is that, though compromise in the shape of just war principles might have been intelligible or even called for in the past, the truly Christian ideal has always remained non-violence, and that our time is challenging us to retrieve a vision of the ideal and to work towards it.

Enda McDonagh and the Theology of Peace and War

Themes such as these have preoccupied Enda McDonagh throughout his career as a moral theologian in the Roman Catholic tradition. The preoccupation has derived in part from an awareness of the conflicts which have threatened or affected humankind and the planet during the era of the Cold War and in a different manner subsequently. But it has derived in a special way from his consciousness of the conflict which has troubled the Northern part of the island of Ireland, especially during the past three decades and a half. So we find him treating of the just war doctrine in reference to war and violence in general, but also with particular reference to revolutionary warfare. We find him exploring pacifism too, and approaches to the non-violent resolution of conflict. A reserve about the adequacy, from a Christian standpoint, of just war doctrine is evident from his earliest treatments, a reserve which in time becomes an impatience, and which latterly has come to appear like an almost total rejection.[1]

Enda McDonagh's treatment of war and pacifism is of course rooted in his theology as a whole, and were this chapter to attempt a comprehensive account and appraisal of his reflections it would have to locate them in the general theological framework in which his work has been conducted. But such a project would require more than a chapter in a Festschrift, and I have not thought of attempting it here. This piece will focus rather on what McDonagh has written about the ethics of war and peace in his principal contributions to discussion of these themes.

I realise that in taking this approach I am also taking a risk. McDonagh's conception of ethics is of a theological ethics which emerges from an interplay between Christian faith and the experience called morality, or – looked at another way – from an interplay between the sources of Christian reflection and the experience of living in today's world. His treatment of the ethics of violence and war and revolution is shaped by some characteristic theological emphases. I hope it will be enough to point to the

---

1. It would be interesting, though it is not here possible, to examine in detail what McDonagh has to say about revolutionary warfare, which he treats extensively in relation to Northern Ireland and to Zimbabwe (then Rhodesia). His strictures and hesitations about the use of violence apply to revolutionary violence as well as to inter-state conflict, and he argues explicitly for the value of non-violent means in situations of institutional oppression; and, as will be seen, intra-state conflict is included in the call for the abolition of war which he and Stanley Hauerwas made at Notre Dame in September 2002. But his treatment of revolutionary violence is more nuanced than that of inter-state conflict, and his caution about 'outsider' comment and analysis more marked. It is perhaps not unfair to say that he is slower to discount the possibility of a just revolution, for reasons apparent in his treatment of it, than he is of the justice of other war. See 'Violence and Political Change' in E. McDonagh, *Doing the Truth: the Quest for Moral Theology*, Dublin: Gill & Macmillan, 1979 (hereinafter DT); also his *The Demands of Simple Justice*, Dublin: Gill & Mcmillan, 1980 (hereinafter DSJ), published in the USA as *Church and Politics*, Notre Dame: Notre Dame University Press, 1980.

most centrally relevant of these and to advert to others as necessary, and that what I offer as a description of his position is at no
point a distortion.

Two pieces frame Enda McDonagh's thinking on war and
peace and related ethical issues. The first is the chapter entitled
'Human Violence: a Question of Ethics or Salvation' in the 1975
book *Gift and Call: Towards a Christian Theology of Morality*,[2] the
second a joint statement with Stanley Hauerwas entitled
Abolishing War? addressed to Christian leaders and theologians
and presented to a conference at Notre Dame University in
September 2002. The first may be taken as setting out the general
framework within which McDonagh has thought about these
matters, but also as providing a starting-point for his reflections
upon particular aspects of the problematic, and for that reason I
shall offer a fairly detailed resume of it here.

Violence, War and Revolution
McDonagh views war as one item in the repertoire of violence
which human beings are capable of inflicting and do inflict on
one another. Violence he understands to be 'the destruction or
damage wrought by man on his fellow-man or human property';[3] the object is always the fellow human being, even when
what is damaged is property or the environment. Adoption of
the term 'violence' rather than the neutral term 'force' allows
him to advert also to other ways in which humans damage humans, including 'institutional' violence.[4] By this is meant that the
social structure into which people are born and in which they
grow up can, as he says, damage and even destroy them. And
'[f]or the development and maintenance of that structure at least
by neglecting its reform some people have or had responsibility.
The people who suffer helplessly from that structure suffer vio-

2. Dublin: Gill & Macmillan, 1975, 138-166. Hereinafter *GC*.
3. *GC* 138.
4. McDonagh is aware of the reasons for speaking of 'force' rather than
violence, especially in reference to the coercion exercised by the state
and its agents, which may then be judged in terms of whether it is legal
or illegal, justified or not; see *DSJ* 69. But he prefers the term violence
and explains why: 'It is of course important to distinguish force from violence. Yet I feel the whole discussion may be pre-empted by the too
nice insistence on this distinction and the definition of violence as the
"unlawful or excessive use of force"'. See *DT* 139-40. It could be asked
whether the use of the word violence might not pre-empt discussion of,

lence. The people who have the power to alter it are inflicting violence.'[5]

Political violence, in the shape of war or revolutionary insurrection, is an age-old phenomenon, and is probably most often considered (and defended) in the first place not in terms of its ethical justification but in terms of its effectiveness. 'Almost any modern or ancient state you care to mention was born either in actual violence or under the threat of it. It has continued in existence, if it has, because it could command sufficient physical violence to defeat or deter its enemies from within and without. A third world war has been prevented and peace or at least the absence of global violence has been paradoxically achieved by the development of terrifying instruments of violence and of the mental willingness to use them in certain circumstances.'[6] A variation on the argument points to the ineffectiveness of other ways, and examples ancient and modern are invoked to show the necessity of violent means.

But McDonagh does not regard these arguments as conclusive. 'On scarcely any issue is the historical assessor driven to conclude that political achievement was achieved exclusively or even predominantly by a particular use of force, still less can he definitively rule out the possibility that the same goals might have been achieved by non-violent means.'[7] In any case a morally sensitive person is unlikely to regard considerations of effectiveness as conclusive; the end does not necessarily justify the means. And so McDonagh turns to the ethics of political violence, in the first place as this was discussed under the rubric of the just war.

The Doctrine of the Just War
Although he sees it as a departure from New Testament and early church tradition, he is not unsympathetic to just war doctrine in the conditions of its emergence: 'The new political context [church, empire and the world outside the empire after Constantine] provided the setting in which a Christian justification of violence developed. It does not necessarily invalidate

---

for example, 'institutional violence' here and elsewhere. I believe not, though what McDonagh has to say about this might be more persuasive to some readers had he made use of the distinction.
5. GC 143.
6. GC 148.
7. GC 149.

the justification itself which depended on a realistic assessment of the need for social protection and defence of the weak against the marauders.'[8] He cites Paul Ramsey's observation that 'in-principled love' may sometimes have to resort to violence to restrain the unjust aggressor and protect the weak and the innocent. And he opines that whatever its immediate source and even if no Christian basis can be found for it, the just war ethic still needs to be evaluated as an ethical project.[9]

Nor does he accept that its principal Christian authors envisaged it as easily endorsing war. For the medievals it was an exception to the commandment 'Thou shalt not kill', and the express intent of Francesco de Vitoria (d 1546), articulator of the fullest early modern theological account of it, was to limit the horrors of war. And of de Vitoria he says that 'even if he did not have immediate influence on the behaviour of his political and military contemporaries, he laid the groundwork for the later development of international law with the possibility of preventing or limiting war more effectively.'[10]

But he has already signalled reservations: 'For all its sophistication and the authoritative minds which developed it, the just war tradition has two large question marks: how far is it a genuinely Christian tradition, given the example and teaching of the founder of Christianity? How far is it a serious moral tradition, given that it has seldom if ever been of practical influence?'[11] And now he spells some of these reservations out: how realistic is an ethic whose application is a matter for the judgment of the

---

8. GC 153.
9. Ibid.
10. GC 154. See also DSJ 65: '... the just war theorists never intended to make it easy to justify war, much less to glorify it. They found themselves, after Constantine, for example, in the position of having to deal with actual warfare and consider the defence of the neighbour by the Empire. Their new-found responsibility led them to take a rather different line from that of their "pacifist" predecessors who were "without" the law of the Empire and certainly accepted no responsibility for its defence. The basis of their new justification of war was also love of neighbour which, in the context of attack on him, demanded that one come to his defence. Defending the neighbour out of love forms the heart of the theological justification of war. Because the aggressor is also to be loved, the various restraining conditions were worked out over the centuries.' But, he adds, how far love of neighbour and of enemy combined to moderate war in fact may be doubted.
11. GC 152.

interested party? How might there be an impartial way of as-
sessing compliance with just war conditions? How far has any
war ever satisfied the conditions? How far did any initiator of a
war consider these criteria in any serious way? And during or
after a war, how often has there been criticism by Christian or
other leaders of its conduct by their own side?

He grants that all moral decision rests with the judgment of
an interested party, but principles ought to help the agent to see
beyond self-interest, and he doubts whether just war principles
do that for those who may be considering resort to war. One reason for this is that '[t]he just cause, last resort and lawful means
criteria are open to widely differing interpretations in the concrete situation,'[12] His verdict on the just war approach at this
point is that, although it embodies a long tradition of reflection
on the problems of political violence, its limitations are serious;
'just war theory has very doubtful Christian antecedents and
very limited ethical significance.'[13]

Non-Violence

What then of the alternative tradition, the rejection of war as a
political instrument? McDonagh sees this as an aspect of what
seems to be without doubt the position of the early Christians,
the rejection of all violence, and he observes that its influence
never entirely disappeared. For one thing it has helped to 'modify the actuality of war', and at the level of reflection it has pro-
voked serious examination of war's justification. And with
Thomas More and Erasmus the protest against war was revived,
and subsequently it developed into a pacifism now associated
especially with what are sometimes called the Peace Churches.
But it was in the twentieth century – 'one of the bloodiest of all' –
that new political instruments of non-violent resistance were
created, as 'the names of Mohandas Gandhi and Martin Luther
King helped create a new consciousness of the political alternative to violence.'[14]

McDonagh does not purport to offer here a comprehensive
ethical assessment of non-violent approaches, and he focuses
only on their core affirmation of the immorality of war and/or
of any kind of violence. Of this he observes that while 'the more

---

12. *GC* 155.
13. *GC* 157.
14. *GC* 158.

subtle proponents' recognise the problems posed by for example domestic violence, and also the need for order in society
which may demand coercion, the fact is that '[h]ow to protect
the weak from vicious attack or generally uphold social order
without resorting to force – at least in extreme cases – has never
been satisfactorily shown.'[15] Many defenders of political non-
violence admit the possible justice of violence in such exceptional
and extreme cases, but remain resolute in their rejection of war.

There is of course an issue of consistency here: 'To admit violence at the domestic level may weaken the claim to New
Testament origins which scarcely concerned itself with politics,
while it creates a consistency problem if no such exceptions are
allowed at the level of inter-group dispute.'[16] But, as with the
just war ethic, there is also a question of its applicability: 'The
campaigns of Gandhi and King and others inspired by them are
of importance here, but whether they owe their strength to very
particular circumstances and very particular leaders it may not
be possible to say yet. Neither can one judge their lasting impact
on the people and situations for which they were developed.'[17]

Nevertheless McDonagh concludes his essay with an account of Gandhi's philosophy and practice of non-violent resistance, though not before inviting consideration of the question
whether the real problem about violence lies deeper than is revealed by ethical analysis alone. He proposes that at a deeper
level the problem of violence is a problem of 'salvation', citing
Lelia Khaled, Padraic Pearse, Frantz Fanon and Georges Sorel,
each of whom in their various ways testified to a 'belief in the
transforming and salvific character of violence.'[18] Gandhi's way
is contrasted with Fanon's in particular, and whereas for the latter salvation was said to come through violence, for Gandhi it
was by non-violent resistance.

There is no need here to recount the detail of Gandhi's approach, except to say that, as McDonagh points out, non-violent
resistance was not for Gandhi a simple passive resistance, nor
was it the non-violence of the weak or the cowardly. And it involves a training, an ascesis, in which specific techniques of defence and resistance are learned and practised. 'Effectiveness

15. Ibid.
16. *GC* 159.
17. Ibid.
18. *GC* 150.

and ethics are now transformed on the deeper level which Gandhi and Fanon have unveiled. It is at this level that man must finally choose. It is a choice for every man in some degree and a choice for mankind which is becoming more crucial by the year.'[19]

What is the connection between this and Christian faith and theology? 'Christianity is not primarily about ethics but about salvation. God's gift of himself to man, in the man Jesus Christ who overcame human violence and the fear and the hatred of which it is born, by love, is continually seeking expression in the world as a saving force, liberating every man from fear and oppression and violence, reconciling men with one another. The Christian call is to co-operate with this divine gift in its saving activity. Christian ethics searches out the ways and means of co-operating.'[20]

It may be, he says, that in special circumstances a holding operation is all that can be achieved and violence done to individuals or groups has to be violently restrained (he says 'forcibly', but the context makes it clear that what is in question is violent force). But if so, a Christian and the Christian community must recognise this as failure, and they must set themselves again to 'let God and his love triumph over the fear and hatred of our oppressive and violent relationships', a process which will be complete only in the eschaton when the reign of God will be fulfilled completely. 'For the interim, salvation, while still incomplete, reveals the value and limitations of an ethics of personal and political relationships in which forcible coercion may be necessary at times but must always be secondary to the loving and non-violent activity of which Jesus was the master and Gandhi the great modern prophet.'[21]

A Preference for Non-Violence
I have summarised this first extended statement of McDonagh's views in some detail because it both intimates the theological vision which informs his approach and articulates a starting-point for reflection upon aspects of his theme to which he was to return in later work. It can be seen that, though appreciative of the positive in just war doctrine, he already had reservations

19. *GC* 166.
20. Ibid.
21. Ibid.

about its fidelity to the Christian vision and about its value as a set of effective ethical principles. But nor did he see the alternative of non-violence as trouble free, especially in its apparent inability to provide a coherent and consistent account and approach as between political and 'domestic' types of violence. Yet it can be said that already at this stage there is signalled a preference for non-violence which becomes more marked with the passage of time.

The basis for the preference is underscored and amplified in later work, sometimes in the shape of growing scepticism concerning the just war doctrine, sometimes more positively in terms of the values inherent in non-violence. In 1979, for example, in a book which was the fruit of a study of the political situation in the then Rhodesia, undertaken at the invitation of the local church, McDonagh was more frankly dubious than earlier about the practical effectiveness of the just war ethic. He contended that its adherents succumbed to exploring the opening for 'moral violence' provided by the just war position more often than they accepted the restraint which it was meant to impose. 'While deferring to the theory of Vitoria, with all its requirements of just cause, last resort and just means, the statesmen, soldiers and even churchmen have followed a very different practice. It would be difficult to point to a war in which these requirements were convincingly fulfilled, but easy to point to churchmen and statesmen who passionately claimed that they were.'[22]

In addition to the reasons already adduced for regarding the just war approach as flawed there appears increasingly a particular doubt as to its usefulness or validity in view of modern (including nuclear) weaponry, especially as regards the principle of discrimination or non-combatant immunity. This is hinted in the essay just considered: 'The limitations on means, by respect for non-combatants and for a certain code even in regard to combatants, have proved very fragile with the development of modern weapons.'[23] It is elaborated in *The Demands of Simple Justice*,[24] and enunciated very forcefully in a 1982 lecture entitled 'Peace and War: a Task for American Moral Theologians.'[25]

22. *DSJ* 61.
23. *GC* 139.
24. *DSJ* 63.
25. See *The Making of Disciples*, Dublin: Gill & Macmillan, 1982, 203-221. Hereinafter *MD*.

There McDonagh speaks of 'the pervasiveness and totality' of war today. Its pervasiveness in the twentieth century he sees exemplified in the two World Wars and in the links between local wars – in the Middle East, South-East Asia, South Africa and South America – and the super-powers. Its totality is shown in the weaponry now available and used or threatened. 'The technical range of means used in Vietnam [for example] equivalently demolished that restraint on the conduct of war which the distinction between combatants and non-combatants maintained in the light of the just war theory.'[26] But in any case, as he points out, that distinction and restraint had already disappeared in the course of World War II, in the Blitzkrieg, in the bombing of Dresden and Hamburg, and above all in the 'final obscenities' of Hiroshima and Nagasaki. His verdict on just war doctrine is now blunt and bleak: 'The irrelevance of just war theory was finally and cruelly exposed.'[27]

The availability of nuclear weapons of course extends and intensifies the problem. McDonagh was writing in the era of the Cold War, in which the arms race between the superpowers gave the possibility of total planetary destruction, while the arms trade increased the destructive capacity of even small and poverty-stricken nations. 'At the level of locally containable violence as well as at the level of possibly universal and total violence the human weakness for mutual destruction threatens every single person today.'[28]

More positive reasons for Enda McDonagh's preference for non-violence are intimated already in *Gift and Call*, especially when he discusses Gandhi's insight into the 'mutual enslavement' which colonial – or indeed any – oppression brought: 'For

26. *MD* 205.
27. Ibid.
28. Ibid. James Turner Johnson makes the point that analyses made out of a perception shaped by Cold War perspectives are dated: 'Though nuclear weapons and other weapons of mass-destructive capability, including chemical and biological agents, continue to cast their shadow on future warfare, the characteristic shape that warfare has actually taken since the end of the cold war is quite different from that envisioned by the prophets of global holocaust. Contemporary warfare has in fact taken the form of local conflicts, more often than not civil wars, in which no great alliances are involved....' Nor, he says, have they been fought with nuclear weapons, or other weapons of mass-destructive capability. He believes that failure to notice this leads to incomplete

him the mutual enslavement involved must be transformed into
mutual emancipation. Salvation must be achieved for both
sides.'[29] The institutionalised violence of colonial rule and the
physical violence which accompanied it could not, in Gandhi's
view, be overcome by opposing violence with violence, for
'[e]ven if such violence should result in a change of masters, the
violent relationships would be perpetuated.'[30] Gandhi's account
of the relationship between ends and means, on which he differed radically from his political contemporaries, has a particular appeal for McDonagh.[31]

In *Doing the Truth* he draws attention to the consonance of the
way of non-violence with the attitudes enjoined in the Sermon
on the Mount and in the New Testament generally: the attitude
of not returning evil for evil, of loving even the enemy, of a generosity of spirit which goes the second mile, of transcending bar-
riers of class, race and gender, of co-operating with God who in
Christ was reconciling all with each other and with God.[32] He
sees it also as retaining a realistic sense of evil, of the evil that
people do to each other and of the demonic elements that are en-
cased in our social and political structures. 'It seeks to exorcise
these and to bring liberation to the captives of society and history
by the means of passive resistance and non-violent direct action....'[33] In Christian terms 'the redemption of the structures of
society by the exorcising of the demonic would be much more
likely to result from the Gandhi philosophy and strategy.'[34]

It is the threat of nuclear war which dominates in McDonagh's
sketch in a 1982 lecture reproduced in *The Making of Disciples*, of
the task for American theologians *vis-à-vis* peace and war. Here
and elsewhere he has shown the value of non-violent methods
in the prevention of local wars, defensive or revolutionary; now

---

and unhelpful analysis and reflection. See Turner, *Morality and
Contemporary Warfare*, New Haven and London: Yale University Press
1999, 3-5. One could take Turner's point and yet wish to urge the dangers which the existence anywhere of weapons of mass destruction
must carry. The situation in North Korea and, in a different way, that in
Iraq is not reassuring.

29. *GC* 164. See *DT* 146.
30. Ibid.
31. *GC* 165. See also *DT* 141, *MD* 207.
32. *DT* 145-6.
33. *DT* 146.
34. Ibid.

he asks what bearing they might have on the threat of nuclear war. Local wars may escalate so their prevention must have a 'multiplier effect' in the promotion of world peace. But he is conscious too of the nuclear superpowers, and he sees that 'there are urgent needs now at the global level which must be met if the nuclear holocaust is not to engulf us through accident or design.'[35]

His scepticism concerning current nuclear deterrence policy is spelled out in a series of observations about its effectiveness and about its morality, culminating in the conclusion that it is imperative that the world be rid of the nuclear menace, 'an enormous but not a hopeless task'.[36] And as nuclear disarmament becomes a possibility, he says, radical changes in methods of defence, in arbitration of disputes and in economic structure will be required. He thinks it unlikely that disarmament can stop at nuclear weapons, for conventional weapons and conventional war must always carry with them the temptation to renew development of nuclear arms. And in the search for new methods of defence, non-violent methods and techniques must come into their own.

An Appeal for the Abolition of War
'The irrelevance of just war theory was finally and cruelly exposed' even in the Second World War, Enda McDonagh wrote in *The Making of Disciples*. It is not therefore surprising that his writing comes more and more to accentuate the value of non-violence; and it is not entirely surprising that his latest public utterance finds him, along with Methodist theologian Stanley Hauerwas of Duke University, calling on Christians of the different traditions 'to join a campaign to abolish war as a legitimate means of resolving political conflict between states and within them'. And although their appeal is in the first place to the Christian community, and more specifically to Christian leaders and theologians, they are confident that there are many who are not part of that community who will wish to join.

The Appeal's goal is nothing less than the abolition of war, and they recognise that their call will appear to some presumptuous, to others theologically flawed, and in practice futile. But they want nonetheless to initiate among Christians 'a serious

35. *MD* 215.
36. *MD* 215-217.

conversation' about the Christian and moral acceptability of war, and to draw 'all concerned human beings' into the examination and development of alternatives, for 'only in such a comprehensive enterprise can the Appeal's final goal of actually abolishing war have any chance of being realised'. And they hope that upholders of just war doctrine will join the conversation, for they too have a stake in making war unnecessary.

Their inspiration is theological: remembering John Paul II's 'War never again' and Tertullian's 'The Lord in disarming Peter disarms every soldier', they face the challenge of the Christian faith and hope that in the death and resurrection of Jesus the destructive powers of this world were radically overcome. 'It is loyalty to the example and teaching of Jesus Christ which summons Christians to renounce war and to seek with the wider religious and human communities to develop alternatives to protect the innocent, to restrain aggressors and to overcome injustice.'

In a paragraph which could serve as a summary of McDonagh's position as set out in the essays referred to above, he and Hauerwas consider the status of the doctrine of the just war. 'Christian attempts at justifying war from the fourth century onwards have always been intellectually and spiritually vulnerable and politically inconclusive. It is very doubtful if any war during that period satisfied the traditional criteria of *jus ad bellum* and *jus in bello*. In more recent times Christian leaders who still endorse the concept of a just war are finding it increasingly difficult to see how the criteria of last resort, non-combatant immunity and proportionality could nowadays be met. In current official church documents and theological analyses there is a discernible unease with the applying of just war theory and even greater unease with its Christian authenticity.'

They make their appeal now, they say, not primarily because of the particular horrors of modern warfare, nor because they think that people nowadays are so enlightened that they will more readily respond. They appeal now, rather, because this time like all time is under God's judgment: 'There is no time like the present (or the past) to say again in John Paul II's words "War never again".' Not that they are under any illusions about the prospect of a speedy end to the use of violent means, which is why they couch the appeal in terms that invite dialogue, and which aim to promote serious conversation and analysis among

Christian leaders about the Christian roots of the peace project. They wish to involve university faculties of theology and of the secular sciences, as well as research institutes, in the quest for a better understanding of the causes and consequences of particular wars and in the search for peaceful alternatives. And they believe that the results of such work should reveal to a wider public that war is immoral and unnecessary.

It is a difficult undertaking, calling for a 'conversation' which might in time become a process of conversion – of Christians to the anti-war dimension of their faith, of others to the peace-making potential of their fellow human beings. The road ahead is hard, yet 'Christian hope must be that this foolishness of God will confound the worldly-wise by persistent witness to peace, by the creative development of peacemaking attitudes and structures, and by achieving non-violent resolutions of particular conflicts.' There are precedents. It was thought once that slavery was part of the natural order and that those who sought its abolition were utopian: 'Let the twenty-first century be for war what the nineteenth was for slavery, the era of its abolition.'

'War never again'?

In the fifty years that separated Jean Renoir's *Grande Illusion* (1937) and Stanley Kubrick's *Full Metal Jacket* (1987), and indeed prior to this period and afterwards, the cinema has offered insight into the true, dehumanising, nature of the sort of war which our times have seen. Before the twentieth century was two decades old, when war was still seen as a glorious thing, Wilfred Owen was writing of 'the old Lie: Dulce et decorum est/ Pro patria mori'. And Siegfried Sassoon addressed the 'smug-faced crowds with kindling eye/ Who cheer when soldier lads march by':

> Sneak home and pray you'll never know
> The hell where youth and laughter go.

As I write there is to hand the newly-published *101 Poems against War*,[37] and it is patent that the new century's poets, too, see through to the horror that lurks beneath the glory. Comparable insights are found in contemporary novels and drama; and what of the likes of Picasso's *Guernica*? Nor do we need to consult the artists, for images from the newspapers and television news, and from documentaries about Bosnia and Rwanda, Kosovo

---

37. Ed. Matthew Hollis and Paul Keegan, London: Faber and Faber, 2003.

and Afghanistan, and other places of recent conflict, remain in the mind, and they merge with the images we retain of Vietnam and Cambodia. What further need is there for argument? Must not warfare be always evil? Why hesitate to cry with Pope John Paul II, 'War never again'?

James Turner Johnson has written of the significance and role of the kind of moral outrage expressed in the art of such as those mentioned above.[38] Moral outrage, he says, may be a proper component of ethical judgment, and he cites Michael Walzer's reliance on examples which illustrate that the judgments underlying moral restraints on war are rooted in experiences of repulsion, outrage and rejection. 'Yet, as *Just and Unjust Wars* also makes clear, moral outrage at a particular horror is by itself not enough; this has to be integrated into a larger system of moral judgment including such fundamental ideals as justice and fairness.'[39]

One might put it differently and say that moral outrage, if it is to be effective, must issue in analysis and argument of the kind exemplified in Enda McDonagh's work, including his analysis of the pros and cons of just war theory and of pacifism. What he and Hauerwas have appealed for is an end to all war, but they have rightly recognised that, powerful as the attraction of non-violence is, powerful as our revulsion against its opposite, its moral superiority will have to be argued for, and its adoption will require 'conversion'.

No More 'Just War'?

People who are already persuaded of the immorality of all warfare will doubtless be impatient, feel frustrated, in face of any defence of just war theory. Defence of just war theory is not of course defence of war, but pacifists may say that to continue to see merit in the doctrine of a just war is to be willing to make terms with violence, and to impede the process of the conversion to non-violence which is called for now, not only for Christians by the example and teaching of Jesus but also by our time's experience of warfare for every man and woman of sensitive conscience and of goodwill.

But men and women of sensitive conscience and of goodwill

---

38. See *101 Poems against War*.
39. Johnson, op. cit., 18. Cf Michael Walzer, *Just and Unjust Wars*, New York: Basic Books, 1977.

may not yet feel it timely to put aside the wisdom which is enshrined in the just war tradition, for it is possible in good faith to think that the world still needs the touchstones of restraint which it offers. Enda McDonagh is no doubt right to be sceptical about the extent to which the doctrine has influenced or influences political leaders. But can it be said that it has had no serious impact at all? At the least some of its most important conditions have worked their way into international law; one need mention here only the Hague and Geneva Conventions and related instruments. How can these have made no difference? Law is not morality, of course, but it may be morality's propaedeutic, as Aquinas among others recognised.[40] And might it not be maintained that current opposition to a war in Iraq, even when it originates in an instinctive revulsion against violence, is nourished, consciously or not, by considerations rooted in just war theory?

No doubt many who marched in Dublin and London and Paris and New York were moved by a sense of the inhumanity and absurdity of all violent conflict, a desire to leave the ways of war behind, a will to search for new ways. And the apparent ease, shocking and frightening, with which it has been concluded that only violence will bring a resolution must force the question whether only a radical stance of non-violence is the right moral response from now on. And yet there are questions. How many are opposed precisely because they are not persuaded of the justice of the cause or the rightness of intention, or that matters have reached the stage of last resort, or that there is any prospect of a meaningful 'success' in the outcome; or because they are horrified by predictions of loss of civilian life on a vast scale, and other *in bello* damage?

Not that these conditions seem to have troubled some of those in leadership who, especially in the United States, are urging war; someone has remarked on the difference between the Presidents Bush as regards invocation or otherwise of just war doctrine in 1990 and now. Even more alarming is the attempt, supported by at least two respected theologians, to interpret a pre-emptive strike against Iraq as defence against 'aggression under way'.[41] One recalls McDonagh's observation that the just

---

40. *Summa Theologiae*, 1a 2ae, Q. 95, art. 1.
41. The phrase captures the spirit of the UN Charter. George Weigel has argued that defence by pre-emption is a legitimate development of in-

cause, last resort and lawful means criteria are open to widely differing interpretations in the concrete situation.[42]

There is, as the US bishops put it, a presumption against war.[43] War is a last resort, and it is always failure. Yet in a world not ready, as it seems, to take the risks of non-violence, a world which has not yet learned non-violent ways (and as Gandhi saw, they require to be learned), the constraints required by just war doctrine may be all that there is in the way of safeguard against barbarism and inhumanity and destruction of life and of mankind's habitat. Hauerwas and McDonagh are right to call church leaders and theologians and the Christian community to lead the search for new ways of making just peace. But the world will not wait until this work is done, and in the holding operation which peace-seekers may have to bear with, the partial wisdom of a flawed tradition may still avail.

herited just war principles, Michael Novak says that it is simply a straightforward application. See G. Weigel, 'Just War and Pre-emption: Three Questions', *Ethics and Public Policy Center Publications*, http://www.eppc.org/publications; M. Novak, 'Iraq: the Moral Case for War', *The Tablet*, 15/02/03, 4-6. Weigel's argument is cautious (though in this writer's view mistaken), Novak's is astonishing.

42. GC 155. The distinction between what is directly and indirectly voluntary or intended is sometimes invoked in a facile way in justification of 'collateral damage'. Insofar as the principle of discrimination relies on the double effect doctrine, it needs to be remembered that an action must qualify under all four conditions required by the doctrine before it can be thought to be justified. So even if the death of civilians or damage to civilian property might plausibly be said to be only indirectly intended, it is nevertheless unjustified if the criterion of proportionate reason is not met. Another way of looking at the matter is to observe that the principle of discrimination *in bello* is to be taken together with the principle of proportionality, and that the application of the direct/indirect distinction is qualified accordingly.

43. *The Challenge of Peace*, Washington DC: USCC, 1983, 22, 26, 27. The assertion of this presumption has been criticised by some commentators – see, for example, Johnson, op. cit. 35. The objection seems strange: a presumption against war is but an application of what one must surely regard as a general presumption against the taking of human life.

Reflections on the 'Appeal to Abolish War'
or
What Being a Friend of Enda's Got Me Into

Stanley Hauerwas

A Visit With Enda

Paula and I were coming to the end of our vacation in Ireland. We had arranged to see Enda on our way to Dublin where we were to leave for home. It is always good to see Enda. We had become good friends during Enda's stay at Notre Dame. Moreover, when Paula and I had come to Ireland for our honeymoon, Enda had arranged a luncheon at Maynooth we will never forget. So I thought our trip to Maynooth would primarily be an opportunity to catch up. In a phone conversation arranging our seeing one another, however, Enda had suggested there was a project he was thinking about that he wanted to talk with me about.

Arriving at Maynooth we were as usual welcomed by Enda's wonderful hospitality. Paula and I enjoy finding out about the many projects with which Enda always seems to be involved. I have always thought that if Catholicism names anything, it names the life of Enda McDonagh. Or put even stronger, if the Catholic Church is the church, the best evidence that it is so is Enda McDonagh. For surely the catholicity of the church is to be found in his life. His is a life at once so deeply at home in Ireland, but one equally at home in Africa – a life dedicated to those that suffer from AIDS, but also sustained by the work of artists who help us see beauty without denying such suffering.

So I am usually not surprised by the wonderful creative mind that Enda is.[1] However, I have to confess I was not prepared when he laid out the project for which he wanted my help. He began by saying he thought he had three to five years of

---

1. For example I think of Enda's book *Gift and Call: Towards a Christian Theology*, Dublin, New York: Gill & Macmillan, 1975, remains one of the most interesting early attempts to rethink what moral theology might look like after Vatican II. In *Gift and Call* Enda reminds us that every gift is also a threat which is as relevant today as it was then.

active life left. He did so with no hint of regret, but rather as a realistic report about his life. He then said that in the time he had left he wanted to devote himself to the elimination of war. He explained that even though he had more or less always assumed a position of just war, he was really more the pacifist. So he thought the two of us ought to draft an 'Appeal to Abolish War.'

Enda went on to explain that two hundred years ago slavery not only existed but many people thought it was also morally unproblematic. Slavery, he observed, still exists; but no one now thinks slavery can be morally justified. The attempt to draft an 'Appeal to Abolish War' would be a beginning in order to start a discussion about war that would make war as morally problematic as slavery. Enda observed war might still exist two hundred years into the future, but at least we could begin the process in which we could hope no one in the future would think war to be a good idea. I confess I was stunned by the simple brilliance of Enda's proposal. I blurted out, 'That is a terrific idea' and happily agreed to work with Enda to write the Appeal.

I do think the Appeal is a 'terrific idea,' but it is an idea that at least presents some difficulty for those, like myself, who are advocates of Christian non-violence. I realise that may seem strange, for what does it mean to be a pacifist if you do not want to abolish war? Those of us committed to Christian non-violence clearly want to work for a world in which war does not exist. But we also believe, at least those of us whose pacifism has been learned from the work of John Howard Yoder, that we are pacifist not because pacifism is a strategy for ending war, but because that is the way we must live if we are to be faithful followers of Jesus. I often try to make this point by noting that Christians are not called to non-violence because we believe non-violence is a way to rid the world of war; but rather in a world of war, as faithful followers of Jesus, we cannot imagine being anything else than non-violent.

An appeal to abolish war might give the impression that the non-violence presupposed by such an appeal is that shaped by humanistic assumptions rather than the christological pacifism I represent. A call to abolish war could be interpreted as a denial of the eschatological presumptions that should shape Christian pacifism. As John Howard Yoder pointed out in his extraordinary essay, 'Peace Without Eschatology':

'Peace' is not an accurate description of what has generally happened to nonresistant Christians throughout history, nor of the way the conscientious objector is treated in most countries today. Nor does Christian pacifism guarantee a warless world. 'Peace' describes the pacifist hope, the goal in the light of which he acts, the character of his action, the ultimate divine certainty which lets his position make sense; it does not describe the external appearance or the observable results of his behaviour. This is what we mean by eschatology: a hope which, defying present frustration, defines a present position in terms of the yet unseen goal which gives it meaning.[2]

If Yoder is right, and I certainly think he is, had I made a decisive mistake in my response to Enda's initial proposal that we develop an 'Appeal to Abolish War?' Was I letting a Roman Catholic moral theologian tempt me to forget my Anabaptist convictions? Put differently, is not a call to abolish war exactly the kind of Constantinianism that any serious pacifist position must disavow? Do I really think that the world, that is all of God's creation that refuses to acknowledge that Christ is truly Lord, is capable of choosing against war? I obviously do not think my signing on to Enda's 'terrific idea' has these implications, but I think it important to say why they do not.

The reason is quite simple. The assumption that christological pacifists could not work to abolish war only underwrites the oft made claim that pacifists may be morally admirable, but they also must disavow political relevance.[3] Yoder spent his whole life trying to challenge that assumption. The eschatological convictions that shape Christian non-violence assume this is God's world. Accordingly, we do not believe that the boundary between church and world is a barrier that cannot be breached. Indeed we believe that the division between church and world is permeable. Therefore I see no reason that an 'Appeal to Abolish War' necessarily betrays the eschatological convictions that shape the Christian witness of non-violence. But it obviously

2. John Howard Yoder, *The Original Revolution*, Scottdale PA: Herald Press, 1971, 56. The original title of this essay was changed to 'If Christ Is Truly Lord' in *The Original Revolution*.
3. Reinhold Niebuhr is, of course, the most powerful proponent of this account of Christian non-violence. See, for example, his essays on pacifism and war in *Love and Justice: Selections From the Shorter Writings of Reinhold Niebuhr*, edited by D. B. Robertson New York: Meridian Books, 1967, 241-301.

makes a difference to whom such an appeal is addressed, as well as the reasons given for why such an appeal makes sense.

Enda and I discussed to whom the appeal should be addressed as well as the substance of the appeal. Enda wrote the first draft to which I only made a few changes. We addressed the 'Appeal' to fellow Christians hoping in particular to elicit response from theologians and ethicists in the Christian tradition, but the 'Appeal' makes clear that the call for an end to war is not restricted to Christians.[4] The reason, however, we believe we can call for an end to war is our conviction that God has in fact abolished war in the cross and resurrection of Christ. There are, of course, many reasons that can be given for calling for an end to war that do not presuppose the apocalyptic presumptions of the 'Appeal,' but we are convinced that the strongest case for the elimination of war entails the christological commitments at the centre of the 'Appeal.'

While we were working on the draft of the 'Appeal,' I began to think a good place to launch the 'Appeal' might be the annual conference on the culture of life and death sponsored by the Center for Ethics and Culture at the University of Notre Dame. These conferences are dedicated to exploring the themes of the culture of life and death at the heart of John Paul II's papacy. The Center's Director, Professor David Solomon, graciously invited Enda and myself to present our 'Appeal' during the Conference at the University of Notre Dame held on October 28, 2002. I shall never forget Enda's eloquent remarks to introduce the 'Appeal' at the Notre Dame conference. He begin quite simply noting that he was neither a pacifist or an advocate of just war, but simply a disciple of Jesus. I thought John Howard Yoder could not have put it better.

Rev Mike Baxter, CSC, and I also made presentations in defense of the 'Appeal,' but neither of us could match Enda's wonderful account of how his experiences with war in Ireland and Africa had convinced him why such an 'Appeal' is so important.

I wish I could reproduce Enda's remarks here because I have

---

4. It is not our presumption that theologians will want to sign on to our 'Appeal', but we hope the very decision not to sign the 'Appeal' will at least challenge those who do not sign to think through why it is they cannot sign. For at the very least we hope the 'Appeal' will occasion reflection about war that too often does not take place until an actual war occurs.

seldom heard a more eloquent defence of non-violence. But my memory is not sufficient for that task. Instead I will reproduce the text of the 'Appeal,' followed by my defence of our text. It may be unusual to reproduce for a Festschrift work written by the one to be honoured, but the 'Appeal,' I believe, honours Enda whose own work has always been an attempt to help us work together.

Moreover, I want to publish the 'Appeal' in this context because we need to use every chance we get to call attention to the 'Appeal'. At this point we can claim little result for our work to have the 'Appeal' discussed, but we recognise that as in the work of peace itself we must be patient. I write this just days (I suspect) before the United States attacks Iraq – a sobering reminder that our imaginations remain possessed by the assumption that war is a noble human undertaking. That we can think of no alternatives to war, I believe, makes the work of the Appeal all the more important.

The Text of the 'Appeal'
An Appeal to Abolish War
to Christian Leaders and Theologians
As Christians called out to serve the church in differing Christian traditions, we appeal to our Christian sisters and brothers to join in a campaign to abolish war as a legitimate means of resolving political conflict between states. Though our Appeal is addressed to the Christian community, we fervently believe that if our witness is true, many not part of that community may want to join our appeal to abolish war. God has after all created us all to desire the Kingdom of Peace.

To many theologians this call for the abolition of war will appear presumptuous on our part (who are these people anyhow?). To others it may seem theologically flawed and practically futile. Yet with John Paul II's phrase from *Centesimus Annus*, 'War Never Again,' ringing in our ears and Tertullian's succinct summary of early Church teaching before our eyes, 'The Lord in disarming Peter henceforth disarms every soldier,' we are driven back to that basic conviction that in the death, resurrection, and ascension of Jesus Christ, the destructive powers of this world, prominent among them War, were radically overcome. It is loyalty to the example and teaching of Jesus Christ which first and foremost summons Christians to renounce war and to seek with the wider religious and human communities to develop alternatives in protecting the innocent, restraining aggressors, and overcoming injustice. Let us study war no more. Let us study peace.

From their fourth century origins, Christian attempts at justifying war have always been intellectually and spiritually vulnerable as well as practically inadequate. It is very doubtful if any actual war during that period fulfilled the traditional criteria of *jus ad bellum* and *jus in bello*. In more recent times Christian leaders and thinkers who still endorse some theory of just war are finding it increasingly difficult to see how criteria such as having exhausted all non-violent means ('last resort'), non-combatant immunity, and proportionality could be observed. In official documents and theological analyses alike there is a discernible unease with the applicability of 'just war theory' but even greater unease with its Christian authenticity.

This Appeal, based primarily on the belief of the incompatibility of war with the teaching and example of Jesus Christ, wishes to draw all Christians into a serious conversation about the Christian and moral acceptability of war and indeed to draw all concerned humans into the examination and development of alternatives to war. Only in such a comprehensive enterprise can this Appeal's final goal of actually abolishing war hope to have any chance of success. We hope those committed to just war reflection will join us in calling for the abolition of war. For it surely must be the case that advocates of just war have, as we do, a stake in making war a doubtful enterprise.

Why now? We do not think so much that the peculiar horror of modern war is the primary reason or that people are so much more enlightened today that they will more readily respond to such an appeal or that alternatives are already in the making, although these may be auxiliary or indeed persuasive reasons for many. Rather, we call for the end of war now because all time is under God's judgment. So there is no time like the present (or the past) to say again in John Paul II's words what has already has been said by God in Christ: 'War never again.' Such a call seems all the more important, however, in a world where the uses of communication and its manipulation make war not only a greater possibility but more hidden.

We have no illusions that our call for the abolition of war will bring an immediate or even quick end to the massacres called

war. So we are phrasing it in terms for interrogation and dialogue, seeking as we have said to promote serious conversation
and analysis among Christian leaders and thinkers on the
Christian roots and possibilities of the project. We hope to enlist
university faculties in the theological and secular sciences as well
as research institutes in the search for the peaceful alternatives
that would be more easily convincing of the immorality of war
for a wider and (non-)Christian public by revealing it as also unnecessary.

This, of course, calls for an energetic and lengthy campaign
of conversation and perhaps better than conversation the conversion of Christians to the true anti-war dimension of their own
faith and the conversion of all to the enriching potential of their
fellow humans. Our call for the abolition of war will hopefully
put us on the long hard road towards the hope of developing
peaceful witness as well as developing attitudes and structures
for resolving conflicts non-violently. We believe the serious
study of the process of peace will only begin once the necessity
of war is denied.

There are encouraging precedents for the larger hope. It was
once assumed that slavery was simply part of 'the natural
order'. Those calling for slavery's abolition were thought to be
foolish utopian dreamers. We are well aware that slavery still
exists in multiple disguises, but no one thinks aloud that slavery
can be justified or that a public profit can be made from it. We
know that what we call war will continue in various guises, but
we trust that in the near future at least no Christian will be
tempted to think that when they say 'war,' they are affirming the
necessity of wars or giving them justification. Let the twenty-
first century be for war what the nineteenth was for slavery, the
era of its abolition, and let Christians give the leadership necessary in achieving that.

September 6, 2002

In Defence of the 'Appeal'
To call for the end of war can reproduce a problem that bedevils
all attempts to think about war in a morally serious manner. The
problem quite simply is whether we know what we are talking
about when we call for an end to 'war'. The problem can be
illumined by asking questions like: 'Why do we continue to call
a war a war if it is not a just war?' or 'Is the kind of war created

by the modern nation state system the same kind of killing that
often occurred between peoples and/or tribes?' Supporters of
war seem quite confident they know what they are talking about
when they defend the necessity of war. We are less confident we
know what we are talking about when we call for the abolition
of war, but it is exactly that kind of confidence characteristic of
the normal discourse about war we hope our appeal calls into
question.[5]

The question whether we know what we are talking about
when we talk about war can be illustrated by asking whether it
is possible to write a history of war. Such a question may appear
to be as odd as whether one believes in the church. One is tempted
to say 'Believe in it? Hell, I've seen it!' So, of course you can write
a history of war because it has been done. John Keegan has a
book entitled *A History of Warfare* so we know it can be done.[6]
Yet Keegan's history of warfare only confirms the difficulty of
knowing what is meant by war.

For example, Keegan criticises Clausewitz for advancing 'a
universal theory of what war *ought* to be, rather than what it actually was and has been.'[7] Accordingly Keegan argues that 'war
is not the continuation of policy by other means,' because 'war
antedates the state, diplomacy and strategy by many millennia.'
From Keegan's perspective war comes close to naming the
human condition. He observes:

Warfare is almost as old as man himself, and reaches into the
most secret places of the human heart, places where self dis-
solves rational purpose, where pride reigns, where emotion is
paramount, where instinct is king. 'Man is a political animal,'
said Aristotle. Clausewitz, a child of Aristotle, went no further
than to say that a political animal is a war-making animal.
Neither dared confront the thought that man is a thinking animal in whom the intellect directs the urge to hunt and the ability
to kill.[8]

Yet it is the same John Keegan who observes in his most recent book, *War and Our World*, that war is a protean activity that
unpredictably changes form. War, he observes, is like a disease

---

5. I use 'we' in this response to indicate that this is a joint project, not
only for Enda and myself but for all Christians.
6. John Keegan, *A History of Warfare*, New York: Vintage Books, 1993.
7. Ibid., 6
8. ibid.

that exhibits a capacity to mutate and mutates fastest in the face of efforts to control or eliminate it. Therefore Keegan offers no more determinative description of war than 'war is collective killing for some collective purpose.'[9]

Keegan's description of war is obviously intended to give an account of war that is morally neutral. But even a description as bland as that offered by Keegan is not successful in avoiding moral implications. For example, his description seems to make any attempts to distinguish between war and terrorism problematic.[10] Moreover, his claim that warfare is as old as mankind surely is overstated. Why does he not say that violence, not warfare, is the mark of our nature? Keegan is trying to provide an account of war that avoids questions of whether war is a good or bad thing. For Keegan war just 'is'. But he fails to see that even the claim that 'war just is' gives a moral status to violence that must be defended.[11]

Keegan's reticence to describe or 'define' war I think is inter-

---

9. John Keegan, *War and Our World*, New York: Vintage Books, 1998, 72

10. The assumption that a clear line can be drawn between war and terrorism often has the result of legitimating war. For example, Wendell Berry observes, 'Supposedly, if a nation perpetuates violence officially – whether to bomb an enemy airfield or a hospital – that nation is not guilty of 'terrorism'. But there is no need to hesitate over the difference between 'terrorism' or any violence and threat of violence that is terrifying. The National Security Strategy wishes to cause 'terrorism' to be seen 'in the same light as slavery, piracy, or genocide' – but not in the same light as war. The Strategy accepts and affirms the legitimacy of war.' Berry is commenting on the recent National Security Strategy published by the Bush White House in September, 2002. Berry notes the most significant statement in the document is: 'While the United States will constantly strive to enlist the support of the international community, we will not hesitate to act alone, if necessary, to exercise our right of self-defense by acting pre-emptively against such terrorists ...' Furthermore the Bust statement claims that the United States is justified in attacking any state that even thinks about developing weapons that may threaten us. Berry's remarks are entitled 'A Citizen's Response' and can be found in the Orion Society website.

11. I think that the position that assumes that war is neither good nor bad but just 'is' is quite interesting. It is so because it helps us to see we continue to have war, because we had war. War turns out to be a habit constitutive of human history that cannot be broken. I have argued something like this in my essay 'Should War Be Eliminated' in my book *Against the Nations: War and Survival in a Liberal Society*, Notre Dame:

esting because it helps make clear that 'war' comes freighted in our speech with normative commitments. Even when we think we are doing no more than 'describing war,' the notion 'war' carries with it (to revert to terms made famous by C. L. Stevenson) a 'pro' or 'con' attitude. But attitude only names habits in which our speech is imbedded that make descriptions seem inevitable and undeniable. War, we believe, is such a habit that shapes us to assume – even if a war is not a just war – a war is still 'war' and as such is an activity which while regrettable remains a moral necessity. In other words, we continue to think that killing in war is somehow morally different than other forms of killing. Yet it is by no means clear why we think war can be so distinguished from unjustified forms of violence.

Our 'Appeal to Abolish War' at the very least is meant to challenge the assumption that it is obvious that war can easily be distinguished from other forms of unjustified killing. Accordingly we challenge those habits of speech that make war such normalising discourse. We want to call into question the assumption made by many that war is often horrible, but we simply have no alternatives in the world as we know it to war. Too many think that as destructive as war may be, war names a necessary practice that we cannot, and perhaps, even should not live without.

In short, we seek nothing less than to have our everyday use of war disciplined by how we must learn to speak as Christians. Christians pray for peace. We often say 'Christ is our peace.' We hear read from scripture Sunday after Sunday that Christians are recipients of the peace only God can give. We celebrate the gift of peace in our hymns which not only call for peace but may be one of the gifts God has given us to be actually at peace with one another. For we do not sing hymns alone; we sing them together in a manner that anticipates the unity that is ours to share.[12] Such unity is what we Christians have learned to call peace.

University of Notre Dame Press, 1992, 169-208. What the church offers the world is not therefore simply a people committed to peace, but a counter history to that which can only tell the story of how we got to where we are at in terms of war.

12. Dennis O' Brien makes this point in his lovely book, *God and the New Haven Railroad (And Why Neither One is Doing Very Well)*, Boston: Beacon Press, 1986. O' Brien observes 'religion is about singing – praying, talking, gesturing – about the humanly unfixable. That is why reli-

For example, consider this stanza from the hymn 435 'O God Of Every Nation' from the Methodist Hymnal:

Keep bright in us the vision of days when war shall cease,
when hatred and division give way to love and peace,
tell dawns the morning glorious when truth and justice reign,
and Christ shall rule victorious o'er all the world's domain.[13]

I think nothing is exceptional about this hymn. My assumption is that you can find numerous hymns in every denominational hymnal that would express quite similar views. But if war is assumed by Christians to be morally unproblematic or even the less of two evils, then how can we sing such hymns? To do so while assuming that war may be a good is to make the Christian desire for peace to be no more than pious sentiment that does no work – it is to make 'peace' some distant ideal rather than an eschatological reality. Our 'Appeal for the Abolition of War' is a call for our theology and ethics to catch up with the church's songs and poetry.

However, it may well be asked if all the Appeal amounts to is a language transforming proposal. We certainly hope it is more than that; but it is at least a call for us to discipline our speech. Moreover, to call for Christians to re-examine how our speech about war may betray the gospel is no small thing. If the Appeal could help Christians speak about war in a manner that does not reproduce the assumption that war is a necessary evil, then a great thing will have been done. At the very least the burden of proof will be on those who support war as the only means for naming the relation between nations and peoples.

Finally, some may be hesitant to support the 'Appeal' because they assume to sign the 'Appeal' would commit them to a pacifist position. But we have carefully worded the 'Appeal' to avoid that conclusion. It is our hope that many who have struggled to make the just war tradition relevant in our world will find themselves able to sign the 'Appeal'. We understand that many assume war is a good necessary to achieve justice. We have no reason to challenge accounts of just war that justify the justice a just war is to pursue. But we hope the 'Appeal' provides

---

gious ceremonies have clustered about the celebration of our chains – the places where we are stuck.' 133.
13. *The United Methodist Hymnal*, Nashville: The United Methodist Publishing House, 1989.

the context for exploring how such an understanding of justice is, as Aquinas maintained, also the subject of charity.[14]

The 'Appeal' is first and foremost addressed to Christian theologians and leaders. We assume and hope that non-Christians may have reasons to support the 'Appeal'. But we believe that Christians, when they are thinking like Christians, will discover they cannot but challenge the assumption that war is one of the necessities of life. When war is so understood, we believe war is but a name for the powers defeated by the death and resurrection of Jesus. So let us no longer serve such 'elemental spirits' but rather be what we are: the church of Jesus Christ. That is why we are bold to call for the abolition of war. We can only do so because we believe war has been abolished through the triumph of the resurrection of Jesus Christ.

---

14. I have probably loaded more into this paragraph than any paragraph can stand, but the point is extremely important. Many just war advocates suggest that just war is an attempt to provide a series of exceptions from the general stance of Christian non-violence. In contrast, Paul Ramsey argued that advocates of just war should not think the object of just war is first of all peace, but rather justice. Accordingly it is a mistake to assume that just war is a strategy to achieve peace because in this time between times peace cannot and should not exist. I think this is the strongest defence that can be given of just war, but I also think that just warriors are seldom candid about whether such an account of just war can be theologically justified. For a discussion of Ramsey's views on this matter see my 'Foreword' to Paul Ramsey's *The Just War: Force and Political Responsibility*, Boston: Rowman and Littlefield, 2002, ix-xiii. For a recent defence of just war as a pursuit of justice see George Weigel, 'Moral Clarity in a Time of War', *First Things*, 129, January 2003, 20-27. Weigel argues that just war understood as a pursuit of justice means that *jus ad bellum* considerations require that a nation is obligated to go to war before any analysis of *jus in bello* concerns are raised. He notes, for example, that many after September 11 2001, have raised questions about avoiding indiscriminate non-combatant casualties in a war against terrorism, 'while little attention was paid to the prior question of the moral obligation of government to pursue national security *and world order*, both of which were directly threatened by the terrorist networks', 23. I have italicised the phrase *and world order* to indicate how just war can quickly become an ideological tool for those that assume that their country knows what is good for 'world order'. What could it mean for such an understanding of justice to be shaped by Christian charity?

A Final Word to Enda

Such is the story of how Enda got me involved in the project to write an appeal to abolish war. I remain extremely grateful that he did so. God knows what effect the 'Appeal' may have, but we cannot pretend that what we are doing is being done for effect. I think we have written the 'Appeal' because we are friends, which is reminder to me how grateful I am to Enda for claiming me as a friend. Such friendship is surely the gift God has given us so that we, that is, the church might be God's alternative to war.

Considering Some Constituents
of Conflict Resolution

Terence McCaughey

Sometimes we speak as though there was a specific recipe for reconciliation, or set conditions for forgiveness. Some have even given the impression that for instance remorse, repentance, forgiveness and reconciliation must follow one another in a certain order if there is to be a genuine resolution of the problem. But in fact we learn that the processes of the human mind are too anarchic and uncontrollable for us confidently to name all the 'ingredients' of reconciliation or lay down the order in which they should be added to the mix.

In the case of political conflict, it has been argued that three distinct stages may be distinguished on the road, i.e. political accommodation, the decision to forgive (sometimes, though not always, accompanied by a decision to ask for forgiveness) and finally the resolve to set out on the journey towards reconciliation. The form and timing of these three steps in any given situation will vary enormously. Cultural considerations will ensure that features of the process which seem very important in one conflictual situation may be less so in another. What is essential to resolution of conflict for instance in a 'shame' culture or in a Buddhist culture may scarcely manifest itself at all in what is called a guilt culture and vice versa.[1]

That being said, however, it is to be observed that projects associated with the facilitation of transition from conflict to relative peace and stability are often founded on the premise that healing and resolution can come only as a result of remembering, re-calling and recording what actually happened during the period of conflict and oppression.

---

1. On the distinction between 'shame' cultures and 'guilt' cultures, see Ruth Benedict, *The Chrysanthemum and the Sword: Patterns of Japanese Culture*, London: Routledge & Keegan Paul, 1967 and Ian Buruma, *Wages of Guilt, Memories of War in Germany and Japan*, London, 1994, 116 et passim.

Remembering itself is inevitable, not optional. It is often un-controllable and it is not for nothing that we speak of memories 'flooding in'. The real questions concern the use to which we put the memories (particularly the collective memories) which we like to repeat, and about how or whether the act of remembering is to be as therapeutic or even salvific as it can be but is not al-ways. The Report of the *Healing through Remembering Project*,[2] is written in the conviction that remembering and articulating are essential to healing. However, the report does record the objec-tions of those who in Northern Ireland contend that the past is 'best left alone' or not 'raked over'. Of course, it is the case that in the North of Ireland, as elsewhere, it is most often those who for-merly exercised what power there was who insist on this point.

However, anyone who has read that report or has worked their way though the first volumes of the report of the South African *Truth and Reconciliation Commission*[3] will readily ac-knowledge the cathartic effect on both perpetrators and victims of owning up to the truth, telling it, hearing it. Such projects go a long way (if not the whole way) towards enabling the past to be what it is, i.e. past, rather than continue to determine or poison our present. But perhaps the following considerations should be borne in mind:

1. The expression of remorse on the part of perpetrators deemed nec-essary to the granting of absolution in e.g. Christian practise, may not be essential in all circumstances: the case of the South African Truth and Reconciliation Commission.

The Promotion of National Unity and Reconciliation Act (1994) established the Truth and Reconciliation Commission in South Africa and laid down the terms under which it should operate. It defined the conditions which would have to be met by any per-son who applied to the Commission for amnesty. It was re-quired that

1. the act for which amnesty was sought should have hap-pened in the period between 1960, the year of the Sharpville Massacre, and mid-1994, the year that Nelson Mandela was inaugurated as President;

2. the applicant had to be shown to have been politically mo-tivated in the action (s)he took, or to have acted in response

---

2. Report of *Healing through Remembering Project*, Belfast, June 2002.

3. *Truth and Reconciliation Commission of South Africa Report*, Cape Town, South Africa & London: Macmillan, 1998 (5 Volumes).

to the orders of a political organisation or of the state or of a recognised liberation movement;

3. the amnesty applicant had to be shown to have made a full disclosure of all facts relevant to the offence; and

4. proportionality had to have been respected, i.e. the means required to have been proportional to the objective.

Provision was made in the legislation for victims to oppose applications for amnesty by showing that the above conditions had not been met. But the legislation did not give them the right of veto over any amnesty granted by the Amnesty Committee of the TRC. Moreover – and most important for the subject under consideration in this short paper – applicants for amnesty were not expected or required to show remorse for their actions, though in fact many did when they appeared before the Hearings Committee.

Archbishop Desmond Tutu, Chairperson of the Commission, has confessed that at the time that its terms of reference were being formulated, he was among those who took the view that applicants should be expected to show remorse. However, by the time the TRC began its work, he had changed his mind on this, recognising just how difficult it is to assess the genuineness or otherwise of any remorse (or, for that matter, apparent callousness) shown by applicants, or to basic conclusions on impressions of their bearing or behaviour when they appeared before the Committee of the TRC. Recognising that 'there's no art to find the mind's construction in the face', those who drew up the Commission's terms of reference decided against there being any such requirement, while insisting on the above-mentioned conditions which have the advantage, at least, of being readily verifiable. Particularly important was the full-disclosure requirement in establishing what have been called 'factual' and 'moral' truth. But when everything has been said that should be said in favour of full and explicit disclosure and the undoubtedly beneficial results that flow from it, there may nevertheless remain a lingering doubt – not so much about the capacity of the truth to clear the air as about the possibility of actually making a full disclosure in all situations. It is arguable that truth commissions have been over-dependent in their procedures on precedents set by the practice of confession in the Christian tradition, whether auricular or general. However that may be, confession at one end of the scale, and psychotherapy at the other, have at least this much in common with the Truth Commissions of South America and South Africa, that they aim to bring subconscious concerns and anxieties to the surface so they can be talked about.[4]

The benefits of this in thousands of cases are unquestionable. However, there are situations where the wounds of conflict have apparently been addressed in less explicit and less verbal ways.

2. The story of the reconciliation of the twin sons of Jacob (Genesis 32-33) does not include any formal, verbal or explicit reference to the conflict, yet it is told by the writer as a classic example of reconciliation, embarked upon and effected.

The cause of the estrangement of the two brothers is told in Genesis 27. The ingenious younger brother Jacob, with his mother's help, cheats the older brother Esau out of his 'birth-right'. Esau is justifiably indignant and, overcome with resentment, he swears to avenge himself on his brother Jacob. So Jacob flees for his life and lives for some years beyond the reach of his brother's anger. He settles down in the household of his uncle Laban, goes into service with him and in due course he marries two of his daughters. After enriching himself substantially in this employment, he later provokes the resentment and jealousy of his uncle and, for peace sake, parts company with him, taking with him the large family and considerable livestock he has acquired. It is at this point that Jacob (Genesis 32:3f) takes the brave though potentially fool-hardy step of sending emissaries to his brother Esau. They are instructed to make a report on what has been happening to Jacob since last the brothers met and to say what wealth he has acquired. Jacob is alarmed when the messengers return and tell him that Esau is coming to meet him with four hundred men. Jacob falls to his knees and prays to be delivered from Esau 'lest he come and slay us all'.

That same night, when darkness falls and Jacob is alone, the narrator tells us he had that visit from an anonymous stranger 'who wrestled with him till the break of day'. The stranger is not 'prevailing against Jacob', so he touches the hollow of his thigh and Jacob's thigh goes out of joint. The stranger prevails on Jacob to tell him his name, but he does not divulge his own.

4. See Priscilla B. Hayner, *Unspeakable Truths, Confronting State Terror and Atrocity*, New York and London: Routledge, 2001, particularly chapter 9.

However, the stranger's identity is clearly implied by Jacob's calling the name of the place Peni-el, i.e. 'Face of God'. For, says Jacob, 'I have seen God face to face and yet my life is preserved.' The significance and force of this is picked up the next morning when, still with Leah and Rachel and the children between himself and the oncoming Esau, Jacob still at a distance, prostrates himself seven times before his on-coming brother. Then the whole atmosphere changes, for Esau breaks into a run, embraces Jacob, falls on his neck and kisses him. He refuses to accept Jacob's gifts, claiming to have no need of them. Jacob, however, persists in his offers, saying: 'If I have found favour in your sight, then accept my present: for truly to see your face is like seeing the face of God, with such favour you have received me.'

After the night spent alone with his conscience and the stranger with whom he wrestles till daybreak, Jacob darkly guesses who the stranger was and he is amazed that he has emerged from the encounter alive. 'I have seen God face to face,' he says, 'and yet my life is preserved.' The next morning he goes forward to meet his estranged brother and is silently embraced by him. Gazing into his face he (as it were) recognises the face he had seen the night before and, not merely is his life preserved, it actually begins again.

Although accompanied by four hundred men, Esau runs (in itself an undignified and vulnerable thing to do) and embraces Jacob. The narrator, however, grants us a glimpse of the sober expectations he entertains even of such a dramatic reconciliation in what he tells us happened next. Although Esau suggests that they proceed on their journey together, they do not in fact do so. They settle in separate parts of the territory they must share – in limited mutual trust. What gives this story of sibling rivalry at this point its particular piquancy is the fact that the writer knew perfectly well that the brothers Esau and Jacob were the eponymous ancestors of Edom and Israel respectively. So the brothers' story is also the story of two peoples living in a single land in tension, and sometimes in hostility, and requiring reconciliation at one another's hands.

The narrative of the reconciliation of the brothers offers several important pointers worth the while of commentators and practitioners of reconciliation to note, even today:

(i) Their rapprochement comes about as the result of a decision, in the first instance of Jacob who is at this point in his life wealthy but more or less isolated and friendless. He has had to part company with the uncle who had earlier been his refuge when the one he feared most was Esau. Now he has no alternative but to make peace, if it is possible, with Esau. So he sends messengers to him as already described – it is the initial step in what in other circumstances we might call a political accommodation. It is not at this stage a move towards reconciliation but, as in many other situations, it is perhaps a pre-requisite of that move.

(ii) The more emotionally draining decision is that of Esau who apparently throws aside years of deep resentment, which must surely be one of the primary ingredients of what we call 'forgiveness', even though that word is never mentioned in this narrative.

(iii) Worthy of note is the fact that whereas Jacob does a lot of scheming and talking, what he keeps talking about (i.e the offer of gifts) is largely ignored and turns out to be beside the point. On the other hand, Esau's response (or should we really say initiative) is entirely non-verbal – 'he ran, fell on his neck and kissed him'.

Interestingly enough, so is the action of the waiting father in Jesus' parable of the prodigal son. In that story all the talking is done by the returning son who approaches his father's gate with a well-rehearsed speech. The father does not even attempt to respond to it or agree about the terms of rehabilitation which the son proposes. He simply also turns and falls on the neck of his boy. It seems that verbal formulations run the risk of coming between them rather than drawing them together.

(iv) Unlike the younger son in Jesus' parable, Jacob does not refer to the unfortunate circumstances that had driven them apart in the first place. It is an important and perhaps surprising aspect of this story, as of the meeting of Joseph with his brothers at which he finally reveals his identity to them, that they do not confess or even ask for pardon – perhaps because there is nothing they could say that Joseph does not know already. It is only when Jacob their father dies and they fear that Joseph may now take revenge on them that they do finally ask for forgiveness of their transgression. But Joseph tells them not to fear (Gen 50:19) and asks rhetorically 'And in the place of God?' One may perhaps compare Esau's words in Genesis 33:10.

(v) It would seem that the spectacular reconciliation of the two brothers and, by implication, the two tribes descended from them, is effected without words of confession or absolution, but is none the less effective for that.

3. Healing which goes beyond the delineation of individual trauma of individual affliction: coming to terms with the self and coming to terms with one's broader social and cultural environment, which itself is devastated by war.

The research done by Alcinda Honwana among rural poor people in Southern Mozambique in the wake of civil conflict in that country between Renamo and Frelimo:[5] her study focuses on the processes of community reconstruction in a country where, unlike South Africa, there has been no Truth and Reconciliation Commission and in the absence of any counselling provided by a national or regional community health service. The people have to some considerable extent been able to draw a line in the sand at a political level. But at the social and psycho-social level that has not been so easy. In the absence of any structures that might enable them to do so, people have sought their own solutions and dug deep within the resources of their communities to find healing. Alcinda Honwana found them doing what they could. She found parents dealing with offspring who were returned child soldiers, family members who had fought on different sides or (due to pressures of poverty) had fought sometimes on one side and sometimes on the other. The distinction between civilian and soldier in such situations is blurred, but this unclear distinction has not served to lower the level of brutality or violence.

In such a situation there is a web of relationships between people going from one side to another, simply trying to survive but, as they do, witnessing (as 'children' often) what adults in most conflicts can often be spared. Alcinda Honwana puts it thus: 'Reconciliation is at once very difficult and very powerful in the sense that it is pursued within the self, within the family … It is intense. It is perhaps more difficult than reconciliation between strangers.'

She notes how acutely aware the people of southern

5. Alcinda Honwana, 'Healing the Social Wounds of War: Case Studies from Mozambique and Angola' in *Transcending a Century of Injustice*, ed. Charles Villa-Vicencio, Rondebosch, South Africa, 2000, 101-111.

Mozambique, among whom she was working, were of the importance of ritual in any effort to restore 'normality' into their lives. The rituals they employ are centred on the belief that life cannot simply go on after the killing as though nothing has happened and, of course, that not just the combatants but also the whole community of the living and the dead has been affected, infected, polluted. Their rituals are centred on a belief in spiritual beings – ancestors of course, but also the actual war dead who are often unburied and continue therefore to be destabilising presences.

We do not need to share this belief system in order to feel the pressure that the conflict's dead continue to exert; we think of the hunger strikers of the Maze Prison or the powerful appeal that can be made to the memory of the dead of the Somme. Furthermore, 'revenge – morally considered – is a desire to keep faith with the dead, to honour their memory by taking up their cause where they left off' (Michael Ignatieff).[6] Ignatieff goes on to say that the problem for reconciliation is precisely that it must 'compete with the powerful alternative morality of violence'. In order to do so, it must address everything in both the individual and the society which has been dislocated and brutalised by the conflict.

The rituals of southern Mozambique which Alcinda Honwana describes attempt to confront bloodshed experienced as pollution not alone of combatants but also of the whole community and the unseen world.

Experience of these rituals, as practised in Mozambique and Angola, suggests that western psychotherapeutic models are not necessarily applicable in all situations everywhere, and must at best be regarded as only one of several ways of effecting post-conflictual healing. However impressive its results, western psychotherapy must be recognised as itself a culturally-conditioned methodology. At its heart is the understanding that the individual can be brought to the point of externalising her/his feelings. The treatment of PTSD (post-traumatic stress disorder) was first identified in the USA in work undertaken with veterans of the Vietnam war. This approach was based on and developed from attempts to understand the condition of American soldiers and veterans who went from civilian 'normality' to war

6. Michael Ignatieff, *The Warrior's Honour, Ethnic War and the Modern Conscience*, London: Chatto & Windus, 1998, 188-9.

and then returned to 'normality'. But this 'normality' is precisely what the boy-soldiers of Mozambique and their families have never experienced.

Given the socio-economic background of many GIs and ordinary British soldiers in (say) Northern Ireland, it is often not their experience either. They are often merely exchanging one abnormal social setting for another. No attempt to enable serving soldiers to accommodate themselves to 'normal life' or to deal with what they have seen and more or less willingly participated in, can afford to be as individually directed as most of our therapy has been.

The rituals described by Alcinda Honwana and others are not aimed at addressing the afflictions, guilt or shame of the individual alone, but rather aim to cleanse the community, the individual and all associated with him, however remotely.

One of her case-studies is the story of a young Mozambique 'veteran'. When he returned to his village he was not hugged or shown affection. Instead, he was taken to the *undumba* ('house of the spirits') where his grandfather thanked the spirits of their ancestors for bringing him back. Then a traditional healer supervised a ceremony aimed at cleansing him from the pollution he would inevitably have suffered. As a part of this the boy was put into a grass hut, carrying his old army clothes. At a certain point the whole hut, including the clothes, was set alight and at the last moment the boy veteran was 'rescued' from the flames. All this took place in the presence of his entire family, and was entirely non-verbal, although the actions were apparently understood by all present. In both Mozambique and Angola the aims of these rituals tend to be frustrated due to the poverty to which the young combatants have returned, but the rituals clearly aim to address the individual's plight in a social catastrophe.

It would be crude and naïve to suggest that such rituals can be copied and transferred to another unrelated society. Nevertheless, important lessons can perhaps be learned:

1. These rituals are performed without regard to what we might be inclined to call the guilt or innocence of the combatants. Rather,

2. they provide a genuine closure on the brutal and horrifying story because they appear to emphasise the pollution involved for the whole community once blood is shed and

3. they are non-verbal and, because they are they do not re-

quire of the more or less traumatised either to repeat formulations that are not their own, nor do they expect them to verbalise experiences which may go, and probably do go, beyond the power of language to express.

Church Politics and HIV Prevention: Why is the Condom Question So Significant and So Neuralgic?

Jon D. Fuller, SJ and James F. Keenan, SJ

As we address the politics of the church in its response to the call for HIV/AIDS prevention, we want to make three preliminary comments. First, we discuss our respective backgrounds, and how contemporary church people like Enda and ourselves have become involved in these policy issues. Second, we briefly review current statistics and forecasts for the HIV/AIDS epidemic so as to appreciate the urgency of working toward HIV/AIDS prevention. Third, we review data on condom effectiveness as critical to the question of the moral means of achieving HIV prevention. We will then move on to the central focus of this reflection, 'A study in the phenomenology of Roman Catholic teaching on HIV prevention.' Here we utilise three narratives to demonstrate how politics, local experience, prior texts and theological method have become interwoven to create the contemporary history of the Catholic approach to HIV prevention.

I. a. Our Respective Backgrounds

Because we share much the same vision of the world, the church and theology with Enda, and because our work with him overlaps precisely on the point of working for HIV/AIDS prevention, we believe it helpful to describe how we came together to work on this topic. Hopefully the reader will see that decisions are often found not in the moment, but as Enda has taught us, in the narrative. Narratives outline how the vocation to pursue moral truth takes us into the world precisely where there is suffering.

Jon Fuller entered medical school in San Diego in 1979, and by the end of his studies four years later had never heard of AIDS. His internship and residency commenced in 1983 at San Francisco General Hospital, and between the time he had interviewed there and arrived several months later, the epidemic had exploded in that city and in that hospital. One week after his arrival the hospital was to open the world's first inpatient AIDS unit. Without anticipating it, he had become immersed in one of the epicenters of the epidemic before there was knowledge of the causative agent or its modes of transmission, before diagnostic tests were available, and before any specific treatments had been developed.

His initial impressions came from two quite different perspectives. On the one hand, the epidemic presented remarkable clinical and scientific challenges as workers tried to comprehend what was happening at a biological level, and then to translate that into effective patient care. On the other hand a raft of thorny questions faced communities of faith as they attempted to respond pastorally to populations who had until that moment been marginalised not only by society but by the churches themselves: gay men and injection drug users.

During the first ten to fifteen years of the epidemic, Catholic pastoral care workers needed to be reminded that when they approached someone sick or dying with HIV, reiterating the Catholic moral teaching about sexuality (or homosexuality) was not what was usually being asked of them, nor what was helpful to their clients. Over time, pastoral workers weeded themselves out: those who were not helpful left the scene, while those who genuinely assisted people to live well and to die well with this disease (and to reconcile themselves with God and often with the church) remained and trained others.

Apart from work being done at the level of individual care, there were also challenges in helping Catholic medical institutions to respond to the epidemic. This, too, was successful: at the present time in the United States, 45% of more than 600 Catholic hospitals provide HIV/AIDS care as compared with only 32% of hospitals overall.[1] Similarly, there was need to assist Catholic religious orders and dioceses in learning to care for HIV-infected members, and in appreciating the complexities of policy development regarding HIV testing for candidates applying for admission to seminaries and religious life.[2]

---

1. Digital Realm Entertainment Group, US Hallmark Cable Channel, cited this statistic in its program 'Sowing Seeds,' 7 April 2002.
2. Keenan, James, 'HIV Testing of Seminary and Religious-Order Candidates', *Review for Religious* LV May-June 1996, 297-314, and Fuller, Jon, 'HIV/AIDS: An Overview', in *Clergy and Religious and the AIDS Epidemic*, Chicago: National Federation of Priests' Councils, 1994, 3-50.

As pastoral and clinical care-givers in this epidemic, the Catholic Church's members have been exemplary. It has been estimated by Vatican officials that the Catholic Church provides 25% of all medical care for persons living with HIV/AIDS worldwide.[3] Yet despite progress in caring for the infected, the question of HIV/AIDS prevention today is arguably one of the most important and problematic issues within the contemporary political life of the Roman Catholic Church.

In an attempt to draw scholarly attention to this question, in 1995 the Reverend Michael J. Buckley, SJ, director of the Jesuit Institute at Boston College, offered the Institute's sponsorship of a seminar of academicians who were to some degree associated with Boston College in order to address the question: what contribution could be made to help the church engage the best of its own tradition in responding to the epidemic? Jim Keenan was one of the members of that seminar, bringing him and Fuller together for the first time.

On one occasion the seminar invited the late Dr Jonathan Mann, a mentor and friend to Fuller, to address the group and to share his insights on how the church might better respond to the epidemic. Dr Mann was the first director of the World Health Organisation (WHO) Global Programme on AIDS, and had helped to establish Zaire's Project SIDA, an enormously fruitful clinical and research collaboration between African and Northern physicians. In responding to the question, Dr Mann, a Jew, recalled his experience at the Vatican meeting on AIDS in 1989: 'The pope said that the person with AIDS should be treated like Christ himself. I thought to myself: "Is this church – which is one of the major care-givers of the world – living up to its own standards?" What impresses me more in trying to move forward is less trying to have you follow my ideas than to hold you to your own.'

His insight gave us a critical starting point and direction: to recognise and to utilise the church's sophisticated, multi-layered way of approaching difficult moral questions. We did not need to go outside the church's tradition to ask how it can respond. We needed, instead, to bring the best of the church's own well developed resources to bear on this issue.

---

3. Lozano, Archbishop Javier, President of the Pontifical Council for Health Workers, speaking to the UN General Assembly's Special Session on AIDS, *Catholic News Service*, 28 June 2001.

Now a little more background on Jim before he joined the Boston College Seminar. He had been studying for a licentiate and a doctorate in moral theology at the Gregorian University from 1982-1987. His basic premise was that the tradition of moral theology in the Roman Catholic Church was richer, more humane and more supple than what was being conveyed on a variety of topics by numerous constituencies in the contemporary Roman Catholic Church.

In December 1987, the Administrative Board of the National Conference of Catholic Bishops (NCCB) in the US published *The Many Faces of AIDS*, a compassionate document that highlighted, among other things, the moral legitimacy of the church's toleration of public educational programmes that included accurate information on condoms for HIV/AIDS prevention.[4] The document cited Augustine's *De Ordine* in justifying its use of the classical moral principle of tolerance in this circumstance.[5] In the document's appendix, the writers took up the case of a health care worker in a Catholic institution who recommends sexual abstinence to a patient who is HIV-positive. After learning that the patient has no intention of being abstinent, the letter advises: 'If it is obvious that the person will not act without bringing harm to others, then the traditional Catholic wisdom with regard to one's responsibility to avoid inflicting greater harm may be appropriately applied.'[6] Several US cardinals, bishops and archbishops subsequently attacked the document precisely because of the condom issue.[7] Their actions, together with Cardinal Ratzinger's later intervention supporting their position, set the stage for a nearly intractable debate (as we will see later in more detail).[8]

Jim returned to the States just as this debate broke. Noting that toleration simply permits an action to occur, and that the health care worker's recommendation is more akin to an act of

---

4. National Conference of Catholic Bishops Administrative Board, 'The Many Faces of AIDS: A Gospel Response', *Origins* XVII/28, 24 December 1987, 482-489.

5. Ibid., footnote 7.

6. Ibid., 488-489.

7. *Origins*, 'Reaction to AIDS Statement', XVII/28, 24 December 1987, 489-493, and *Origins*, 'Continued Reaction to AIDS Statement', XVII/30, 1 January 1988, 516-522.

8. *Origins*, 'Cardinal Ratzinger's Letter on AIDS Document', XVIII/18, 7 July 1988, 117-118.

material co-operation, he wrote a lengthy, technical article out-
lining the applicability of the principle of co-operation as the
more appropriate moral principle to apply in this circumstance.[9]

Keenan's article became the first of many that he and other
moral theologians would write which applied seventeenth-
century moral principles to demonstrate the compatibility of
magisterial teaching with effective HIV/AIDS prevention methods. In particular, these theologians highlighted that in the case
of HIV the condom was not being used as a device for contraception, but as a prophylactic against transmitting a deadly disease. They showed how traditional principles acknowledged the
legitimacy of such a distinction, and defended condoms for
HIV/AIDS prevention while upholding – or at least not contesting – the validity of church teaching on contraception.[10] That
distinction – between the therapeutic and the contraceptive – is
found in *Humanae Vitae* itself: 'The church does not consider at
all illicit the use of those therapeutic means necessary to cure
bodily diseases, even if a foreseeable impediment to procreation
should result therefrom – provided such impediment is not directly intended for any motive whatsoever' (paragraph 19).

Similarly, the distinction had earlier been applied to the birth
control pill. In that case, moralists and bishops recognised that
the church's condemnation of contraception did not extend to
the use of 'the pill' to regulate a woman's abnormal menstrual
cycle. That is, recognising that the pill could be used for purposes
other than contraception, many authors noted that church teaching only condemned intentionally contraceptive activity.[11]
Moral theologians were now making use of a similar distinction

9. Keenan, James, 'Prophylactics, Toleration and Cooperation:
Contemporary Problems and Traditional Principles', *International
Philosophical Quarterly* XXIX/2, 1988, 205-221.

10. Keenan, James, ed., assisted by Lisa Sowle Cahill, Jon Fuller, and
Kevin Kelly, *Catholic Ethicists on HIV/AIDS Prevention*, Continuum,
New York, 2000, 21-29. The most significant argument for condoms and
against the teaching on birth control comes from Kelly, Kevin T., *New
Directions in Sexual Ethics: Moral Theology and the Challenge of AIDS*,
Geoffrey Chapman, London, 1998. For a survey of the principle's appli-
cations, see Fuller, Jon and Keenan, James, 'Condoms, Catholics and
HIV/AIDS Prevention', *The Furrow* LII, 2001, 459-467.

11. Ford, John C., and Kelly, Gerald, 'Sterilizing Drugs,' in *Contemporary
Moral Theology, Volume II, Marriage Questions*, The Newman Press,
Westminster, Maryland, 1963, 338-377.

to afford their bishops a way of discussing and promoting HIV/AIDS prevention strategies without in any way compromising the teaching on birth control.

However, no matter how much this distinction had been proposed, little progress was being made in moving toward a consensus on the question. Therefore, in 1997 we invited four others to meet with us to consider specifically the issue of HIV/AIDS prevention: Lisa Sowle Cahill, Professor of Moral Theology at Boston College; Rev Kevin Kelly, a senior moral theologian from Great Britain; Rev Robert Vitillo, ACSW, former Director of AIDS programmes with Caritas Internationalis in the Vatican and currently Director of the Catholic Campaign for Human Development of the US Bishops' Conference; and Rev Enda McDonagh. That meeting led to the publication of *Catholic Ethicists on HIV/AIDS Prevention*.

Having described how our personal experience and our work with Enda has focused us sharply on the question of HIV prevention from the perspective of the Catholic moral tradition, let us now turn our attention to the glaring facts of the epidemic itself.

I. b. The Demographics of the HIV/AIDS Pandemic

Although it was recognised only in 1981, by 1999 AIDS had become the fourth greatest cause of death in the world, accounting for 4.8% of all deaths worldwide and three million deaths per year (8,000 each day). In Sub-Saharan Africa AIDS is the leading cause of death, accounting for more than one-fifth of all deaths and twice as many as the second cause of death.[12] Today, with forty two million people living with HIV/AIDS and twenty five million persons having died, sixty seven million persons have had their lives dramatically changed by this viral epidemic. Nearly 14,000 new infections occur every day, with the vast majority of these occurring in developing countries, through heterosexual transmission, by persons who are largely unaware of their HIV status. Half of new infections occur in women, and 2,000 per day in persons younger than 15. The disease is not spreading evenly, however. Between 1999 and 2001, percentage increases of HIV-infected persons in various regions of the world ranged from a negligible increase in Australia and a 4% in

---

12. World Health Care Report, WHO, 2000.

North America, to an 89% increase in South/Southeast Asia and a 138% increase in Eastern Europe and Central Asia.[13]

AIDS has had a dramatic impact on duration of life, with adult life expectancy dropping by fifteen to thirty three years in some countries.[14] Although as recently as 2001 the UN had estimated that by mid-century the world's population would be reduced by at least 300 million because of the AIDS epidemic, that reduction has recently been revised to 480 million, with forty seven million of the increased number of deaths expected to come from India and forty million from China.[15]

In 2000, one fifth of African orphans had lost at least one parent as a result of AIDS. That proportion is currently 50%, and is expected to grow to 70% by 2010, when one in ten children in sub-Saharan Africa will have lost one or both of their parents to AIDS (accounting for twenty nine million AIDS orphans). Countries such as the Central African Republic have closed more than 100 schools as a result of teacher deaths, and illness of parents often causes children (especially girls) to be pulled from school both because of lack of school fees and because their efforts are needed to manage family farms.[16]

In response to growing numbers of unparented or poorly parented AIDS orphans living in large cities, in recognition of shrinking economies due to AIDS, and with HIV prevalence in some military populations as high as 60-90%,[17] the UN security council has met to discuss AIDS not to consider its health ramifications, but because of the security implications of these numerous dramatic changes.[18]

I. c. HIV Prevention
Given the relentless spread of HIV around the world, and particularly in economically underdeveloped situations, preventing new infections must obviously be a paramount concern. Many

13. UNAIDS.
14. UN Department of Social and Economic Affairs, 2002, World Population Prospects, the 2000 Revision.
15. Naik, Gautam, 'HIV's Impact is Seen by UN as Worsening,' *Wall Street Journal*, 26 February 2003.
16. UNAIDS, December 2001.
17. Morin, Richard and Deane, Claudia, 'AIDS Takes Toll on African Militaries,' *Washington Post*, 4 March 2003.
18. Crossette, Barbara, 'Gore Presides Over Rare Security Council Debate on AIDS,' *New York Times*, 11 January 2000, A3

governments and church organisations have adopted an approach to the sexual transmission of HIV known as the ABC approach. First, A: Abstain; delay onset of intercourse until marriage. If you can't abstain, or are already in a sexual relationship, then B: Be faithful to that partner. If you choose (or do not have the freedom to say 'no' to) sexual relations, then C: use a Condom.

Is this good advice? Many have argued that condoms are not 100% reliable in preventing HIV infection, and any expert would be foolhardy not to acknowledge this fact. Condoms can break; they can degrade under improper storage conditions or with inappropriate (petroleum-based) lubricants; they can be improperly manufactured and improperly used. However, arguments that HIV is smaller than latex pores and therefore that condoms provide no protection are obviated by studies involving their actual use among humans.

The largest analysis of published, peer-reviewed studies looking at the question of condom effectiveness was produced by the National Institute of Allergy and Infectious Diseases of the National Institutes of Health, USA, in July, 2001.[19] As that meta-analysis noted, it must first be appreciated that HIV is a very inefficiently transmitted infection when compared with other common sexually transmitted diseases. For example, a single exposure to gonorrhea causes infection in 60%-80% of women. In contrast, after a single exposure to HIV, only 0.1%-0.2% of women become infected. The study found that use of condoms reduces the already low transmission rate of HIV by 85%. If one applied these data to 10,000 persons being exposed to HIV during sexual intercourse over a period of one year, in the absence of condoms 670 would become infected, while that number would be reduced to 90 if condoms were used consistently and correctly. The conclusion is clear: condoms are not perfect, but for those who choose (or are forced into) sexual contact, significant protection is afforded by this method.

---

19. National Institute of Allergy and Infectious Diseases, National Institutes of Health, Department of Health and Human Services, 'Scientific Evidence on Condom Effectiveness for Sexually Transmitted Disease (STD) Prevention', 20 July 2001 (available at http://www.niaid.nih.gov/dmid/stds/condomreport.pdf).

II A study in the phenomenology of Roman Catholic Teaching:
The case of the evolving position on HIV prevention
Having described the epidemic and having presented data supporting the effectiveness of condoms for HIV infection, we now
turn to our major subject: the development of church positions
and practice regarding HIV prevention 'on the ground'. We present narratives from three cases dealing with HIV prevention in
different periods and places: the United States, the Vatican, and
South Africa. While we note the results that were attained, we
are interested especially in highlighting methods and arguments that proponents (and opponents) of HIV/AIDS prevention have employed. We present these cases so as to see how
moral arguments go forward politically in the life of the church
and of the world. We also present them so as to engage the reader
in the process of appreciating that arguments in favour of condom use are cogent and both respectful of and consistent with
the tradition. While discussing these cases, we will also briefly
review relevant statements made in other parts of the world in
order to argue that there is more episcopal support for a pro-
condom position than has been widely recognised or appreciated.

II. a. The US Case
In the US, the first episcopal letters discussing HIV/AIDS were
published in April, 1987. The California Catholic Conference
urged its readership to read and study the US surgeon general's
report on AIDS: 'Written in "plain English," this document provides a clear biological and medical explanation of the nature of
AIDS and AIDS-related complex, how the disease is transmitted, and how its spread can be prevented.'[20] Although the bishops'
letter did not explicitly mention condoms, the recommended
surgeon general's report certainly did.

In the same month, Archbishop Anthony Pilla of the Catholic
Diocese of Cleveland published guidelines regarding AIDS
education. The letter instructed teachers to 'discuss specific
medical facts about AIDS. Be very direct, and as thorough as
possible ... If the person cannot or will not refrain from the sexual
intercourse behaviour that would transmit AIDS, be explicit in
presenting the fact that for those who ignore church teaching
condoms are recommended by some experts in other fields as a

---

20. California Conference of Catholic Bishops, 'A Pastoral Letter on
AIDS,' *Origins* 1987; XVI/45, 23 April 1987, 786-790.

means of preventing AIDS ... You are to inform them of a fact, from medical science, that condoms are recommended to protect against AIDS. This is information "about" condoms; it is not a recommendation "for" condoms.'[21]

As already noted, in December 1987, the Administrative Board of the NCCB, chaired by Cardinal Joseph Bernardin, issued 'The Many Faces of AIDS: A Gospel Response'. Despite its praiseworthy pastoral approach, one passage became especially neuralgic: 'Because we live in a pluralistic society, we acknowledge that some will not agree with our understanding of human sexuality. We recognise that public educational programs addressed to a wide audience will reflect the fact that some people will not act as they can and should; that they will not refrain from the type of sexual or drug abuse behavior that can transmit AIDS. In such situations educational efforts, if grounded in the broader moral vision outlined above [that is, the Catholic understanding of human sexuality], could include accurate information about prophylactic devices or other practices proposed by some medical experts as potential means of preventing AIDS. We are not promoting the use of prophylactics, but merely providing information that is part of the factual picture.'[22]

Immediately after its publication, the archbishops of Boston, New York, and Philadelphia publicly opposed the moral validity of such programmes, while several California bishops, including the archbishops of Los Angeles and San Francisco, went on record in support of the NCBB statement.[23] One year later, Cardinal Ratzinger supported the opposition position in a letter he wrote to the US apostolic pronuncio (Archbishop Pio Laghi), which was passed on to the NCCB president Archbishop John May and to each member of the NCCB. Cardinal Ratzinger's letter first emphasised the need for episcopal unity:

The lively discussion, widened and sometimes distorted by the press worldwide, which followed the publication of the NCCB Administrative Board's well known document ... has

21. Pilla, Bishop Anthony M., 'Recommended Guidelines for Teaching About AIDS and Contraceptives in the Diocese of Cleveland', 3 April 1987.
22. National Conference of Catholic Bishops, 'The Many Faces of AIDS', 486.
23. *National Catholic Reporter*, 'Attack on Bishops' AIDS Report Called Harmful', 25 December 1987, 4-5 and 'California Churchmen Say Condom Education is Realistic', 25 December 1987, 4.

generated in many of the faithful, and not only in the United States, a good deal of confusion regarding the authentic Catholic position on the moral problems involved. The Holy See wishes, therefore, to express its deep concern that the unity so necessary among the bishops in the teaching of Christian moral doctrine be clearly and publicly demonstrated. In the first place, and on a more general level, one must keep in mind the problem posed by the worldwide reaction which accompanies certain documents issued by various episcopal conferences. This requires a particular sense of responsibility and prudence in the choice of things to be treated and in the manner in which these statements are published, not to mention a careful composition of the texts themselves. At least in some cases, when the subjects under discussion are of interest to the universal church, it would seem advisable to consult in advance with the Holy See.[24]

The cardinal saw unity threatened not by the three opposing cardinals, but by the committee chaired by Cardinal Bernardin.

Cardinal Ratzinger went on to discuss whether 'toleration' was the appropriate moral principle to invoke in the case of condoms for HIV prevention: 'In the case under discussion, it hardly seems pertinent to appeal to the classical principle of toleration of the lesser evil on the part of those who exercise responsibility for the temporal common good of society. In fact, even when the issue has to do with educational programs promoted by the civil government, one would not be dealing simply with a form of passive toleration but rather with a kind of behavior which would result in at least the facilitation of evil.' In this criticism of the applicability of the principle of toleration, the cardinal was not necessarily rejecting the letter's conclusion but rather the principle being invoked. That is, as Keenan had already noted, the principle of co-operation is the more appropriate principle to be applied here.

The cardinal concluded, 'In a society which seems increasingly to downgrade the value of chastity, conjugal fidelity and temperance, and to be preoccupied sometimes almost exclusively with physical heath and temporal well-being, the church's responsibility is to give that kind of witness which is proper to her, namely an unequivocal witness of effective and unreserved solidarity with those who are suffering, and at the same time, a

---

24. *Origins*, 'Cardinal Ratzinger's Letter.'

witness of defense of the dignity of human sexuality which can only be realized within the context of moral law.'

In 1989, in a demonstration of the unity that Cardinal Ratzinger urged, the entire NCCB published a second letter entitled 'Called to Compassion and Responsibility: A Response to the HIV/AIDS Crisis'.[25] Although they did not refer to the previous document, nor did they officially retract the language of the previous document, they did reverse themselves. Referring to educational programmes that discussed 'safer sex' methods of prevention, they wrote: 'We fault these ['safer sex'] programs for another reason as well. Recognizing that casual sex is a threat to heath, they consistently advise the use of condoms in order to reduce the danger. This is poor and inadequate advice, given the poor failure rate of prophylactics and the high risk that an infected person who relies on them will eventually transmit the infection in this way. It is not condom use which is the solution to this problem, but appropriate attitudes and corresponding behavior regarding human sexuality, integrity and dignity.'[26]

Despite the fact that many US moral theologians have written articles upholding chastity, abstinence, the teaching on birth control, as well as the condom as a final prophylactic recourse in HIV/AIDS prevention (see footnote 10), the US episcopal conference still stands in tacit opposition to HIV/AIDS prevention programmes that even include condom information.

The bishops' position, reflected in the comments from Cardinal Ratzinger, emphasised the integrity of sexuality, a concern that those who promote prevention do not ignore. But none of the cardinals who opposed the Bernardin stance address the greater threat, not to sexuality or chastity, but to life. Noticeably absent in the concerns of those who resist adequate HIV/AIDS prevention strategies is an acknowledgment that the present crisis is ultimately and most importantly a threat to life itself, and not just a threat to sexual mores. The issue of protecting life, the heart of HIV/AIDS prevention strategies, does not appear to be at the forefront of their priorities. Out of their concern for the principle of chastity, which appears to override concern for the sanctity of life, these church leaders see condoms as part of the problem, not part of the solution.

25. National Conference of Catholic Bishops, 'Called to Compassion and Responsibility: A Response to the HIV/AIDS Crisis', *Origins* XIX/26, 30 November 1989, 421, 423-434.
26. National Conference of Catholic Bishops, 'Called to Compassion', 429.

II. b. The Vatican Case

Part of the reason we have felt free to speak about the need to promote HIV/AIDS prevention is that for many years there have been bishops and cardinals who have recognised the unique and serious threat posed by HIV infection, and who have in many cases acknowledged the legitimate use of condoms to prevent such transmission. In 1985 the bishops of Papua New Guinea and the Solomon Islands wrote that 'both the government and the churches must ... give honest and complete information to everybody, because everybody has the right to know what HIV/AIDS is and what are the ways of transmission of the virus and what are all possible means of protection'.[27] In 1996, the Social Commission of the French bishops' conference proposed a variety of preventive means as appropriate: 'It is this trilogy – condom, limitation of the number of partners, and abstinence – which offers a balanced and coherent message ... To oppose the condom by promoting only fidelity, or the contrary, is ineffective ... Presented as the minimum preventative means necessary, the condom must be recognised as a very first step towards becoming responsible.'[28] Cardinal Adrianus Simonis of the Netherlands, commenting on the case of an HIV-infected husband and his uninfected wife, stated: 'In this precise condition and only in the realm of marriage the condom may be seen as a form of self-defence.'[29] Archbishop (now Cardinal) Christoph Schönborn of Vienna said, 'Love can never bring death ... in given situations the condom can be seen as the lesser evil.'[30] In a World AIDS Day public television interview in 1988, Jean-Marie Cardinal Lustiger of Paris commented: 'You who suffer from this illness, you who cannot be chaste, use the means that are proposed to you, out of self-respect and out of respect for others. You must not cause death.'[31] The German bishops' conference wrote that 'before the deadly menace which the AIDS virus ef-

27. Bishops of Papua New Guinea and Solomon Island, Pastoral Letter on STD and AIDS, 1995.

28. La Croix, Xavier, 'AIDS: Challenge for the World,' in *La Société en Question* (AIDS: Society in Question), Paris: Bayard Editions, 1996, 156-157

29. *Catholic News Service*, 'Dutch Cardinal Says Condoms OK When Spouse has AIDS', 16 February 1996

30. *Catholic News Service*, 'Vienna Archbishop Says Condoms Morally Acceptable to Fight AIDS', 3 April 1996.

31. La Croix, 'AIDS: Challenge'.

fectively represents, it is necessary to do everything to avoid contamination ... The information must be complete, broad-based and honest, without ceasing to be balanced. It must not become a disguised invitation to sexual licence.'[32]

Unfortunately, these statements are not well known. Even though cardinal archbishops have endorsed HIV/AIDS prevention, that fact – and their authority – is rarely acknowledged, either in the Catholic or the secular press. Rather, the common perception is of a monolithic Roman Catholic front against any tolerance or acceptance of condoms. Nonetheless, it is worth noting that with the exception of the first NCCB letter, none of these (predominantly European) statements have prompted a public Vatican reaction contesting either their theological legitimacy or the episcopal authority of their authors.

There has been even stronger evidence of implicit tolerance from the Vatican on this topic. In 1996, Monsignor Georges Cottier, OP, theologian of the papal household and president of the International Theological Commission, was asked in an interview with Vatican Radio whether condom distribution might qualify as a 'lesser of two evils' approach. He responded: 'This is the question that moralists are asking themselves, and it is legitimate that they ask it.'[33]

Our intuitions regarding Vatican tolerance appeared to be even more firmly bolstered in 2000 with the publication in L'Osservatore Romano of an article by Monsignor Jacques Suaudeau of the Pontifical Council for the Family.[34] We believed that Suaudeau's article conveyed important insights about Vatican curial thinking on HIV prevention. Why? First, that the article was published in L'Osservatore Romano, the official newspaper for the Vatican curia, implied that the article's content represented a substantive constituency of curial thinking. Second, it endorsed abstinence and the proper understanding of Christian sexuality as the safest and most human preventive approach against HIV transmission. Third, it did not attack the endorsement, promotion, distribution or use of prophylactics.

---

32. *La Documentation Catholique*, 1998, No 2176, 191-195.
33. *Catholic News Service*, 'Papal Theologian: AIDS-Condoms Issue Legitimate to Debate', 15 February 1996.
34. Suaudeau, Monsignor Jacques, 'Prophylactics or Family Values? Stopping the Spread of HIV/AIDS', *L'Osservatore Romano*, English Edition, 27 September 2000, 2.

Rather, in introducing a novel distinction between containment and prevention, it claimed only that prophylactics alone are inadequate prevention, but explicitly noted their effectiveness in containing the pandemic. Fourth, while noting that further studies regarding the adequacy of prophylactic usage for HIV prevention are still needed, it did not categorically deny their effectiveness. Fifth, it acknowledged the positive function that prophylactics have had in two populations critically affected by the HIV epidemic (in Uganda and Thailand). Sixth, it explicitly referred to the use of prophylactics as a 'lesser evil,' a traditional theological principle used to describe morally permissible though regrettable action. Finally, it concluded by recognising the need for more fundamentally human, life-enhancing programmes to prevent HIV transmission.

In response to his article (which had received little notice), we wrote a short essay for *America* magazine drawing attention to Msgr Suaudeau's arguments.[35] While we never suggested that the Vatican had changed its position, we did say that Msgr Suaudeau's article appeared to recognise the legitimacy of arguments already put forward by numerous theologians who had similarly used principles including 'lesser evil' to support the use of condoms within HIV prevention programmes.

The essay unleashed a remarkable reaction. In an Associated Press report, Msgr Suaudeau called our article 'a pretence to relaunch the argument. This is a manipulation. It is blown up and exaggerated.'[36] In a subsequent interview with *Catholic News Service* Msgr Suaudeau said his use of the term 'lesser evil' was not so unusual, indicating that the phrase had been commonly used by moral theologians and church leaders like Cardinal Jean-Marie Lustiger of Paris.[37] However, in a clarification published in *L'Osservatore Romano*, Msgr Suaudeau noted that 'the expression "lesser evil" ... was used in the strictly medical sense

35. Fuller, Jon and Keenan, James, 'Tolerant Signals: The Vatican's New Insights on Condoms for HIV Prevention', *America* CLXXXIII/8, 23 September 2000, 6-7.
36. Simpson, Victor L, 'Vatican Official: Opposition to Condoms Unchanged', *Associated Press*, 19 September 2000.
37. Norton, John, 'Theologians Say Condom Use OK in Certain Cases, Not as Policy', *Catholic News Service*, 22 September 2000.

of public health ... and must consequently be understood not in the moral sense, but exclusively in an epidemiological sense.'[38]

Among many other respondents, Cardinal Bernard Law commented in his column in the Boston archdiocesan Catholic newspaper, *The Pilot*:

> The newspapers recently carried a story about a forthcoming article in a national magazine by two Jesuit priests who are located in the Boston area. These priests claim to have found, in an article published last April in *L'Osservatore Romano*, a change in church teaching. Today's *New York Times* quotes the author of that *L'Osservatore Romano* article as being very perplexed that such an interpretation should have been placed on his writing. Church teaching on fundamental matters of faith and morals is not going to change. It cannot change. Furthermore, it is ludicrous to make it appear that such a change can be sought out like cues for a treasure hunt. The Jesuit authors of the forthcoming article would do well to review *Veritatis Splendor*. It does not represent a change in church teaching, but it expresses in a very compelling way how it is that we approach the splendor of truth. It might also be helpful for them to review *Fides et Ratio* (Faith and Reason). These two encyclicals of Pope John Paul II are exceedingly important for the church today.[39]

Wanting to give as accurate a presentation of Msgr Suaudeau's argument as possible, *America* magazine issued a press statement in reaction to criticisms of our article, trying to situate our claims about Suaudeau's essay in a larger context:

> The central issue is whether the use of condoms can be understood to be a 'lesser evil'. In Catholic moral theology this term denotes regrettable activity that nevertheless can be tolerated, or may even be mandated. Bishops from the United States, Brazil, France, South Africa and Papua New Guinea have argued that the use of condoms to prevent HIV transmission is a lesser evil, and the same language was used by Monsignor Suaudeau in *L'Osservatore Romano*. Although this argument is based on traditional Catholic moral reasoning,

---

38. Suaudeau, Monsignor Jacques, 'Prophylactics or Family Values?: Stopping the Spread of HIV/AIDS', *L'Osservatore Romano* XVI, English Edition , 19 April 2000, 9-10.

39. Law, Bernard Cardinal, 'Dominus Iesu is Addressed to Catholics', *The Pilot*, CLXXI/36, 22 September 2000, 2.

in the past, no Vatican official or agency has used the language of 'lesser evil' in talking about condoms and AIDS. Nor has any Vatican official or agency ever indicated that condoms in some instances have 'good results' in the prevention of sexually transmitted diseases. For these reasons the authors found it hopeful that Monsignor Suaudeau, after close observation of the catastrophic realities emerging from Africa and Asia, signaled a willingness to acknowledge the orthodoxy of local bishops who have invoked the principle of lesser evil in addressing the role of condoms in the context of HIV prevention.[40]

But even this straightforward response prompted another severe reply. Bishop Raymundo Damasceno Assis, secretary general of the Brazilian bishops' conference, labelled as 'a flat lie' our statement that 'Bishops from the United States, Brazil, France, South Africa and Papua New Guinea have argued that the use of condoms to prevent HIV transmission is a lesser evil.' Bishop Damasceno 'rejected any claim that Brazilian bishops have ever supported the use of condoms as morally acceptable to prevent AIDS.'[41] We responded by citing an Associated Press story by Harold Olmos (13 June 2000) which quoted Bishop Eugênio Rixen of Goias, a member of the Brazilian Catholic Church's Health Pastoral, as proposing the use of condoms to prevent HIV transmission as 'the lesser of two evils'. We also telephoned Bishop Rixen who confirmed our claim, while he also acknowledged that this language was subsequently not endorsed by the entire bishops' conference. We also telephoned Mr Olmos who indicated that he had confirmed the story with the press office of the Brazilian bishops' conference before filing his report.[42]

Despite resistance from at least some bishops, moral theologians continued to apply the resources of the tradition to the condom question. In fact, even some very conservative moral theologians subsequently weighed in with their particular applications. John Norton's *Catholic News Service* story of 22 September, 2000 recounted a leading moral theologian for the

---

40. *America* magazine Press Release, 20 September 2000.
42. *Zenit News Service* (Rome), 'Condom Claim "A Flat Lie", says Brazilian Bishop,' 22 October 2000; also carried in *The Tablet*, 28 October 2000, 1460.
43. Fuller, Jon and Keenan, James, 'Our Truthful Claim', *The Tablet*, 25 November 2000, 1598.

Legionnaires of Christ who made applications not unlike those made by Cardinal Lustiger of Paris and Cardinal Schönborn of Vienna.[43] Moreover, Norton also reported that Franciscan Father Maurizio Faggioni, a physician, a professor of moral theology at Rome's Alphonsianum university, and a consultant to the Congregation for the Doctrine of the Faith, said that condom use might be justified when one of the spouses has AIDS, as long as the 'exclusive and primary' intent was to defend the healthy partner from infection and not to prevent pregnancy: 'This is a classic application' of the Catholic moral principle of 'double effect,' he said.

While others admittedly took opposing points of view, what is noteworthy is how, by referring to the moral tradition, many conservative and mainline theologians have continuously found within the tradition a variety of principles relevant for HIV/AIDS prevention strategies that do not undermine church teaching on life and sexuality. Still, even with these most conservative claims, most bishops remain unable to acknowledge the apparent validity of these endeavors.

II. c. The South African Case

Redemptorist Bishop Kevin Dowling of Rustenberg, South Africa, was chairperson of his episcopal conference's national AIDS office. Through a *Catholic News Service* report by Tracy Early on 29 June 2001, we learned that Bishop Dowling, a trained moralist, was prompting the South African bishops to wrestle with the question of HIV/AIDS prevention. (South Africa, with 4.5 million persons HIV infected, is estimated to have more infected persons than any other country in the world.) Bishop Dowling noted in the interview that South African bishops emphasised prevention through abstinence. But he also said that 'we are in a world where people choose not to live according to these values,' and in that context, condoms were not a means to prevent the transmission of life but 'to prevent death.'[44] Bishop Dowling further explicated his position in an interview published in South Africa's *Sunday Times*, in which he indicated how much the challenging position he was taking was based on his pastoral experience: 'My personal stance on

43. Norton, John, 'Theologians Say Condom Use OK.'
44. Early, Tracy, 'Bishop says AIDS Crisis Prompts Need for New Thinking on Condoms.' *Catholic News Service*, 29 June 2001.

this issue comes out of much reflection, not to say anguish over the enormity of the suffering of people in the AIDS pandemic, of the complex issues which have to be faced, all of which I have experienced in a very personal way in my own ministry and support of AIDS programmes in the diocese here.'[45] Using sanctity of life argumentation, he reflected on someone infected with HIV who chooses to enter into a sexual relationship, who is forced into liaisons in order to survive financially, or who is in a marital relationship and wishes to engage in intercourse with an uninfected spouse. While agreeing that abstinence before marriage and faithfulness to one's partner in marriage is 'the only complete safeguard against infection,' he also proposed that where abstinence was not chosen or not possible, infected persons must be made aware of the responsibility to use a condom to avoid spreading the virus. 'In that context, the use of a condom can be seen not as a means to prevent the "transmission of life" leading to pregnancy, i.e., as contraception, but rather as a means to prevent the "transmission of death" or potential death to another.' Similarly he made an appeal to mercy: 'If we simply proclaim a message that condoms cannot be used under any circumstances, either directly or through not trying to articulate a proper response to the crisis we face, then I believe people will have difficulty believing we are committed as a church to a compassionate and caring response to people who are suffering, often in appalling living conditions. The fact that condoms are not 100% safe in every case cannot be advanced, in my view, as an argument that they should never be used in any circumstance. We live in an imperfect world, and sometimes even imperfect results at least can save some lives.'

Bishop Dowling's comments were made in anticipation of the episcopal conference's meeting to be held on 24 July. In response to his remarks, Cardinal Wilfred Napier, OFM, president of the conference, told the South African Press Association that the plan will 'have to be weighed up against the backdrop of not only the church's traditional teaching, but also current scientific evidence about the quality, effectiveness, and actual usability of condoms in situations which pose the greatest risk of infec-

---

45. *Sunday Times* of South Africa, 'Statement by Bishop Kevin Dowling of Rustenburg, Issued Before the Bishops' Meeting at the End of July 2001, Explaining his Position on Condoms,' 9 July 2001.

tion.'[46] Archbishop Dennis Hurley, retired bishop of the Durban diocese, said he supported condom use, but only in very limited circumstances such as when one spouse was infected with HIV and the other was not: 'I just can't see how it fits in with true obedience to God's will to endanger the other spouse when it'd be easy to avoid such danger by use of a condom. It's a clash of moral values, and in such clashes people should be free to choose, especially to choose the more important value, in this case the life of a spouse.'[47] *The Southern Cross*, a Catholic newspaper in South Africa, endorsed Bishop Dowling's stand on condoms and said that condoms provide one way – albeit an imperfect one – of stemming the AIDS epidemic. It called on the church 'to reconcile its total ban on prophylactics with the philosophy of the sanctity of life. No civil organ is doing more to fight Aids in Southern Africa than the Catholic Church. Bishop Dowling's comments should be seen as an attempt to balance Catholic doctrine with the need of the church to be compassionate to the most ostracised and vulnerable people in our society.'[48] Like Bishop Dowling, the editorial also viewed the use of condoms for HIV prevention as a prophylactic, not a contraceptive. In response, the Vatican's representative in Southern Africa, Archbishop Francisco Colacco, said that he expected the episcopal conference would not approve the proposed changes to the church's policy on condoms.[49]

After they met, the South African Bishops' Conference issued a statement entitled 'A Message of Hope' which attacked condoms in its opening paragraphs: 'The bishops regard the widespread and indiscriminate promotion of condoms as an immoral and misguided weapon in our battle against HIV-AIDS ... Condoms may even be one of the main reasons for the spread of HIV-AIDS. Apart from the possibility of condoms being faulty or wrongly used, they contribute to the breaking down of self-control and mutual respect.'[50]

46. Nessman, Ravi, 'Africa Bishops Mull Easing Condom Ban,' *Associated Press*, 12 July 2001.
47. Ibid.
48. *The Southern Cross*, 'The Condom Debate,' (editorial), 18 July 2001.
49. Podger, Corinne, 'Plea to Church on Condoms', BBC News Online: World: Africa 17 July 2001.
50. Southern African Bishops' Conference, 'A Message of Hope from the Catholic Bishops to the People of God in South Africa, Botswana and Swaziland', July 30, 2001.

Despite this seeming outright rejection of condoms early in their statement, Bishop Dowling's and Archbishop Hurley's positions were implicitly accepted later in the document, where it was acknowledged that in the case of married couples in which one member was infected, taking means to protect against infection was appropriate: 'There are couples where one of the parties is living with HIV/AIDS. In these cases there is the real danger that the healthy partner may contract this killer disease. The church accepts that everyone has the right to defend one's life against mortal danger. This would include using the appropriate means and course of action. Similarly where one spouse is infected with HIV/AIDS they must listen to their consciences. They are the only ones who can choose the appropriate means, in order to defend themselves against the infection.' This is not unlike the application of the principle of double effect as argued by Fr Faggioni above.

In a subsequent interview, Cardinal Napier confirmed that the allowed protection that married couples could choose to use referred to condoms.[51] Curiously, some bishops as well as some in the media did not understand the distinction between a condom being used as a prophylactic as compared with its use as a contraceptive, nor the specific application of the principle of double effect in this instance. For instance, in his interview Cardinal Napier insisted that married couples using condoms for HIV prevention must nevertheless abstain from sexual relations when the woman was ovulating so that the condom would not also prevent conception.[52] This condition was not present in the bishops' original statement.

Responses to the bishops' statement varied considerably. Looking at the glass as 'half full,' *The Southern Cross* editorialised from a positive perspective: 'Only a few months after the Vatican's head of health care, Archbishop Javier Lozano Barragan, ruled out condom use as "never ethically permissible", the bishops of Southern Africa – whose region covers three of the world's most AIDS affected countries – virtually endorsed condom use in marriages where one partner is HIV-infected. This decision ... was courageous and compassionate.'[53]

51. Nessman, Ravi, 'African Bishops Rule Out Condoms', *Associated Press*, 31 July 2001.
52. Ibid.
53. *The Southern Cross*, 'The Church and Condoms', 4-10 December 2002.

However, an impassioned letter published by the Sisters of Justice of Johannesburg took issue with the fact that the bishops only allowed consideration of condom use within stable married couples: 'We ask ourselves for whom the SACBC statement is in fact a message of hope? For many women, the SACBC message in its present form will not be one of hope ... The condom issue is only a surface issue. What is on the table now is about much more than condoms. It is about the kind of church we would like to be as we reach out in compassion, as disciples of Jesus, to those who are in mortal danger and have no other means of protecting themselves. It is about the way we feel for people in complex socio-cultural-economic situations; people who do not live in regular, equal and loving relationships ... It is about how we search humbly and sincerely for truth, justice and compassion without seeing everything in 'black and white' terms as though there are no grey areas in between. And finally, it is about gender imbalance in society and church, about the on-going injustice, violence and discrimination against women.'[54]

III. Conclusion

In the evolution of the teaching on condoms and HIV/AIDS prevention, a variety of issues have emerged that call for our attention. First, it is evident that the tradition of moral teaching possesses a wealth of insights and principles that can empower us to solve novel and thorny contemporary problems. Second, it is precisely those who are most familiar with this tradition that have developed supportive arguments on behalf of condoms for HIV prevention over the years. While the initial insight to differentiate the condom's contraceptive purpose from its prophylactic one remains a central issue, the later insight to appeal to the principle of the sanctity of life arose when it was noted that some bishops and curial leaders seemed singularly concerned about chastity. That is, the moralists responded to the bishops' concern by drawing attention to another, even more central value. Third, rarely does it seem that bishops who were critical of tolerant positions responded in kind, and only infrequently do they show evidence of understanding the arguments being proposed. Why is this? Was it due to a general suspicion of

54. Sisters for Justice of Johannesburg, 'Continuing the Conversation,' 16 August 2001; cited in *The Tablet*, 'Condoms as a Lesser Evil', 25 August 2001, 1218-19.

moral theologians or of casuistry? Was it their inability to consider that there was any other issue at stake than the birth control teaching? Was it that they are simply surrounded by persons who encouraged them not to entertain the arguments?[55]

Whatever the reason(s), there are few moments when, despite the efforts of those working in HIV/AIDS prevention, opposing bishops recognised or responded in good faith to the arguments and complaints of moralists. Many bishops have overridden this argumentation by simply reiterating their concerns about chastity, and by saying (this much was an echo of the moralists themselves) that condoms alone were not the solution. The concern of moralists to save lives, and to have the tradition move forward while responding to the AIDS crisis, has simply not been shared by many bishops.

Inasmuch as bishops in their own localities and in the Vatican participate in the magisterial teaching of the Roman Catholic Church, the present 'stalemate' has to give us pause about notions like 'communio', 'authority', and 'moral truth'. For some reason there is presently an impediment in the church's ability to formulate moral truth, at a time when this impediment is potentially putting millions of lives at risk.

IV. Postscript
Whether there is any *bona fide* dialogue in this debate seems to be a valid question, but as we submit this essay in tribute to the ongoing work of Enda McDonagh, two recent developments draw our final attention. First, in a remarkable article in *The Southern Cross* that was subsequently cited in *The Tablet*, Archbishop Denis Hurley of South Africa wrote, 'By and large, artificial birth control no longer seems to be a matter for confession on the part of married couples, much to the relief of confessors. Does this mean that the laity, in so many parts of the world, have taken the matter into their own hands, and while doing so have not been disturbed by the clergy? Why then all this fuss about condoms in certain circumstances involving HIV/AIDS?'[56] While moralists proposed principles to afford bishops an accommodation of both a good HIV/AIDS prevention strategy

---

55. Black, Peter and Keenan, James, 'The Evolving Self-understanding of the Moral Theologian: 1900-2000', *Studia Moralia* XXXIX, 2001, 291-327.
56. *The Tablet*, 'Why the Fuss About Condoms?', 1 February 2003, 29.

and the birth control teaching, bishops insisted on opposing the condom and they rejected the offer. Now Archbishop Hurley, writing from a major AIDS region, acknowledges that just as Catholics dismissed episcopal teaching on birth control, similarly they are doing the same with episcopal teaching on condoms for HIV prevention. Inevitably, one has to ask: Are the bishops seriously undermining the credibility of their own teaching authority?

Finally, an interesting report comes from a Catholic theological meeting ('Responsibility in a time of AIDS') held in Johannesburg 5 to 7 February 2003. Among several claims made in the conference's final statement, two are germane to our reflection. First, HIV/AIDS 'should not be dealt with in a framework of individual moral values but in the framework of social justice.' Second, the church was reprimanded for inadequate education work and messages about condoms which 'have tended to confuse the issue, since they are tied to teachings about contraception, whereas the goal here is to defend oneself against a deadly disease.'[57]

Additional Bibliographical Resources
'African Bishops Slam Condom Use in AIDS Fight', *Reuters*, July 30, 2001.
Catholic News Service, 'South African Bishops to Discuss AIDS, Condom Use,' 11 July 2001.
Fuller, Jon, 'AIDS Prevention: A Challenge to the Catholic Moral Tradition,' *America* CLXXV 28 December 1996, 13-20.
Fuller, Jon, 'Needle Exchange: Saving Lives,' *America* CLXXIX, 18-25 July 1998, 8-11.
Fuller, Jon and Keenan, James, 'Catholic Answers to AIDS', *The Tablet*, 30 June 2001, 942-943.
Keenan, James, 'Applying the Seventeenth Century Casuistry of Accommodation to HIV Prevention', *Theological Studies* LX, 1999, 492-512.
Keenan, James, 'Catholics Fighting the Spread of HIV: Exposing and Encountering the Same Problems in the Virgin Islands as Around the World', *Catholic Islander* XIV, 1999, 13.
Keenan, James, 'The Return of Casuistry', *Theological Studies* LVII, 1996, 123-129.
Whitney, Craig, 'French Bishops Support Some Use of Condoms to Prevent AIDS', *New York Times* 13 February 1996, 5.

---

57. *The Tablet* 'Bishops Tackle Mbeki Over Aids Policy,' CCLVII/8474, February 22, 2003, 38.

Linking Ethical and Globalisation

Mary Robinson

We do not know the way out of the marasmus of the world, and it would be an expression of unforgivable pride were we to see the little we do as a fundamental solution, or were we to present ourselves, our community, and our solutions to vital problems as the only thing worth doing.[1]

I blame Enda for my presumption in linking the words ethical and globalisation! He has had an inspiring influence on me throughout my working life, and when I was elected President of Ireland, he was an obvious choice as chaplain. Over the years we have discussed many topics, from art to politics to human rights to poetry, and – through it all – he has woven an ethical dimension to provide an overall coherence.

In 1995 I was honoured to be asked by Professor Hans Küng to contribute to a book he was compiling, *Yes to a Global Ethic.*[2] I had read some of his work, and was interested in how he was seeking to identify common values among all the world's religions and faiths to define a global ethic. But Enda knew him personally, as he seems to know so many key thinkers of our time, and he gave me insights into the person I would subsequently grow to like and admire deeply. Hans Küng's vision impressed me, the idea of finding a universal common ground among religions that would provide humanity with a common value system. Writing in 1999, he explained it this way:

> The globalisation of the economy, technology, and the media means also the globalisation of problems: from financial and labour markets to the environment and organised crime! What is therefore also needed is the globalisation of ethic. Again: not a uniform ethical system ('ethics'), but a necessary minimum of shared ethical values, basic attitudes and standards to which all regions, nations, and interest groups can

---

1. Václav Havel, 'The Power of the Powerless' 1978 in *Open Letters: Selected Writings 1965-1990*, selected and edited by Paul Wilson London: Vintage Books, 1992
2. Hans Küng, ed., *Yes to a Global Ethic*, London: SCM Press, 1996

subscribe – in other words, a shared basic ethic for humankind. Indeed, there can be no new world order without a world ethic, a global ethic.[3]

The philosopher Peter Singer, in his book *One World: The Ethics of Globalization*,[4] argues that how well we come through the era of globalisation will depend on how we respond ethically to the idea that we live in one world.

As is often true of philosophers, Professor Singer is ahead of the times in highlighting that just as globalisation has underscored the commonality of all nations, it has also enlarged the ethical sphere of responsibility of individuals. He notes that while it is natural for individuals to prioritise their social obligations, from family to friends to compatriots, one implication of an increasingly interconnected world is that the circle must be expanded to encompass people of other nations.

Speaking at Yale University in September 2002, Secretary General Kofi Annan framed the idea in this way:

Whether it is the area of crime, health, the environment or the fight against terrorism, interdependence has ceased to be an abstract concept. It has become a reality in our own lives. This poses a real challenge, not only to political leaders, but to civil society, non-governmental organisations, businesses, labour unions, thinkers and citizens of every nation. We need to rethink what belonging means, and what community means, in order to be able to embrace the fate of distant peoples, and realise that globalization's glass house must be open to all, if it is to remain secure.[5]

Starting with the Universal Declaration in 1948, and carried forward in the body of international law that has been painstakingly developed over half a century, the world has expressed through human rights a legal framework of shared commitment to the values of dignity, equality, and human security for all people. Our challenge is to give those values practical effect both in our own communities and in the global community of nations. We each have a responsibility to help realise the vision of

---

3. Hans Küng, 'Project for a Global Ethic 1999', *International Journal of Politics, Culture and Society*, Vol 13, 1999, 16.
4. Peter Singer, *One World: The Ethics of Globalization*, Yale: Yale University Press, 2002.
5. Speech at Yale University 30th September 2002.

the Universal Declaration, in Eleanor Roosevelt's words, to make human rights matter 'in small places, close to home'.

That leads me to a theme that was constant for me while High Commissioner for Human Rights and which will remain such in my current work. Simply described, it concerns implementation and delivery. How do we move on from proclaiming the rights of people and the obligations those rights give rise to on the part of states and the international community, towards the realisation of those rights and obligations in practice, on the ground? How do we use the great steps that have been taken to date both to define rights and commit states to those definitions, into truly effective collective action at national and international levels to secure those rights for everyone in our world, without distinction?

Under the banner 'all human rights for all', the Vienna Conference on Human Rights in 1993 endorsed the strong link between human rights, democracy and development.

We began the twenty-first century with an important affirmation of that link. The largest gathering ever of government leaders expressed, through the United Nations Millennium Declaration, the international community's renewed commitment to the principles of justice and international law. Indeed, during the three-day special session of the General Assembly in September 2000, a total of 273 new treaty actions took place – 187 signatures and 86 ratifications or accessions – on instruments such as the Optional Protocols to the Convention on the Rights of the Child on the involvement of children in armed conflict, and the Convention on the Elimination of All Forms of Discrimination against Women, the Rome Statute of the International Criminal Court, and the International Convention for the Suppression of the Financing of Terrorism.

The Millennium Declaration stressed the need for sustained efforts to create a shared future, based upon our common humanity in all its diversity. It identified as the priority: 'to make globalisation work for all the world's people'.[6] The moment was marked by a spirit of re-dedication to international law and institutions as the best hope for the twenty-first century.

But just one year and three days after this historic declaration was adopted, the terrible events of September 11, 2001 in the United States set the world on a different and much less hopeful

---

6. www.un.org/millennium/

course. Since that day, the commitments which ushered in the new century have been increasingly overshadowed by the threats of terrorism, by fears and uncertainties about the future, and by questions about the viability of open societies joined by international norms and values. The war in Iraq has been the most recent and extreme test to date of the international system's legitimacy and relevance in this new global environment.

Yet it is also painfully evident that the events of 9/11 did not, in fact, change much in the lives of most people on the planet. Human insecurity, alas, was a daily reality before 9/11 for the hundreds of millions who live in absolute poverty or in zones of conflict, and it remains so. For these people, insecurity is not equated with where a terrorist might strike, but instead, with where tomorrow's only meal will come from, or how a job will be found that will produce enough income to provide shelter for a family, or purchase life saving medicines for a dying child.

During my extensive travels throughout the developing world as High Commissioner I witnessed this stark, unacceptable divide. Again and again I saw that the reality of living in absolute poverty is to be deprived of all human rights and human dignity. Journalists who liked to ask what, in my view, was the worst human rights problem were often surprised that I replied 'absolute poverty'.

When I completed my mandate in September 2002, I set out with a small group of colleagues to bring the experience of working at the international level in human rights to bear directly on the priority that the world leaders had identified in the Millennium Declaration, that is, 'to make globalisation work for all the world's people'.

The project we are developing – the Ethical Globalisation Initiative (EGI)[7] – seeks to work with those who are committed to bringing the values of international human rights to the tables where decisions about the global economy are being made. EGI is driven by the conviction that in order to build a world in which security is underpinned by sustainable development and social justice, and where globalisation works to the benefit of all the world's people, it is vital that multilateralism and respect for international law – in particular, international human rights law – work as well.

EGI's aim is to seek in a low-key, targeted way, to be a pro-

7. www.eginitiative.org

moter of good practices or model projects, of how human rights approaches can produce results. It also plans to be a 'chorus leader,' linking local activists and networks with academics and policy development, which together can produce the analysis and recommendations needed to influence decision makers at different levels in government, international organisations, the business sector and civil society.

For example, one of the issues to be tackled from a human rights perspective is health, access to life-saving treatments and HIV/AIDS. One of the first projects EGI is developing (in co-operation with the Center for Research on Women, the International AIDS Trust and the Center for the Study of AIDS at the University of Pretoria) is to engage with African parliamentarians, beginning with a meeting in Botswana in September 2003, to reduce women's vulnerability and to combat stigma in the HIV/AIDS pandemic in Africa. It is important to build greater understanding that HIV/AIDS could be more effectively addressed by adding the dimension of a women's rights issue, both from the perspective of women as victims of the disease as well as as primary caregivers for the sick and orphaned. As one slogan has put it – 'The best investment in an AIDS vaccine is an investment in protecting women's rights.'

EGI is also developing, in co-operation with the Respect Group in Europe, a new 'Business Leaders Initiative on Human Rights' which was launched in May 2003.[8] It involves senior business leaders from multinational corporations in a consultative process with different stake holder groups to better define the extent of business responsibilities for human rights, particularly in countries facing problems of extreme poverty and deficient governance. The corporations involved have identified three specific areas – poverty, governance and health – on which they will explore the role and responsibilities of corporations and where the border lies with the responsibility of states and of international institutions.

Another model of business leadership is being developed by a group of fifteen companies in Sweden who have established a network called Plural[9] to explore ways of developing a strong business case for valuing cultural diversity. Given the level of xenophobia, racism and anti-semitism in many European coun-

8. www.respecteurope.com
9. www.respecteurope.com

tries today, this is a refreshingly positive approach which could be replicated by similar networks in other EU countries. It would be timely to have a business initiative in Ireland which could lift the current debate on issues of discrimination against refugees, asylum seekers and migrants to a positive valuing of diversity as a business asset.

Civil society at grassroots level is also finding new ways to network and share experience of addressing social issues both regionally and internationally. There is an increased emphasis on the importance of economic and social rights in tackling poverty, and I felt honoured to participate in the launch in Thailand in June 2003 of an international network of some 300 activists on economic social and cultural rights, called ESCR-Net.[10]

This network builds on the way that environmental activists, development experts and human rights advocates in every region are learning to use the commitments of their governments, in ratifying human rights covenants and conventions, as a means of securing transparent and participatory decision making on the whole range of human rights issues: economic and social as well as civil and political.

Those working on child rights are analysing budgets and recognise that the finance ministry in the government has a crucial role in relation to the education and health of children. They are engaging business in addressing in a responsible and effective way the problem of child labour. Women's groups are focusing on land issues, access to credit and the importance of having a 'critical mass' of women in parliament to secure legislation on domestic violence and the reform of rape law. Environmental activists and poverty groups are strengthening their campaigns on access to water by drawing on the jurisprudence of courts in India and South Africa, and on the general comment on the right to safe water of the Geneva-based Committee on Economic, Social and Cultural Rights.

This process reached new levels among civil society groups at the Johannesburg World Summit on Sustainable Development in 2002, where their rallying cry was 'no sustainable development without human rights.' Development and environmental activists have recognised that the path to sustainable development requires explicit respect for international human

10. www.escr-net.org

rights standards. Unfortunately, this affirmation was largely resisted by governments in the official texts of Johannesburg. But the reality is that the debate has moved on ahead of them. In Johannesburg, the broad human rights agenda, covering civil and political as well as economic, social and cultural rights was pressed by civil society as being of direct relevance to many of the issues on the Summit agenda, from access to clean water to fighting HIV/AIDS, to better defining the responsibilities of non-state actors for social and environmental protection. This momentum will be carried forward by a range of bodies such as ESCR-Net.

The intention is to build broader alliances with, for example, social movements, with those who are fighting for debt relief, with committed allies on global reform within the UN agencies and certain governments, with economic analysts such as Amartya Sen and Joseph Stiglitz, and with groups working for social justice – such as women's organisations in the informal sector – who may not have identified themselves as human rights groups.

The network recognises that the traditional state-based framework of human rights obligations has become less than fully adequate in a world in which the fulfillment of rights, in developing countries in particular, often depends on the political and economic institutions of developed states, the role of transnational corporations, and the structure of international institutions. In significant ways, power has shifted from the public to the private, from national governments to multinational corporations and international organisations. This has resulted in a gap in accountability for human rights protection, a lack of transparency, and an absence of broad public participation in critical policy decisions.

There is an increasing frustration among many people about their lack of means through which to participate in, and structure, the decisions that affect their communities and nations. Finding ways to enforce human rights standards in these new environments is often quite difficult. That is why networks such as ESCR-Net are so essential in sharing information, testing new approaches and mobilising diverse groups into joint actions.

Human rights work – whether at the level of theory or in the implementation of policies – has reached a stage of maturity where it can integrate the insights and tools from disciplines and professions other than the purely legal. In other words, implementation of international human rights standards is no longer just a lawyer's preserve. There is space and need for much broader intellectual and scholarly attention to the subject, as well as for integrating human rights into the practical and policy programmes that seek to advance human development and human security.

Significant progress has been made in this direction. Looking back over my five years as High Commissioner, I have seen important breakthroughs, crucially beginning with the mainstreaming of a rights-based approach throughout the UN system. It is also to be seen in the strong links now made between human rights and human security in the recent report of the Commission on Human Security co-chaired by Amartya Sen and Sadako Ogata, *Human Security Now*.[11] There is a real opportunity to take up the Commission's broader approach to human security as an entry point to economic and social rights. I understand the concern that human security can be seen as an attempt to dilute the focus on human rights. However, the summary to the Report emphasises:

> Human security means protecting vital freedoms. It means protecting people from critical and pervasive threats and situations, building on their strengths and aspirations. It also means creating systems that give people the building blocks of survival, dignity and livelihood. Human security connects different types of freedoms – freedom from want, freedom from fear and freedom to take action on one's own behalf. To do this, it offers two general strategies: protection and empowerment. Protection shields people from dangers. It requires concerted effort to develop norms, processes and institutions that systematically address insecurities. Empowerment enables people to develop their potential and become full participants in decision-making. Protection and empowerment are mutually reinforcing, and both are required in most situations.[12]

The two concepts of 'protection' and 'empowerment' are core human rights values. This more rounded approach to human security, which is not just focused on addressing the symptoms

---

11. Amartya Sen and Sadako Ogata, *Human Security Now*, Report of the Commission on Human Security, 2003.
12. Ibid, 1.

– important as that is – by taking measures to prevent acts of terrorism, but which recognises the need to address the deeper divides in our world, enables the broader agenda of human rights to reinforce human security. Human rights, after all, provide the legal standards for protection and the tools for empowerment.

To fulfil the priority of world leaders in the Millennium Declaration of 2000, of making globalisation work for all the world's people, we must have a more values-led process. Many of us will continue to consult the 'oracle' Enda for wise advice on how to strategise for a more ethical globalisation, and we will bear in mind Václav Havel's heartening words at the conclusion of 'The Power of the Powerless':

> *For the real question is whether the brighter future is really always so distant. What if, on the contrary, it has been here for a long time already, and only our own blindness and weakness has prevented us from seeing it around us and within us, and kept us from developing it?*[13]

---

13. op. cit., 214.

It's great to be alive:
retirement and human flourishing

Kevin T. Kelly

Some people dread retirement. They see it as the end of their useful life. It suggests that they are past their sell-by date. It is the final down-hill stage of life before facing death.

Others long for retirement. It promises the luxury of being able to choose how they spend their time, what they do and where they go. It offers the prospect of having the opportunity to do those things they have always longed to do.

For those dreading it, retirement may be a self-fulfilling prophecy. Seeing nothing positive in it, they may progressively give up on life and go steadily down-hill physically, mentally and even spiritually. By lacking any will to live, they may actually hasten their own death.

Longing for retirement, though it might sound a more positive approach, could be a sign that a person might be failing to make the most of present reality. They could be losing touch with what some writers describe as 'the sacrament of the present moment'. The grass can always seem greener on the other side.

Perhaps the healthiest approach to retirement is to see it as a continuation of one's life journey, looking forward to its new opportunities for growth and development but also facing realistically the various losses which will inevitably accompany it.

Of course, a happy and long retirement is not simply the product of a positive state of mind. Poor health, sickness and disease can make serious in-roads into the quality of life of people of advancing years, as can social factors which increase their feeling of being vulnerable, marginalised and insecure.

Some Reflections on My Own Experience
Since I am on the threshold of moving into the process of retirement myself, I will start from my own experience. At the beginning of a retreat I made recently, I was very struck by a phrase in a book I was reading: 'Sit with your reluctance, and see it for

what it is.' For some reason, it made me think about two reactions I had shortly before my retreat. In the first instance, someone asked me, 'What are you most looking forward to?' 'Retirement' was what immediately came into my mind. And the very day before my retreat, I received a letter inviting me to a meeting with my archbishop – along with other priests round about my age (seventy in June 2003) – to help us think about the practical implications of retirement, whenever that might be in the future. Again, my own reaction was significant. Far from feeling threatened, a bit of me was feeling – wouldn't it be good if the archbishop invited me to retire!

I shared these feelings with my retreat director, since I was disturbed lest whether these two reactions were an indication of some kind of 'reluctance' on my part, a resistance to my ministry as parish priest in St Basil's, a yearning to escape from all the responsibility and work involved. Yet I knew I didn't want a move to another parish. I felt very much at home in St Basil's. Was my reluctance due to some kind of ingrained laziness or a longing to be rid of all the responsibilities involved and a yearning for an easier life? I did not think it was just about that – not totally anyway. Was it linked to a feeling of being overworked – feeling there is no end to the long lists of things to be done? I have to admit that, when I am on my own, I rarely sit down and relax. I always feel there are more things I could be doing.

My retreat director advised me to stay with my feelings about retirement during the retreat – but perhaps to see them in a positive light rather than negatively. She even suggested that 'retirement' could be a kind of metaphor for reflection during the whole retreat. I followed her advice and I gradually began to understand retirement as a process. In my case that process needs to begin now. I am already in the process of retiring even as I write this article. In fact, the research and reflection involved in it have turned out to be a very valuable element in my own retirement process.

One of the wonderful gifts of the parish I am in is the way so many people share in the ministry, activity and running of the parish. In Vatican II language, there is plenty of 'collaborative ministry'. Together we share responsibility both for the running of the parish and for the various forms of ministry which make up the life of the church. It began to dawn on me during my retreat that the process of my retiring as parish priest could be a further important step in the development of collaborative ministry in the parish. In some way or other, all the parishioners should be involved in my retirement process. For the whole parish to take a full part in this retirement process could be an important growth experience for everyone, myself included. Obviously, all dimensions of the life, ministry and mission of the parish would need to be looked at to ensure that these were being properly catered for in the process of my 'letting go'.

However, the process would need to go far beyond making sure that all the structures of parish ministry are properly maintained. One of the challenges for any parish today lies in coming to terms with its mission as church in the local neighbourhood and town, as well as its social responsibilities, national and international. We are living in exciting times in the church. God's spirit seems to be calling us to greater vision and a renewed commitment to share our faith and bring gospel-values into everyday life at all levels. If my retirement process is to be a 'growth experience' for the whole parish, the parishioners need to do far more than keep things ticking over. They need to grow even more alive and show greater dynamism and vision. It would also be important that young people should feel part of the process and be given the freedom to make their unique contribution, however disturbing some older ones (like me!) might find it.

In God's providence, part of the uniqueness of St Basil's is that we share the same church with the Anglican parish, All Saints. In fact, both communities usually call themselves by the same name, St Basil and All Saints. Over the past twenty years since our purpose-built shared church was opened, our two communities have tried to share deeply in all sorts of ways, gradually growing more and more together as one community. I look on the vicar, Guy Elsmore, and his wife and family as very precious friends and we collaborate very closely in our pastoral and liturgical planning and decision-making. Our lives, ministry and mission are bound up with the people of each other's parish, as well as with the life of the local community. If my retirement process is to be a growth experience for St Basil's, it needs to have a similar impact on Guy and the parishioners of All Saints. Hence, they too should be intimately involved in my retirement process.

At present, a relatively small group of parishioners are responsible for much of the organised life and pastoral ministry in the parish. If the only outcome of the kind of retirement process I am envisaging is that these willing people end up taking on extra work and responsibility, it would be far from beneficial to the parish. There is no way most of these people could do any more. That is why as many parishioners as possible need to be involved in the retirement process. In turn, that might call for an organised programme of lay-formation to equip people for the kind of ministries they will be undertaking. Since such a programme could help people to see how their involvement fits into the wider picture of ministry, thus increasing their sense of contributing and belonging, maybe one of my top priorities in the next few years should be getting a wide-ranging programme of lay-formation and ministerial training off the ground. People already retired in the parish would seem obvious candidates for this kind of involvement. However, ironically, many such people find their time 'to do what they want' severely limited by their child-minding commitments as grandparents (though looking after their grandchildren – within limits! – is exactly what they want to do).

I could imagine some parishioners thinking, 'Such a retirement process is fine while Kevin is still with us. What about when he finally goes? Will our increased ability to look after most aspects of parish life on our own be leaving ourselves open to a succession of older parish priests nearing retirement?' In reality, regardless of any positive retirement process, that is almost bound to happen, given the increasing age of priests in the archdiocese – and in the UK and Ireland as a whole. That makes greater collaborative ministry even more important and urgent.

However, if the retirement process I envisage is even moderately successful, St Basil & All Saints' could contribute towards providing a helpful model for parish life, not just ecumenically but also at the level of pastoral ministry. What would matter most would not be the age of the parish priest but the active involvement and co-responsibility of the parish community. In fact, the parish could end up by seeing more younger faces around, if one fruit of an effective retirement strategy was that a pastoral placement here became a valuable optional component in ministerial formation in the archdiocese. Moreover, it goes without saying that such formation would be as much the responsibility of the parishioners as of the parish priest.

It is possible that this shared retirement process might work out so well that I would be able to continue even longer as parish priest, despite my increasing limitations due to age and poor health. However, I suspect it would be better for the parish – and for me – if I were to go sooner rather than later. After all, for myself I envisage retirement not as giving up priestly ministry, but as growing into a different mode of being a priest. Who knows what that might be! More writing perhaps? Or more CAFOD involvement? Or being available as a kind of theological or pastoral sounding board for people? Or perhaps just sitting back and enjoying life and the wonderful people God has shared with me as part of my life?

Life After Retirement – Stagnation or Growth?
It is sometimes said that when we retire we can do what we always wanted to do. That is hardly flattering about the way we have exercised our freedom up to this point in life. A good friend of mine always insists that all through life he has tried to do what he wants to do. And he suggests that is true of most people. A mother sitting by the hospital bedside of her desperately ill child is doing what she wants to do. At that moment, in that particular situation, there is nowhere else she would want to be. Admittedly, when her daughter is back home and better again, by that hospital bedside is the last place that mother would want to be. Loving exposes us to a lot of pain and makes us very vulnerable. Yet loving is what we have chosen to do. In that context, disengagement for more radical engagement suggests that we become more focused in our loving. Perhaps, in that sense, it might be true to say that retirement offers us the opportunity to do what we have always wanted to do. Our changed circumstances, though they may be more limiting in some respects, enable us to concentrate on what we regard as the most important priorities in our lives. That is why retirement can be a most enriching time of life. We do not retire from life; we retire deeper into life. In fact, retirement is sometimes described as a process of disengagement for more radical engagement, a time for refining one's priorities.

A lot of things change in the life of a person who retires. Though some of these changes may be very welcome, at least in the early years of retirement, others will be experienced as losses which touch a person quite deeply. For instance, many losses are linked in some way or other with leaving one's normal occupation, whether this be the workplace, school, hospital, university and even parish. A loss of personal self-esteem and even identity may be felt when one leaves a position where one's competence is recognised and most of one's social contacts are based and which has provided the basis for one's financial security. One may even feel the loss of an ordered structure to one's daily life when one loses the discipline of a daily timetable and the creative stress born of the expectations of others.

If retirement is to be a time of personal growth, it is essential that these losses be acknowledged, properly grieved over and in this way laid peacefully to rest. Where these losses leave some important human needs unfulfilled, as far as possible they need to be compensated for. Denial that there are any losses involved could be a recipe for disaster.

Christians are familiar with the gospel image of the seed falling in the ground and dying so that new life and growth can emerge. Maybe that image can throw light on the process of retirement. Disengaging to re-engage involves a reordering of priorities. No longer are we tempted to dance to the tune of the expectations of others. We can look more deeply into the meaning of life and thus focus on the things we see to be most important. In a sense, retirement can spark off a further stage of growth in our more authentic self. In a society which bases personal worth on such indices as economic achievement and capacity as a consumer, facing up to retirement can help us to be more aware that we are more than what we do. Our self-identity goes much deeper than our activity.

Many retired people say how much they appreciate the freedom of their new situation in life. Maybe that is a sign they have passed beyond the grief of their loss of work and all that entails and laid it peacefully to rest. However, greater freedom is about more than having ample free time and the ability to set one's own agenda. It is not just about freedom from external constraints. It offers the opportunity for a deeper level of freedom, a freedom for the more important things in life. This can take various forms. For some it may leave them free for prophetic risk-taking. Seeing more to the heart of things, they can challenge laws, procedures and rituals which have lost or come adrift from their meaning. In that sense, retired people can be powerful advocates for change. They have a sufficiently rich treasury of memories to avoid being imprisoned by the rigidities of an un-historical past. Like the ageing Simeon and Anna, they can inter-pret the past as a seed-bed of hope and promise. So they are able to read the signs of the times and believe in a future which is in God's gift but in which God has called us to share as his artisans in building.

The Jesuit, Patrick Purnell, prefers the expression 'sabbath people' to the more politically correct 'senior citizens'. He is not suggesting that retirement is a time for rest, in the sense of sit-ting back and doing nothing. Although the Bible pronounces the sabbath holy precisely because God rested on that day, God's rest was not a long sleep-in but consisted in enjoying the good-ness and beauty of his creation. Our consumer culture is a rest-less culture. Advertisers are so busy trying to create new 'wants' with which to whet our appetites for the latest gadgets or com-puters, people have little time or inclination to sit back and sim-ply enjoy the wonder, beauty and simplicity of life.

Another expression for the retired is 'Ulysses people'. This highlights another essential ingredient of a happy retirement, namely, to continue our life-long voyage of discovery by having a searching mind and heart. People also stress the importance of the mind-body interaction and insist that a healthy lifestyle with exercise appropriate to one's age holds the key to maintaining mental alertness throughout the ageing process.

As human persons we are essentially social beings. Eugene C. Bianchi in his essay 'Living with Elder Wisdom' writes that 'creative elders oppose the ageing stereotype of withdrawal from social involvements' and quotes some inspiring examples, including one lady who insisted, 'My aches and pains are less important than my agenda.'[1] All stress that inspiring social con-tacts and strong social support groups come high on the agenda for making retirement a continuing growth experience. For some, these groups will offer motivational inspiration and help people to maintain their social commitments. For others, they can help to compensate for the loss of former friends. New friendships can also offer a further stimulus for personal growth in retirement. A retired person's increasing dependence on oth-ers can in some cases result in the blossoming of new and very profound friendships.

1. Eugene C. Bianchi, 'Living With Elder Wisdom', *The Way Special Issue on Ageing*, April 1996, 93-102, at 98.

Retiring Grace-fully: Towards a Spirituality of Retirement
I am always a little suspicious of spirituality language. I well remember being at a meeting with Enda McDonagh in which someone remarked that the key to spirituality lay in discovering one's inner self. Enda commented: 'When I look within myself, I can never find any inner self. All I can find is a cluster of relationships.'

Made in the image of a trinitarian God, we are essentially relational beings. If spiritual growth has any meaning, it must be about growth in the way we live out the truth of all the relationships, human and divine, which lie at the core of our being human persons. That growth needs to continue all through life, including the years of retirement. A whole variety of factors specific to the retirement and ageing process will affect the way we grow during these years. In that sense it is possible to speak in terms of a spirituality of retirement. However, what we are talking about ultimately is how we grow as human persons during the retirement process.

Retirement can be a time for contemplation, looking at life with eyes of wonder and enjoying its goodness. In a sense, prayer and contemplation are retirement activities. In fact, it could even be argued that retirement offers a very privileged opportunity for experiencing in an even deeper way the mind-blowing truth that we are made in the image of God. It can give us the opportunity to grow as sabbath people, that is, people who are thankful for the giftedness of life and for the gift of other people – and ourselves. Appreciation of such giftedness lies at the heart of contemplative prayer. All is sheer gift – and God is all-giving, for-giving. Human growth in the period of retirement will often take the form of a deepening of prayer-life into contemplative prayer, though it might not be recognised as such. The contemplative prayer life of some may perhaps be glimpsed in the way they talk about the great pleasure they get from gardening and how it brings them closer to nature. For others who take up painting or poetry in retirement, it might be seen in the way these creative activities take them out of themselves. For others who are grandparents, their experience of contemplative prayer might be found in the wonder of the gift of their grandchildren and the love they awaken in their grandparents. For others it might be in the way they experience a deeper dimension of life on a long walk, or while listening to a piece of music, or reading a good book. Contemplative prayer enables people to see beneath the surface of life.

And it is not only the beauty and wonder of life they face; they become more aware of the suffering and tragedy that seems so much a part of life. This 'God's-eye view' can make them more tolerant of situations of ambiguity. Similarly, seeing beneath the surface of life can help people to appreciate the goodness of diversity, whether in cultures, or lifestyle, or even in religions. This can even lead to a change in their image of God or the divine. A God of laws and institutions can give way to a more compassionate God whose being is shrouded in mystery rather than enunciated in the precision of dogmatic formulae.

Although initially retirement usually offers a person greater independence, factors such as diminishing strength, mobility, eyesight and hearing along with greater likelihood of sickness and hospitalisation may eventually increase the level of a retired person's dependence on others. Active acceptance of dependence need not be seen as giving up the ghost or entering on a period of second childhood. Active acceptance of dependence can be a very important human characteristic, provided it is matched by the dependability of those on whom one is depending. Throughout the whole of our lives, we live in a state of interdependence on each other. That is why dependability (reliability, faithfulness etc.) is such a central Christian virtue. God is the utterly dependable one, the faithful one. A powerfully moving expression of this comes from Pedro Arrupe, the former General of the Jesuits. Towards the end of his life, when severely disabled by a stroke and hardly able to speak, he said in a message to his brother Jesuits:

> More than ever, I now find myself in the hands of God. This is what I have wanted all my life, from my youth. And this is still the one thing I want. But now there is a difference: the initiative is entirely with God. It is indeed a profound spiritual experience to know and feel myself so totally in his hands.[2]

Mary Elizabeth Kenel, in her article, 'Preparing for Retirement', draws attention to this phenomenon:

> ... encouraging others to demonstrate an appropriate level of care toward us and to do so in such a way that the very act of accepting care is in itself an act of caring. Caring behaviour

2. *Documents of the 33rd General Congregation of the Society of Jesus*, St Louis; Institute of Jesuit Sources, 1984, 93.

does not denote a one-side dependency. Instead, it is a complex interchange that defines an enduring relationship between persons. Accepting care and resources from another does not transform the recipient into a needy, passive burden. As we prepare to enter the retirement phase of life, let us ask ourselves whom we allow to grace us with the gift of caring.[3]

Retirement and Theology

Is there a theology of retirement? That is a question I was tempted to explore in this article – and it is certainly worth exploring. However, the more I got in touch with the real-life experience of retirement, whether through conversation or reading or personal reflection, the more I came to see that it would be much more interesting to explore retirement as a source of theology. To be even more specific, I began to suspect that, for many theologians, embarking on the process of retirement seems to have had a significant impact on their theology. It is almost as though experiencing the human process of retirement is itself a theological source. Maybe this should not be surprising. After all, if theology is more an activity ('theologising') than a finished product (e.g. book, article etc), then it is only natural that a major human experience such as the retirement process should strongly influence a theologian his or her doing theology. In these days when the subject tends to be seen as centre-stage, that is only to be expected.

'Retirement theology', if I may coin a phrase to describe this phenomenon, is likely to reflect a number of those features which we have seen to be associated with the retirement process itself. I would suggest that 'retirement theology' might exhibit some of the following characteristics:

more focused – in line with 'disengaging to re-engage', it is likely to be a theology which is not interested in peripheral matters and goes to straight to the fundamental issues to be faced;

a greater sense of the preciousness of time (kairos) – a theology which is not afraid to recognise the need for change in life as part of the on-going process of liberation from oppression; and so a theology with a definite sense of urgency, prepared to seize the present opportunity;

---

3. Mary Elizabeth Kenel, 'Preparing for Retirement', in *Human Development*, Vol 23, Summer 2002, 13-18, at 17.

more experience-based – a theology with a greater awareness of and trust in the action of God's spirit in the lives of people;

more pastoral – a theology which is deeply concerned about the pastoral dimensions of theological issues, acknowledging that, in the final analysis, theology is not about abstractions but about living relationships, human and divine;

ready to take risks – a theology which is prepared to think creatively and imaginatively, rather than be held back by an over-cautious fear of possible consequences – and so a theology with a greater faith in the future;

more tolerant of diversity – a theology nourished by long and rich experience of life, and so one which is more open to the positive salvific role of other faiths and more likely to emphasise that our primary encounter with God lies in the reality of everyday life rather than in liturgy;

more open to ambiguity – a theology which is prepared to start from where people are and which is more aware of the growth process in life, with all its ups and downs, light and shade; so a theology more prepared to accept en-route pastoral solutions despite their being tinged by compromise and ambiguity;

more contemplative – a theology which goes below the surface of things and interprets life in a deeper context; hence, one which accepts the giftedness of reality as something to be responded to in terms of gospel values rather than legal and administrative technicalities

sabbatical – a sabbath theology linked to the contemplative dimension of retirement; a theology flowing from the experience of wonder before the incomprehensibility of God and our own sheer 'giftedness' as creatures; the very activity of theologising itself being our sharing in the divine activity of 'seeing that it is good' and thus at the heart of our being made in the image of God;

a more humble theology – one which recognises that ultimately we are in the hands of God and that, in its fullness, God's kingdom is pure gift of God and not some human making.

It would require another article to explore how far these characteristics are reflected in the theological contribution Enda McDonagh has made to the life of the church in Ireland and worldwide in recent years, as well as to the whole arena of social justice and peace and justice, at home and abroad. Without attempting such a task, I cannot resist making a few comments.

Over the past decade I have increasingly noticed Enda's great gift for being a kind of contemplative presence at various meetings. He has developed a knack for discerning the really crucial underlying concerns in any discussion and can put his finger on just where the heart of the gospel touches these issues. I have seen that at meetings of moral theologians or people involved with HIV/AIDS, especially in the developing world. He has highlighted the urgency of the latter issue through his constant insistence that we are living 'in a time of AIDS'. He has also shown himself prepared to take risks, as for instance, when he floated the proposal that baptisms in Northern Ireland should only be celebrated on an ecumenical basis; or when, in September 2002, he joined forces with Stanley Hauerwas (hardly a natural bed-fellow!) to launch an 'Appeal to Christian leaders and theologians' to make the twenty-first century 'be for war what the nineteenth was for slavery, the era of its abolition.' Likewise, some of Enda's recent outspoken and courageous articles in *The Furrow* on the current painful situation of the Catholic Church in Ireland are not afraid to speak of the sinfulness and woundedness of the church, though in a spirit of deep humility and discernment. I am also thinking of how the development of his whole approach to moral theology has exhibited the traits of being more experience-based and practical and also more open to ambiguity and appreciative of diversity. One final example: Enda's 'theology from the edges' is a striking example of the profoundly sabbatical quality of his theology.

Conclusion

The retirement activity of disengagement for re-engagement in a more focused way sounds rather like a description of the process of conversion and renewal. If that is so, perhaps retirement is not just a passing phenomenon in the church due to the increasing numbers of ageing priests and religious. Maybe the life-giving potential inherent in the retirement process is actually a sign of the times for the church in our day. It could be that God's spirit is calling the church into a new phase of its continued growth rather akin to the retirement process. Perhaps there has to be a lot of letting go in the church in all sorts of ways, especially as regards power and structures and even traditional styles of liturgy and church life. If this is true, such losses will need to be named and owned and even grieved over, if we are to let go of them in a life-giving way.

In writing this article I have been helped by two talks by Patrick Purnell SJ and Mannes Tidmarsh,[4] and by the latter's excellent pamphlet, *Vocation to Retirement*.[5] Above all, I would like to acknowledge that some of the key ideas in this article have been greatly influenced by the thinking of my good friend, Fr Austin Smith CP. At the end of 2002 he was awarded an honorary doctorate in Law by the University of Liverpool in recognition of his creative and imaginative ministry as a priest in Toxteth, Liverpool, where he has pushed forward the boundaries of Christian ministry and mission in an area of serious social deprivation and discrimination. Through his respectful presence he has been witnessing to the action of God's spirit in their lives and relationships as they struggled to be true to their individual and collective dignity in the face of unjust and dehumanising pressures at many levels. I mention this purely because the conferral of such an honorary doctorate is relevant to retirement theology. It is no mere coincidence that Austin, as part of the process of disengaging to re-engage, is embarking on a reflective study of priesthood and its broader ramifications in the light of his own 50 years experience as a priest within the Passionist congregation. That promises to be a work of retirement theology *par excellence*. No doubt we can look forward to something similar from Enda. Retirement theology promises a rich future!

---

4. Patrick Purnell SJ and Mannes Tidmarsh talks recorded on audio-cassette at Upholland Northern Institute in the 1980s.
5. Mannes Tidmarch, *Vocation to Retirement*, Occasional Paper No 6, Christian Council on Ageing, Epworth House, Stuart St, Derby, England.

An Appreciation

Imogen Stuart

When I think of Enda McDonagh my inner eye sees somebody who radiates a deep joyfulness. This joy is something that I imagine was a quality the early Irish monks had and kept through all their harsh and ascetic lives, and in their tumultuous years of raids and other disasters and which they retained. It shows a kind of spirituality you acquire through loving nature – seeing God all around you – seeing God in all living creatures and having an understanding of human frailty. All this is enveloped by Enda's intelligence or, better said, wisdom.

You think I know him very well – over many years – having spent hours in his company? Not so. I don't know when we first met, but I know if I had met him earlier in my life when I had many queries on spiritual and scriptural matters there would have been no better person than Enda. I know we have a kind of dialogue: he in his words and I through my sculpture.

He is one of the very few people who have realised and taught how interwoven Christianity and art is.

Enda McDonagh's Moral Theology

Charles E. Curran

Enda McDonagh's vocation has been as a Roman Catholic moral theologian situated primarily at St Patrick's College, Maynooth. This essay will discuss four major points: his catholicity, the development of his thought, his understanding of moral theology, and a further evaluation of his work.

McDonagh's Catholicity

Everyone rightly takes for granted McDonagh's catholicity but two aspects of his catholicity stand out. First, Catholic with a capital 'C' includes catholic with a small 'c'. Small 'c' catholic is universal and all-embracing. His concerns and interests have been inclusive, extensive, and broad. He has been more than familiar with theology, philosophy, and ethics; but, in addition, he has a deep appreciation and feel for politics, art, poetry, and drama. This festschrift testifies to his catholicity. There has never been a festschrift for a Catholic theologian that has brought together so many different people from the fields of politics and art and all its dimensions. Enda McDonagh is catholic in his concerns, his interest, and his knowledge.

Second, the Catholic theological tradition with its emphasis on the catholic, the inclusive and the all-embracing has insisted on a 'both-and' approach rather than an 'either-or' approach. Karl Barth complained that his primary difficulty with Roman Catholic theology was its 'and'. Barth has pointed out what, in my judgment, is the most distinctive aspect of Catholic theology but also has indicated some problematic aspects about it.[1] Recall that Catholic theology insisted on scripture and tradition, not scripture alone; on grace and works, not grace alone; on faith and reason, not faith alone; on Jesus and the church and Mary

---

1. From a Catholic perspective, see Hans Urs von Balthasar, *The Theology of Karl Barth* , New York: Hope, Rinehart, and Winston, 1971, 40-41.

and the saints, not Jesus alone. The problem has been that at times the Catholic tradition has given too much attention to the aspect after the 'and' and has seen it somewhat independently of the first aspect. McDonagh himself, in one brief allusion to the Barthian position, agrees with the problematic aspect of the Catholic understanding in the past.[2] But all have to agree that the 'both-and' are characteristic of Catholic theology. An approach that is Catholic is by definition inclusive and universal and thus insists on a 'both-and' type of approach.

The basic Christian understanding has always seen the disciples of Jesus related both to God and neighbour in a community of discipleship. McDonagh, however, has developed the Catholic 'and' in fascinating ways and in the process has broken significant new ground. No contemporary Catholic moral theologian has recognised and emphasised more the essential connection between liturgy and moral life than Enda McDonagh. He was the obvious choice to write the article on liturgy and Christian life in the *Dictionary of Sacramental Worship*.[3]

An early essay shows how both the liturgy and Christian life have Trinitarian, convenantal, and community aspects. In addition, life, like liturgy, has dimensions of worship, thanksgiving, and petition.[4] The basic principle of the relationship is quite clear: 'The fulfillment and transformation of humanity and cosmos through the creative and saving presence of God is what Jesus announces and inaugurates with the kingdom. The already, the continuing but ambiguous, the yet-to-be are all dimensions of the creation-transformation which Jesus, church, and sacraments express and realise.'[5] McDonagh then applies this understanding in creative ways. Baptism is the right of initiation and entrance into the one church of Christ. But in Northern Ireland, baptism signifies baptism into a historical community in opposition to another particular Christian community.

2. Enda McDonagh, *The Making of Disciples: Tasks of Moral Theology*, Wilmington, Del: Michael Glazier, 1982, 107.
3. Enda McDonagh, 'Liturgy and Christian Life,' in *New Dictionary of Sacramental Worship*, ed. Peter E. Fink, Collegeville, Minn: Liturgical Press, 1990, 742-53. This essay is reprinted in Enda McDonagh, *Faith in Fragments*, Dublin: Columba Press, 1995, 92-108.
4. Enda McDonagh, *Invitation and Response: Essays in Christian Moral Theology*, New York: Sheed and Ward, 1972, 96-108.
5. Enda McDonagh, *Between Chaos and New Creation: Doing Theology at the Fringe*, Wilmington, Del: Michael Glazier, 1986, 86.

Should we stop the practice of baptism in these circumstances when reality contradicts the very meaning of baptism itself? McDonagh here raises a very significant question without coming down firmly on the side on discontinuing baptism.[6] Recently, McDonagh has proposed the need for joint ecumenical baptisms and Eucharists in Ireland.[7] Both in theory and in practice he has emphasised the ecumenical dimension of the church that is another aspect of his catholicity.

In his later writings, the now retired Maynooth professor relates the communion of the sacraments and of the Eucharist especially to the consumerism so prevalent in First World countries. We consume our environment, we consume one another, the rich consume the poor, and the powerful consume the powerless. In fact, the historical Jesus was consumed by the political and religious leaders of his time – *consummatum est*. But the communion of the sacraments and the Eucharist is a sharing in the bread of eternal life and the cup of salvation. The symbol and reality of sacramental communion radically confront the sinful consumption present in so many aspects of contemporary life.[8]

Father McDonagh also brings together prayer and politics in the light of the Catholic 'and'. Prayer is the liberation of God in our hearts, our lives, and our world. To pray is to bring this transforming and liberating love of God into our lives and into the world. To pray is to accept our political vocation to help transform society. It is true that many other theologians have mentioned the movement from prayer to politics, but what about the other movement from politics to prayer? Many involved in politics have no interest in either God or prayer. Even most Christians see no movement from politics to prayer. But, in the light of the Catholic 'and', McDonagh also insists on this movement and relationship. Social and political commitment is based on the existence and the needs of others. In political involvement, we open ourselves to the transforming mystery of the other with attitudes of wonder, awe, thanksgiving, humility, and forgiveness. These are the same characteristics of prayer, but the 'and' is even stronger. The openness to the other by its inherent dynamism leads to openness to the transcendent God

6. Ibid., 85-86.
7. Enda McDonagh, 'Dear Michael and John,' *Céide*, April 2002, 7-8.
8. *Faith in Fragments*, 104-07.

as the one who is mediated in and through the human other. Social and political activity for the Christian should lead to prayer.[9]

A later essay even adds a third element – poetry – to prayer and politics. This essay insists on a deeper relationship of unity and distinction, challenge and convergence, between prayer as awareness of, and response to, God the ultimate reality and poetry as the human expression of reality even and perhaps especially in its tragic dimension. Here too prayer and poetry deal with mystery, inspiration, and the search for adequate and beautiful form. At first sight politics seems to be closer to prose than to poetry. But politics needs the imaginative and the creative that is found in poetry. Healthy politics needs the protest of art against any kind of social tyranny, but it also needs the celebration of art and poetry. Prayer, poetry, and politics are three *loci* of creative and redeeming activity which the theologian must recognise and connect.[10] In the light of the darkness facing the church in Ireland, McDonagh maintains that the poetic imagination in the midst of darkness can help faith people in Ireland to move through that same type of creative imagination from darkness to life.[11]

The Catholic 'and' comes through in McDonagh's understanding of anthropology although he never develops anthropology in depth in any one place. The self exists only in relationships with God, others, various communities, and the cosmos. Note all the 'ands' that form the complex reality of the human person. Such an anthropology strongly rejects the individualism which continues to be so prevalent in the ethics and life of many first world countries and now seems to be ever more present even in Ireland.[12] Previous discussions of liturgy and prayer and their relationships to life point out the essential relationship of the person to God. From his earliest writings, Professor McDonagh has emphasised the person or self in relationship to

---

9. *Making of Disciples*, 99-111; See also Enda McDonagh, *Church and Politics: From Theology to a Case History of Zimbabwe*, Notre Dame, Ind: University of Notre Dame Press, 1980, 79-87.
10. Enda McDonagh, *The Gracing of Society*, Dublin: Gill & Macmillan, 1989, 123-38.
11. Enda McDonagh, 'Faith and the Cure of Poetry: A Response to the Crisis in the Catholic Church in Ireland,' *Céide*, September 2001, 8-11.
12. Many of the essays in *The Gracing of Society* address the problem of individualism.

the other. In fact, an essay in the 70s sees the moral obligation in terms of a call that has an unconditional character about it. The source of the call-obligation is another person or group of persons who call the person to recognise and respond. In transcending self to reach out to the other, a certain disintegration of the subject occurs; but there follows a re-integration of the subject in relationship to others and to other communities.[13] The presence of the other is a gift that draws us out of ourselves and enables us to transcend ourselves. The striving and achieving dimension of our response to the other is subordinated to the gift dimension of the other. But, in this sinful world, we also experience the other at times, not only as gift, but also as threat. The predominance of gift over threat is what calls us to conversion and true liberation. Too often contemporary Catholic thinkers see moral development only in terms of self-development and fail to see personal development in terms of our relationships with others.[14]

A chapter in *Faith in Fragments* insists that the recovery of the other/stranger 'both human and divine' is at the heart of the renewal of ethics and of God's place within it. God is the stranger God, and we who believe that the stranger God has come to us must likewise embrace the human stranger both in the form of individuals and of groups. Too often both Christian life and Christian thought have emphasised the exclusion of the other. Economic, cultural, social, political, and gender exclusions have consistently prevailed in our world. The word and work of Jesus, however, was always open to the stranger and especially the poor, the sinner, and the outcast. The stranger God calls for all believers in that God to embrace and include the human stranger.[15]

From his very earliest writings, McDonagh insists on the importance of community. One could only become a human person within human communities. Theology itself, like all study, also has a community dimension.[16] A later essay insists that one becomes a person only in community thereby changing the communities of family, school, neighbourhood, city, nation, world. Community is formed and reformed by persons. Only such a

---

13. Enda McDonagh, *Gift and Call: Toward a Christian Theology of Morality*, Dublin: Gill & Macmillan, 1975, 39 ff.
14. *Making of Disciples*, 71-79.
15. *Faith in Fragments*, 137-45.
16. *Invitation and Response*, 6-8.

community dimension can deal with the problems facing our society – war, devastation, waste, pollution. Our ethics both philosophical and theological as well as our moral education have been too individualistic. The community dimension must become primary.[17]

The later writings bring in more the relationship to creation, cosmos, and ecology, especially in the light of a world threatened by ecological devastation. The Creator who made creation saw that it was good. The Creator maintains a communion of respect and care for creation. We are called to the same respect and care for all creation. Communion rather than consuming should characterise our relationship to the created world.[18] The emphasis on the person, the other, communities, and cosmos strongly oppose the individualism so present in thought and practice in contemporary first world societies. Note, however, that McDonagh does not develop in any detail the various communities to which we belong and their influence on us as persons and our influence on them.

The retired Maynooth professor also recognises the need for both the particular and the universal. He has dealt extensively with the particularity of the Irish situation and the Irish church in the light of the broader tradition of the universal church. Post-Vatican II Catholic theology rightly made a move from the universal to the particular. Even Vatican II itself proposed a universal theology, but the seeds of differentiation were already sewn. Liberation theology in South America was the first of the theological moves to a more particular approach. Now we realise that the so-called universal theology itself was in reality a very particular theology – the theology of white, rich males. The universal easily became a cloak for theological imperialism. Historical consciousness insists on the importance of particularity and the social location of all theologians and thinkers. This move to particularity is perhaps the greatest single change in post-Vatican II Catholic theology. At times, however, the temptation still exists to make one particular theology a model for all others thus resulting in a new imperialising universalism. But the move from the universal to the particular does not abolish the value of the universal or general although it does qualify that value very considerably. We still must communicate theologically across

---

17. *Making of Disciples,* 77-79.
18. *Faith in Fragments,* 147-55.

the boundaries of culture, history, society, politics, race, gender, and economic class. Particular communities of the disciples of Jesus share commitments of faith, understanding, and practice that are common to all of them.[19]

McDonagh's insistence on Catholic inclusiveness and the Catholic 'and' comes through in his recognition of three complex roles of the church and of church teaching – the priestly, the prophetic, and the wisdom roles. Some will be tempted to emphasise, either exclusively or primarily, one of these functions; but the Maynooth professor insists on all three. All three are necessary, but also all three are subject to distortion and temptations. The priestly role is tempted to assume a worldly style of power; the prophetic is tempted by destructive exaggeration; the wisdom role is tempted to make worldly compromises. All the roles and functions are necessary and help to correct the possible deficiencies and temptations in any one of the three.[20]

Throughout his writings, Enda McDonagh insists on faith and morality, reflection and action, theory and practice. In terms of the sources of wisdom and knowledge, he emphasises faith and experience rather than the more traditional Roman Catholic faith and reason. The insistence on human experience is both broader and more particular than the older insistence on human reason. Experience can include many different aspects of the human, but it also includes the experience of particular persons or groups. All these three aspects come together in his approach to theology where he fears that the Catholic 'and' (as in dogmatic and moral and sacramental theology) has fragmented and separated what should be a whole. A future section will develop in detail his understanding of moral theology.

Discontinuity and Change

The insistence on inclusiveness and the Catholic 'and' has been present throughout McDonagh's writings although different emphases have emerged at different times. But his approach to moral theology has developed considerably over the years. His inquisitive, creative, and restless mind has moved from one

19. *Between Chaos and New Creation*, 91-122.
20. Enda McDonagh, 'Prophecy or Politics? The Role of the Churches in Society,' in *Faithfulness and Fortitude: In Conversation with the Theological Ethics of Stanley Hauerwas*, ed. Mark Thiessen Nation and Samuel Wells, Edinburgh: T & T Clark, 2000, 306-08.

approach to another. His own understanding of moral theology has gone through four different stages from the time he was a student to the present.

Pre-Vatican II Approach. The first stage was the pre-Vatican II approach to moral theology. He was trained in this theology, but from the beginning of his teaching and writing moved away from it. Even as a student, he was dissatisfied with the pre-Vatican II approach to moral theology.[21] In his own words, 'The fortress church with its stone ramparts of precise teaching and Latin liturgy and with its granite doctors of divinity enjoyed (if that be the word) its most powerful period from the 1860s to the 1960s.'[22] The teacher handed on to the student the authoritative answers given by Rome and found in the textbooks.[23] 'Textbook theology tended to indoctrinate rather than inspire.'[24] In moral theology, the textbook was called the manual of moral theology. These textbooks came into existence in the post-Tridentine period to train confessors for the sacrament of penance especially to judge the existence of sin and above all the gravity of sin – mortal or venial. At this time, this practical moral theology became closely associated with canon law that proposed the laws that Catholics should follow in their life in the church. Moral theology thus saw the moral life primarily in relationship to negative laws pointing out what was sinful. The manuals often used the Ten Commandments as the basic structure and then added in the requirements of canon law. The scope and approach of the manuals was act-centred, legalistic, minimalistic, and casuistic. There was no attempt even to connect the many laws with the primary law of love of God and neighbour.[25] Enda McDonagh was obviously sent to get a second degree in canon law at Münich in order to prepare himself to follow in the footsteps of his ecclesiastical predecessors at Maynooth to teach both moral theology and canon law. From my somewhat removed and distant perspective it seems that McDonagh was already strongly disenchanted with such an approach and purposely wrote his dissertation in canon law not on a narrow topic of canonical

---

21. Ibid., 288-90.
22. *Faith in Fragments*, 36.
23. *Making of Disciples*, 22.
24. *Faith in Fragments*, 34.
25. *Making of Disciples*, 22-24; *Invitation and Response*, 16-19.

legislation but on the much broader and more important issue of church and state in Ireland!

Post-Vatican II Approach. His early post-Vatican II writings recognise the newer approach to moral theology heavily influenced by Vatican II, but, as he correctly points out, efforts at renewal had begun with the Tübingen School in Germany in the nineteenth century and were developed by Fritz Tillmann in the 1930s and more so by Bernard Häring in the 1950s. One can only assume that he became aware of these developments as he was studying in Germany in the early 60s. Vatican II presented the impetus that brought about the demise of the manuals of moral theology and called for a life-centred moral theology (not an act and sin-centred approach), nourished by the scripture, the liturgy, and the universal call of all Christians to holiness. The biblical, theological, and ecumenical movements of the time provided a new context for a moral theology that is biblical, Christ-centred, and charity inspired.[26]

His 1972 book, *Invitation and Response*, brings together previously published essays that attempted to integrate moral theology more closely with dogmatic theology, scripture, and liturgy. His book emphasises the covenantal structure of morality (notice the call-response theme from the very beginning of his work) as centred on Jesus Christ.[27] Early in this period McDonagh thought that this renewed moral theology, for all its limited beginnings, seemed destined to grow in the coming decades and perhaps would be synthesised later in a way comparable to that of Thomas Aquinas in his day.

A Theology of Morality. But by the time *Invitation and Response* was published in 1972, McDonagh was already pursuing a different approach to moral theology that he called a theology of morality.[29] *Gift and Call*, his 1975 collection of essays, develops this approach especially in its first four chapters. A theology of morality is distinct from a moral theology and begins with the human experience of morality and not with revelation. We experience the moral call as unconditional, involving the call of the other both as person and as groups. Notice the community aspect coming through. The gift and call of the other must ulti-

---

26. *Invitation and Response*, 18-20.
27. Ibid., viii-ix.
28. Ibid. 20
29. Ibid., 18.

mately overcome the threat and fear character of the other. The Maynooth professor sees this approach as complementary to the covenantal approach emerging from the Vatican II context. One has to wonder here how his own earlier approach of invitation and response based on Christian revelation influenced his understanding of human moral experience which has the same basic structure as his theologically based approach. Perhaps an apologetic concern is also expressed here, for such an approach defends and supports his own understanding of moral theology but does it via the human experience of all. In his subsequent development, he emphasises particular experience and opposes the emphasis on universal human moral experience.

Theology at the Fringe. The theology of morality, the third stage in his own development of moral theology, quickly gave way to a final stage in his development – doing theology at the fringe. A number of factors contributed to this new stage. First, he gradually came to see the weakness of the renewed Vatican II moral theology associated with prominent theologians such as Bernard Häring and Josef Fuchs. This moral theology emphasised the person as subject and agent, and not just the particular moral act; the historical dimension of Christian and human existence and theology; and the theological dimension of moral theology. But McDonagh has reservations about how this renewed theology incorporated these three achievements of Vatican II. First, the emphasis on the person has been so strong that the community awareness and understanding have been neglected and not analysed or developed. Second, the historical dimension of the theory and practice of morality rightly overcame the non-historical orthodoxy of pre-Vatican II theology but accepted an understanding of history as gradually developing in a progressive manner and did not give enough importance to the tragic and transformative sense of history.[30] In this context, he realised that Vatican II itself tended to be too optimistic, as illustrated in the Pastoral Constitution on the Church in the Modern World. Occasionally, McDonagh quotes the second phrase in the Pastoral Constitution on the Church in the Modern World – '*luctus et angor.*' The title, *Gaudium et spes*, coming from the first two words of the document, fails to recognise the struggles and the tragedy of human existence.[31]

---

30. *Gracing of Society*, 19-21.
31. *Between Chaos and New Creation*, 183-95.

The understanding of history mentioned above leads into his third criticism of post-Vatican II moral theology as not being theological enough. The realities of sin, grace, redemption, and eschatology do not seem to be that present. At best, post-Vatican II moral theology emphasised the connection with creation but did not give that much sustained attention to the broader theological aspects. (It seems to me this criticism is more apropos with regard to Fuchs than it is with regard to Häring.) McDonagh illustrates his own more theological approach by describing a transformative notion of justice concentrating on the needs of the poor, the marginalised, and the oppressed rather than the Thomistic notion of justice that was more of a managerial than a transformative type.[32]

In keeping with his own methodological understanding of the role of experience and of theology, it seems that both these aspects influenced his criticism of post-Vatican II moral theology. From the viewpoint of experience, all recognise that the 60s throughout the world were a very optimistic time. Vatican II brought the Catholic Church into a sympathetic dialogue with modernity and its technological developments. But in the late 60s and afterward people came to experience much more the problematic aspects of modernity, the tragic aspects of human existence, and the growing injustices throughout the world. Modernity was not all it was cracked up to be. The poor, especially in the third world, cried out in a loud voice. McDonagh's particular experience, the Irish situation, reinforced his recognition of the tragic and the non-progressive nature of human history. Too often in Northern Ireland religion became a support for violence, hatred, and separation. During this post-Vatican II era, many Irish missionaries in the developing world became strong supporters of the need for justice for the poor and the marginalised. Our author learned from their experience. McDonagh became familiar with the South African scene and especially with the experience of Zimbabwe in the 1970s that he studied extensively with a focus on the issue of revolutionary violence. His later experience with the pandemic of AIDS in Africa only confirmed his emphasis on the poor and the marginalised and the need to do theology from the fringe.[33]

The role of experience in McDonagh's theology is the basis

---

32. *Gracing of Society*, 21-27.
33. 'Prophecy or Politics,' in Nation and Wells, 298-306.

for his recognition of the autobiographical aspect of theology. His first collection of essays refers to the inescapably autobiographical character of theology.[34] Theology is a personal exploration of the reality of the Christian life internal to the explorer and thus a personal relationship.[35] But the person obviously is influenced by the historical situations and context within which one exists. As a result of the social aspects, McDonagh refers to sociobiography rather than autobiography.

McDonagh develops the new stage in his theory in a 1986 collection of essays, *Between Chaos and New Creation: Doing Theology at the Fringe,* that was written 'in the context of a world in crisis and of an Ireland sharing that crisis but in its own fashion.'[37] The author dedicates the book 'for Bekan,' a fringe Irish village where he was born and brought up. Writing these essays obviously brought back memories of his experience of life in this small village in Western Ireland. 'Theology as autobiography moves inexorably on.'[38]

McDonagh is familiar with the most significant theological developments in contemporary Christian thought. A narrative theology forms and challenges the community of disciples. But narrative must give way to praxis, performance, and experiment.[39] Our author recognises that all theology is metaphorical, symbolic, and analogical and now adopts the metaphors of chaos and new creation.[40] But there is no doubt that the political theology of John Baptist Metz and especially the liberation theology of South America had the strongest influence on McDonagh and paved the way for this final stage of his development. Liberation theology emphasises the social aspect of theology with special emphasis on the role of the poor, the marginalised, and the deprived. Our author thus moved to doing theology at the fringe. Such an approach also stresses the tragic aspect of history and human existence and not the optimistic

---

34. *Invitation and Response,* viii.
35. Ibid., 2.
36. Enda McDonagh, *Doing the Truth: The Quest for Moral Theology,* Notre Dame, Ind.: University of Notre Dame Press, 1979, 1-13, 187-207.
37. *Between Chaos and New Creation,* 3.
38. Ibid., 9.
39. Ibid., 101-05.
40. Ibid., 4.

approach of the Enlightenment, modernity, and even of Vatican II.[41]

Under the influence of liberation theology, McDonagh now gives a central place to the metaphor of the reign of God. Earlier writings refer to the kingdom of God but he later shifts to the reign of God in keeping with others who see the concept of kingdom as too hierarchical and patriarchal. He always mentioned the kingdom of God in earlier writings but, from the middle 80s, he gave central importance to this metaphor in the light of liberation theology. The reign of God gives a special role to the poor, victims, marginalised, and those on the fringe. From the perspective of those on the fringe, the tragic aspect of human existence comes to the fore. His new theological vision insists on the movement from chaos to new creation. Chaos refers to the pre-creation or post-fall states described in Genesis. Chaos and creation, fresh chaos and new creation, convey much of the rhythm of dialectic of the Hebrew scriptures but also of the work of Jesus and the community of his disciples. Jesus in his suffering, death, and resurrection overcame chaos, sin, and destruction. But Christians after Jesus live out the tension involving the intrusion of the transhistorical eschaton and the time laden human response still required in history. Humankind and the cosmos, despite the presence of the reign of God and the new creation, remain vulnerable to the return of desert and chaos. At the heart of human destruction and chaos is the presence of the God of Genesis and Golgatha. God is faithful to God's people despite their failure and remains compassionate and co-suffering. This compassionate, co-suffering, forgiving, and reconciling God is continually doing a new creative thing. The utter weakness and chaos of Calvary became the symbol and source of new power and the new creation.[42]

The End of Moral Theology
The four stages in his development indicate a dissatisfaction not only with the moral theology of the pre-Vatican II manuals, but also with the post-Vatican II moral theology as it developed within the Roman Catholic Church. His primary critique of the manuals was their failure to be theological because of their heavy emphasis on philosophy, casuistry, and individual acts.

41. Ibid., 183-85; *Gracing of Society*, 83-92.
42. *Between Chaos and New Creation*, 3-9.

Unfortunately, theology was divided into various branches or specialties – scripture studies, dogmatic theology, and moral theology. Yes, some division of theology is necessary in order for students and others to study it, but the unity and distinctiveness of theology have been lost.[43] The 1982 *Making of Disciples* calls for the end of moral theology even in its post-Vatican II form. There is still need for an integrating theology trying to bring together scripture, dogmatic theology, and moral theology. Theology reflects on the truth and life of Christian discipleship. Perhaps dogmatic theology has suffered even more than moral theology in its separation from Christian living. Dogmatic theology became a self-enclosed discipline dealing with the study of historical formulas and philosophical discussions about these and failed to bring the saving gift of God in Jesus Christ through the Holy Spirit to Christian living. 'The end of moral theology, provided it is accompanied by the self-enclosed dogmatic theology, could prepare the way for rebirth of an integrated theology … In the other sense of end as purpose, the end of moral theology and of the moral theologian must be to provoke and promote such conscientisation among theologians in general and provide some guidance to how a new integrated theology of Christian truth and life might emerge.'[44]

The essays collected in *Between Chaos and New Creation* (1986) and *The Gracing of Society* (1989) continue the insistence on a more integrated theology with the emphasis on the community of the disciples of Jesus announcing, discerning, promoting, and bearing witness to the reign of God which is the new social existence of human beings.[45] Since the reign of God gives a central place to the outcast, the marginalised, and the poor, a theology based on such an understanding must be a theology at the fringe. His writings and interests from the late 70s on have centred primarily on society. The earlier writing, as exemplified in *Invitation and Response*, dealt primarily with fundamental moral theology.[46]

In his writing on society, McDonagh insists not on a social ethic that gives too great a role to philosophy but a theology of society. One essay in *The Gracing of Society* illustrates how he has

43. *Invitation and Response*, 14-21.
44. *Making of Disciples*, 2.
45. *Gracing of Society*, 4.
46. *Invitation and Response*, viii.

tried to rethink the course in social ethics to emphasise the theological and radical social aspects.[47] His primary concern is the
gracing of society and a theology of society.[48] The Maynooth
professor points out the four kingdom values that should be
present in society – freedom, justice, peace, and truth.[49] Note the
close relationship with the four values of society proposed on
the basis of a natural law approach by Pope John XXIII in *Pacem
in terris* – truth, justice, charity (solidarity), and freedom. *Pacem
in terris* sees peace in its fullest sense as resulting from the presence of these other four values.[50] Since peace is more than the
absence of war, it seems to require the presence of these other
values. McDonagh might have been better to follow *Pacem in terris's* approach by seeing peace as resulting from the other values
and by incorporating solidarity as a special value of its own.

McDonagh's theological understanding of these kingdom
values, however, differs from the natural law approach of *Pacem
in terris*. *Pacem in terris* primarily sees justice as regulating the relations between states and our world by recognising the rights
and duties of all concerned with a special concern for minori-
ties.[51] McDonagh criticises this concept of justice in the light of
the biblical concept of justice (*sedaqah*) which is a characteristic
of God which overlaps with fidelity, loving kindness and mercy.
God's justice becomes a standard and a challenge for God's people. Unlike the Aristotelian and Thomistic views of justice, the
prophetic tradition in the Hebrew Bible shows the essentially
social character of covenantal justice. Amos and the prophets
decry the injustice of society as a whole that results in the oppression of the weak by the strong, the wealthy, and the powerful. Jesus preached this kind of justice. History must still continue
its ambiguous way, but the gift of God's justice and mercy, the
eschatological breakthrough of God's justice, has already occurred. We must let that justice come into our world and carry
out its transforming role. *Sedaqah* justice is radical, visionary,
and transformative in comparison to Aristotelian justice that is

---

47. *Gracing of Society*, 48-80.
48. Ibid., 1-18.
49. Ibid., 61-76.
50. Pope John XXIII, 'Pacem in terris,' no. 80-129, in *Catholic Social
Thought: The Documentary Heritage*, ed. David J. O'Brien and Thomas A.
Shannon, Maryknoll, N.Y.: Orbis, 1992, 144-51.
51. Ibid., no. 91-97; 145-47.

managerial. Transformative justice goes to the underlying structures and calls for change so that the poor and the marginalised
of this world will be liberated. Managerial justice is not a pejora-
tive term and it can deal with some problems facing our world,
even the forgiveness of debts by poor countries; but it cannot attack the underlying structures that imprison so many people in
our world. However, McDonagh never develops what these
new structures are and how they should come into existence.[52]

Further Evaluation
Catholicity. The strong catholicity of McDonagh's interests and
approach constitutes a very positive aspect of his theology. The
danger today in many academic writings including theology is
that disciplines are so complex that one is forced to become narrower and narrower going into the discipline in depth and not
able to connect to the other human and Christian aspects. The
inclusion of poetry, politics, spirituality, sacramentality, dogmatic theology, and biblical theology into moral theology provides a broad and holistic view that all too often is missing. The
need for a broad human dialogue was the motivation behind his
helping to launch the journal *Céide* in 1997.[53] The same appealing inclusiveness comes through in McDonagh's method. In
fact, he fears that the Catholic 'and' in the past resulted in moral
theology being cut off from all other aspects of theology, and he
strives now to bring all theology together. In our limited world,
however, choices also involve some exclusions and aspects that
do not receive as much emphasis.
Essay format. The format of his writing obviously has influenced
his approach. Format and content are related. The Maynooth
professor has never written a detailed monograph in moral
theology. The closest to such a monograph is his *Church and
Politics: From Theology to a Case History of Zimbabwe.* But even the
first half of that reads more like a collection of essays.
Throughout his writing career he has been the master of the
short insightful theological essay often appearing in *The Furrow*
or similar type publications. McDonagh early on perceptively
realised that what a theologian produces, and I might add especially a moral theologian in the post-Vatican II church, depends
'on the demands made upon him in the course of his erratic hist-

---

52. *Gracing of Society*, 21-27.
53. Enda McDonagh, 'Margin to Margin,' *Céide*, September 1997, 4.

ory and on the resources he can command to meet these demands.' The author recognises both of these limitations, but without such limitations it is hard to see how theologians would produce any real theology at all.[54] Recall that for McDonagh the theologian reflects from within on the life of Christian discipleship in its particular situations. The theologian learns from the community and tries to provide the community with some intellectual insight as the total community itself tries to respond in its own circumstances. Without doubt, the essay requested by others forms the principal vehicle for McDonagh's theology. In these essays he has had many insightful things to say to the community about Christian vision and praxis as well as the particular subject addressed but, again, such an approach has its limitations. The Maynooth professor has never attempted to develop a systematic moral theology. Also, by definition, these essays, despite fascinating insights, ordinarily do not delve deeply into the specifics of how the community should react in a particular situation.

Theological dimension. Our author's emphasis on the theological dimension of moral theology has also been a very significant contribution. The theological aspect and the inclusion of all theology should rightly characterise any Christian moral theology. More than any other contemporary, the Maynooth professor has developed the theological aspect of the discipline.

Here too form and content interact. The short insightful essay presenting theological perspectives supports such an emphasis on the theological. A more synthetic approach would have to bring together all the other aspects of philosophy, experience, and the human sciences that enter into a truly systematic approach. Especially from a traditional Catholic perspective, theology includes all those aspects that help us to understand the human. The divine is mediated in and through the human and all its aspects. Nothing human is foreign to the Christian and the theological. Since McDonagh has not attempted a synthetic and systematic theology of Christian life and society, he has not had to flesh out and develop his theological perspectives.

In his longer essay on teaching the theology of society, our author also recognises the need to bring in the philosophical as-

---

54. *Invitation and Response*, viii.

pect as well as other human aspects.[55] However, even in this essay, the approach remains quite general and does not develop or integrate the human into the theological in that much detail.

The two areas that McDonagh has discussed in some depth – peace and AIDS – definitely bring more aspects of the human into the equation, but still the fully human aspect remains undeveloped. Two essays in this festschrift volume deal with McDonagh's approach to peace and violence. As pointed out, he has always been skeptical about the just war theory and has recently joined with Stanley Hauerwas of Duke University calling on Christians of different traditions in the light of their witness to Jesus 'to join a campaign to abolish war as a legitimate means of resolving political conflict between states and within them'. Since this 'appeal to abolish war' is written in the style of a manifesto it does not go into great detail. The appeal, which is addressed to the Christian community but with the hope that many others will join the appeal, recognises the need 'to develop alternatives in protecting the innocent' and the long hard road of 'developing attitudes and structures for resolving conflicts nonviolently'.[56] It seems to me, however, in keeping with some of McDonagh's earlier discussions and emphases that two important human aspects need to be developed in much greater depth if we are to abolish war – the role of public society in general and the role of political structure.

From his earliest writings on religious freedom, Professor McDonagh has recognised the significant distinction proposed by John Courtney Murray between society and the state. The state is the narrow part of public society that has the power of coercive law. The broader public society embraces all those individuals, institutions, and groups (e.g., media, educational institutions, religious groups, voluntary associations of all kinds) that try to build a better society.[57] McDonagh has used this distinction in emphasising that the primary role for the church should be in convincing the broader society through discussion and witness and not trying to use the coercive power of law.[58]

---

55. *Gracing of Society*, 48-82.
56. See the Hauerwas essay in this volume.
57. Enda McDonagh, *Freedom or Tolerence? The Declaration on Religious Freedom of Vatican Council II*, Albany, N.Y.: Magi Books, 1967.
58. 'Prophecy or Politics,' in Nation and Wells, 292-94.

He also discusses this distinction in his work on peace and violence in Zimbabwe.[59]

To abolish war both the broader public society and the political structures of the world have a most significant role to play. As noted in the Hannon essay in this volume, McDonagh has frequently appealed to the non-violent tactics and approaches of Gandhi and Martin Luther King. Much work needs to be done in peace thinking, peace building, and the development of strategies of non-violence in the public sphere if our world is to abolish war.

But public attitudes, tactics, and non-governmental involvement are not enough. The state or the political order has a role to play. All recognise that we need more adequate political structures that will try to bring about peace in our world. Personally I do not think that we can ever have – or even should have – world government in the light of our great diversity, limitations, and sinfulness, but we need more adequate political structures than we have today. The Second Gulf War has reminded us all of the inadequacy of the present international political structures.

To try to abolish war, one must work in a concerted way for a change of attitudes, strategies, tactics, and approaches in the broader society and for a more adequate international political system. Peace will never come in our world without such significant and important changes. The appeal to abolish war would be more effective if it gave greater recognition to what has to happen in the broader public society and in the international political order. The theological needs to be mediated in and through the human.

Theology at the Fringe. McDonagh's particular theological perspective is most appropriate today – a liberationist theology of the reign of God from the fringe with a special emphasis on the poor, the marginalised, and the excluded in the light of the metaphor between chaos and new creation. Such an approach highlights perhaps the major problem facing our world and people in it – the great number of people who are poor, marginalised, oppressed, and excluded.

Professor McDonagh has used this approach with great effectiveness also in his discussion of the church especially in the

---

59. *Church and Politics*, 29-43.

light of the problems of the Catholic Church in Ireland.[60] One can summarise his approach in three steps. First, the church is the herald or servant of the kingdom or the reign of God. McDonagh does not develop this aspect in great detail but constantly mentions it and thus focuses on a significant ecclesiological understanding. In my judgment, even post-Vatican II Catholic ecclesiology often suffers from a triumphalism of the church that readily and quickly identifies the church with the word and work of Jesus. As the servant of the kingdom, the church itself stands under the challenge and judgment of the reign of God. The church will always fall short and be in need of forgiveness and reconciliation. The church is a pilgrim church always in need of reform.

Second, theology at the fringe calls special attention to those who are excluded or who are on the fringe of the church. The Maynooth professor has frequently emphasised in his writings the people who are marginalised and excluded in the Catholic Church. In the last twenty years, he has especially insisted on the inclusion of women. One can also notice his growing use of inclusive language in the light of the Christian feminist movement. In addition, he frequently mentions the divorced and remarried, the travellers, the poor, and gays and lesbians.

Third, McDonagh often in the 1990s has addressed the role and response of the church in Ireland in the light of its travails and problems. The leadership of the Irish church has held onto a triumphalistic notion of the church stressing its power in and over society, but this has not had good results. The rapid decline in numbers of vocations to the priesthood and religious life and the considerable drop-off in the number of those celebrating Sunday Eucharist indicate the problems the church in Ireland is facing. Then the child abuse scandals in various religious institutions and the sexual abuse of children by priests and religious, together with the efforts on the part of hierarchy and leaders to cover up these abuses, have added to the darkness and despair in the Irish Catholic Church. McDonagh has tried to address this situation in the light of his metaphor between chaos and new creation. The church should not be bogged down in scapegoating or name-calling. The church needs to act creatively to strive to bring some light in the midst of darkness. McDonagh makes

---

60. *Faith in Fragments*, 18-89; see also Enda McDonagh, 'A Shared Despair,' *The Furrow* 53, 2000, 259-62.

some specific proposals as to how the church can more creatively respond in the midst of the present situation.

His particular theological emphasis of theology at the fringe thus addresses very adequately some of the crucial problems facing society and church. However, such an emphasis is too narrow to serve as the basis for developing a more systematic moral theology and also does not adequately address many problems facing our world. Recall that Catholic social teaching recognises the preferential option for the poor but stresses the preferential aspect in order that other aspects might also be brought into consideration. In addition, the metaphor 'between chaos and new creation' also raises some questions. McDonagh himself admits that sometimes we also go from new creation to chaos.[61] Thus, it is a two-way street, but his illustrations invariably go from chaos to new creation. How much 'new creation' can we expect before the fullness of the reign of God at the end of time? The new creation will never be fully present in this world.

This essay has studied the contributions of Enda McDonagh over a period of more than forty years to Catholic moral theology. Looking back over one's life, it is easy to see that social location has influenced the approaches taken but also the limitations necessarily involved in such choices. Our author, however, perceptively recognised the importance of social location early in his vocation as a moral theologian. One does theology in response to particular situations and demands and in the light of one's own concerns, abilities, and interests.[62] No one can do all aspects of theology. Enda McDonagh has not developed a systematic and synthetic moral theology nor has he developed in depth many particular issues.

McDonagh might very well characterise his own approach as 'moral theology in fragments.' His last collection of essays bears the title *Faith in Fragments*. Both in the world at large and in the social and political life of Ireland and in the Irish church, we are living in dark and fragmentary times. All recognise the problems existing in the north of Ireland, but the south is also suffering despite the economic boom of the early 90s. Drugs, poverty, a growing gap between rich and poor, a leaving behind of many people who do not feel a part of society, all challenge Irish soci-

---

61. *Between Chaos and New Creation*, 4.
62. *Invitation and Response*, viii.

ety today. The leadership of the Irish church has failed to address the realities of the present time, and child abuse scandals
and cover-ups have racked the church. The estrangements, exclusions, and excommunications in person, church, and society
lead to very fragmentary times for all. But how are faith and
communion even possible in the midst of such fragmentation?

Unity and community seem incompatible with fragmentation, but not so in reality. Communities in history, from family
to nation to church, are formed from uneasy and unstable com-
binations of fragments.[63]

In an analogous way, in my judgment, the fragments of
moral theology help the communities of church and world
achieve some unity and community in their respective lives. All
recognise that times of stress, darkness, and fragmentation are
not fertile soil for a synthesis. Postmodernism with its emphasis
on diversity and particularity eschews any possibility of a synthesis. Our author's understanding of theology as reflection on
the life of the Christian community and as a service to that community help to situate the proper role for the theologian.
McDonagh seldom develops a detailed casuistry for guiding the
community in what it should do. The total community together
must decide how to act and respond, but it can be helped by the
insights provided by the theologian. Thus, the function of the
theologian is precisely to provide those imaginative and helpful
fragments that will be of service to the fragmented communities
of our world as they strive for greater solidarity. From this perspective, moral theology in fragments constitutes an apt and
insightful understanding of McDonagh's approach to moral
theology.

In my judgment, these fragments of moral theology are quite
significant and not mere crumbs. If we may invoke the biblical
image, these fragments fill up twelve baskets. Enda McDonagh
has provided the pilgrim community of the disciples of Jesus
with an all-inclusive Catholic understanding, a resolutely theological approach to life and society, a corrective Christian vision
and praxis from the margins, and perceptive insights of what
church and society need in our times.

---

63. *Faith in Fragments*, 62.

Select Bibliography

'The One Fold', *The Furrow*, Vol 9, October 1958, 646-653.

'The One Fold' in *The City: Essays on the Church*, Maynooth: A Furrow Book, 1960, 13-19.

'Religious Freedom and The State', in *Christian Unity: Lectures of the Maynooth Union Summer School 1961*, Maynooth: The Furrow Trust, 1961, 140-157.

'The Christian Life-XI/Tolerance', *The Furrow*, Vol 12, January 1961, 49-55.

Roman Catholics and Unity, London: Mowbray & Co. Ltd., 1962.

'Marriage and Virginity' in *The Meaning of Christian Marriage*, edited with an Introduction by Enda McDonagh, Dublin: Gill, 1962, 164-178.

'Peter', in *Praying for Unity: A Handbook of Studies, Meditations and Prayers*, edited by Michael Hurley, Maynooth: The Furrow Trust, 1963, 117-119.

'The Layman in the Church', *The Furrow*, Vol 11, November 1963, 683-690.

'Moral Theology: The Need for Renewal' in *Moral Theology Renewed*, edited by Enda McDonagh et al, Dublin: Gill & Son, 1964, 13-30.

'The Primacy of Charity' in *Moral Theology Renewed*, edited by Enda McDonagh et al, Dublin: Gill & Son, 1964, 130-151.

'Moral Problems and Christian Personalism, Recent English Literature on the Moral Theology of Marriage', *Concillium*, Vol 5, 1965, 130-154.

'Penance & Charity', in *Sin & Repentance, Papers of the Maynooth Union Summer School* edited by Denis O'Callaghan, Maynooth: 1966, 93-108.

'A Roman Catholic Comment' in *Ecumenical Studies: Baptism & Marriage*, edited by Michael Hurley, Dublin: Gill & Son, 1967, 208-219.

Freedom or Tolerance? The Declaration on Religious Freedom of Vatican II, London, New York: Darton, Longman & Todd 1967.

'Morality: Man's Response to God', in *Truth and Life*, edited by Enda McDonagh et al, Dublin: Gill & Son, 1967, 34-39.

'Conscience: The Guidance of the Spirit', in *Truth and Life*, edited by Enda McDonagh et al, Dublin: Gill & Son, 1967, 121-137.

'Hope: Going Forward in Christ', in *Truth and Life*, edited by Enda McDonagh et al, Dublin: Gill & Son, 1967, 198-213.

'Christian Marriage in an Ecumenical Context', *The Furrow*, Vol 19, January 1968, 3-11.

'An Approach to Morality', *The Furrow*, Vol 19, June 1968, 307-317.

'Theology in the University', *The Furrow*, Vol l9, December 1968, 676-685.

'The Question of Identity', *Priest: Person and Ministry: Papers of the Maynooth Union Summer School*, edited by Gerry Meagher, Dublin: Gill & Macmillan, 1969, 1-14.

'Coresponsibility and the Theologian', *The Furrow*, Vol 20, April 1969, 172-184.

'Theology of Vocation', *The Furrow*, Vol 21, May 1970, 292-297.

Invitation and Response, Dublin, New York: Gill & Macmillan, 1972.

'The Learning Community', *The Furrow*, Vol 23, July 1972, 391-398.

'The Role of Mary', *The Furrow*, Vol 25, September 1974, 488-493.

Gift and Call, Dublin, New York: Gill & Macmillan, 1975.

'Why Do They Leave?', *The Furrow*, Vol 26, November 1975, 652-667.

'Church, State and Morality/Comment', *The Furrow*, Vol 27, June 1976, 324-327.

'J. G. McGarry: Editor of The Furrow, 1950-77', *The Furrow*, Vol 28, December 1977, 793-746.

'Politics of Dishonour', *The Furrow*, Vol 28, December 1977, 776.

'An Irish Theology of Liberation?' in *Ireland: Liberation and Theology*, edited by Dermot A. Lane, New York: Orbis Books, 1977, 22-31.

'Violence and Political Change', *The Furrow*, Vol 29, February 1978, 76-88.

Doing The Truth, Dublin: Gill & Macmillan, 1979.

Social Ethics and the Christian, Manchester: Manchester University Press, 1979.

'Conversion and Mission', in *A New Missionary Era*, edited by Padraig Flanagan, New York: Orbis Books, 1979, 3-8.

'Theology and Irish Divisions', *The Furrow*, Vol 30, January 1979, 19-30.

'Prayer and Politics', *The Furrow*, Vol 30, September 1979, 543-554.

'*Redemptor Hominis* and Ireland', *The Furrow*, Vol 30, October 1979, 625-640.

'The Priest as a Christian', *The Furrow*, Vol 31, June 1980, 351-357.

The Demands of Simple Justice, Dublin: Gill & Macmillan published in the USA as *Church and Politics: From Theology to a Case History of Zimbabwe*, Notre Dame, Ind.: Notre Dame University Press 1980.

'A Personal Relationship with Jesus Christ', *The Furrow*, Vol 32, December 1981, 763-771.

The Making of Disciples, Dublin: Gill & Macmillan, 1982 .

'Ireland's Divided Disciples', *The Furrow*, Vol 33, January 1982, 22-28.

'Vision and Values – Public Philosophy and the Recent Election', *The Furrow*, 33, March 1982, 137-151.

'The Grace of Remembering – On the Death of a Friend', *The Furrow*, Vol 33, April 1982, 212-215.

'Set Free for Freedom – The Letter to the Galatians', *The Furrow*, Vol 34, February 1983, 82-88.

'The New Words – Liberation', *The Furrow*, Vol 34, October 1983, 639-640.

'The Grace of Unbelief', *The Furrow*, Vol 35, February 1984, 75-84.

'British Responsibility and Northern Ireland - A Theological Reflexion', *The Furrow*, Vol 35, November 1984, 681-692.

'Decree on Ecumenism – Twenty Years Later', *The Furrow*, Vol 35, December 1984, 790-793.

'A Church for the World' in *Freedom To Hope? A Festschrift for Austin Flannery, OP*, edited by Enda McDonagh et al, Dublin: Columba Press, 1985, 82-93 .

'Peadar O'Donnell – Challenge to Irish Christians', *The Furrow*, Vol 36, November 1985, 693-700.

'Northern Ireland and Irish Responsibility', *The Furrow*, Vol 36, June 1985, 345-354.

'Reconciliation in Jewish-Christian Relations', *The Furrow*, Vol 36, September 1985, 564-568.

'Between Heaven and Bekan Cross' in *Bekan: Portrait of an East Mayo Parish*, Connaught Telegraph, Castlebar, 1985, 119-120.

Between Chaos and New Creation, Dublin: Gill & Macmillan, 1986.

'An Irish Theology and the Influence of Particulars' in *Irish Challenges to Theology, Papers of the Irish Theological Association Conference 1984*, edited by Enda McDonagh, Dublin: Dominican Publications, 1986, 102-129.

'The Cross and the Critical Mind', *The Furrow*, Vol 38, April 1987 243-247.

'Pray this Poem', *The Furrow*, Vol 38, June 1987, 403-405.

'Human Spirit -Holy Spirit', *The Furrow*, Vol 38, August 1987, 526-528.

'Faithful to the Future', *The Furrow*, Vol 38, September 1987, 587-593.

'Faith at the Fringe I – Poets, Players and Prophets', *The Furrow*, Vol 39, April 1988, 235-241.

'Faith at the Fringe II – Doubting Christians: the Grace of Unbelief', *The Furrow*, Vol 39, May 1988, 309-314.

'Faith at the Fringe III – Powerless Christians', *The Furrow*, Vol 39, June 1988, 367-372.

'Faith at the Fringe IV – Forgotten Christians', *The Furrow*, Vol 39, July 1988, 442-446.

The Gracing of Society, Dublin: Gill & Macmillan, 1989.

The Small Hours of Belief, Dublin: Columba Press, 1989.

'Liturgy and Christian Life' in *New Dictionary of Sacramental Worship*, edited by Peter E. Fink, Collegeville Minn.: Liturgical Press, 1990, 742-753.

'Moral Theology and Transformative Justice', in *History and Conscience: Studies in Honour of Sean O'Riordan*, edited by Raphael Gallagher and Brendan McConvrey, Dublin: Gill & Macmillan, 1989, 73-84.

'Between Westport and Asia Minor', *The Furrow*, Vol 41, April 1990, 231-238.

'A Passionate God?', in *Faith and the Hungry Grass: A Mayo Book of Theology*, edited by Enda McDonagh, Dublin: Columba Press, 1990, 163-174.

'Between Westport and Asia Minor' in *Faith and the Hungry Grass: A Mayo Book of Theology*, edited by Enda McDonagh, Dublin: Columba Press, 1990, 7-13.

'Let the Dance Continue', *Trinity Jameson Quatercentenary Symposium: The Dancer and the Dance*, edited by Eda Sagarra and Mireia Sagarra, Dublin: Trinity College Dublin, 1991, 110-117.

'Ten Questions for the Irish Catholic Church', *The Furrow*, Vol 43, June 1992, 331-333.

'Should the Healing Begin at Christmas...?' *The Furrow*, Vol 43, December, 1992, 651-655.

'Shall We Hope?', in *Salvation or Survival: A Second Mayo Book of Theology*, edited with an Introduction by Enda McDonagh, Dublin: Columba Press, 1993, 248-255.

'Teaching in the Mission of the University' in *The Role of the University in Society: Proceedings of the NUI Conference held in Dublin Castle, May 1994*, 95-102.

'Moral Theology in Communication' in *Mass Media & the Moral Imagination*, edited by Philip J. Rossi & Paul A. Soukup, USA: Sheed & Ward, 1994, 281-288.

'The Winter Name of Church', *The Furrow*, Vol 46, January 1995, 3-12.

'And the Stone was Made Flesh – A Bicentenary Meditation on Maynooth', *The Furrow*, Vol 46, June 1995, 349-354.

'Bruised Reeds and the Mystery of the Church – in Memory of Tommy Waldron', *The Furrow*, Vol 46, October 1995, 543-553.

Faith in Fragments, Dublin: Columba Press, 1996.

'A Church Vulnerable to Life and Love', *The Furrow*, Vol 47, February 1996, 76-74.

'The "Christening Man" and the Priestly People', *The Furrow*, Vol 47, October 1996, 523-535.

'Margin to Margin', *Céide*, Vol 1, No 1, 1997, 4.

'Inhabited by the Others, After the Plays of Frank McGuinness', *Céide*, Vol 1, No 4, 1997, 12-14.

'The Graves of Omagh', *Céide*, Vol 2, No 1, 1998, 3.

'Invite and Encourage – A Millennial Proposal for Sharing the Eucharist', *The Furrow*, Vol 50, January 1999, 18-25.

'Beyond "Pure" Theology', *The Furrow*, Vol 50, November 1999, 579-586.

'Letter to Sarah', in *Sources: Letters from Irish People on Sustenance for the Soul*, edited by Marie Heaney, Dublin: Town House Books, 1999, 101-105.

The Irish Review, 2000, A Post-Christian Ireland?, edited with an Introduction by Enda McDonagh, Cork: Cork University Press, 2000.

'Prophecy or Politics? The Role of the Churches in Society', in *Faithfulness and Fortitude: In Conversation with the Theological Ethics of Stanley Hauerwas*, edited by Mark Thiessen Nation and Samuel Wells, Edinburgh: T& T Clark, 2000, 287-309.

'Unopened Ground – *The Furrow* of the Future', *The Furrow*, Vol 51, February 2000, 68-79.

'For What We are About to Receive – Grace Before Seventy', *The Furrow*, Vol 51, June 2000, 341-350.

'The Risk of Priesthood', *The Furrow*, Vol 51, November 2000, 592-601.

'Our Ellis Island', *Céide*, Vol 3, No 5, 2000, 4-5.

'The Reign of God: Signposts of Catholic Moral Theology' in *Catholic Ethicists on HIV/AIDS Prevention*, edited by James F. Keenan et al, New York and London: Continuum, 2000, 317-323.

'The Republic of Learning', *Céide*, Vol 3, No 3, 2000, 17-19.

'Theology and Modern Irish Art', *Céide*, Vol 3, No 4, 2000, 35-36.

'Does Church Unity Matter and to Whom', *Céide*, Vol 4, No 2, 2001, 27-28.

'Faith and the Cure of Poetry', *Céide*, Vol 4, No 5, 2001, 8-10.

'Guns into Ploughshares – An Ecumenical Challenge', *The Furrow*, Vol 52, March 2001, 147-149.

'Seeing Salvation in Creation', *Céide*, Vol 4, No 4, 2001, 26-27.

'A Shared Despair?', *The Furrow*, Vol 53, May 2002, 259-262.

'Dear Michael and John', *Céide*, Vol 5, No 5, 2002, 7-8.

The Reality of HIV/AIDS, written jointly with Anne Smith, Dublin: Trócaire, Veritas, CAFOD, 2003.

'Church-State Relations in Independent Ireland' in *Religion and Politics in Ireland at the Turn of the Millennium*, Essays in Honour of Garret Fitzgerald on the Occasion of his Seventy-Fifth Birthday, edited jointly with James P Mackey, Dublin: Columba Press, 2003, 41-63.

Series Editor: *Theology for a Pilgrim People*, Dublin: Gill & Macmillan, 1987 – 3 volumes.

Series Editor: *Christian Perspectives on Development Issues*, Dublin: Trócaire, Veritas, CAFOD, 1998 – 7 volumes.

The Contributors

CHARLES E. CURRAN, a priest of the Diocese of Rochester, New York, is the Elizabeth Scurlock University Professor of Human Values at Southern Methodist University. He has served as president of three national academic societies – the American Theological Society, the Catholic Theological Society of American, and the Society of Christian Ethics. His most recent publications are: *Catholic Social Teaching 1891-Present: A Historical, Theological, and Ethical Analysis*, 2002 and *The Catholic Moral Tradition Today: A Synthesis*, 1999 both from Georgetown University Press.

GABRIEL DALY is a member of the Order of St Augustine. He has been a Lecturer in Systematic and Historical Theology at Trinity College Dublin for many years and is an Honorary Fellow of the college. A former Chairman of the Irish Theological Association he has published widely. His books include *Transcendence and Immanence: A Study in Catholic Modernism and Integralism*, Oxford: Clarendon Press, 1980 and *Creation and Redemption*, Dublin: Gill & Macmillan, 1988.

BARBARA FITZGERALD, having completed a BA (Hons) degree in Trinity College as a mature student in the late 1980s, began working with a North/South reconciliation body called The Irish Association where she organised conferences, meetings etc in Northern Ireland and in the Republic for twelve years. She has been involved with the Glenstal Ecumenical Conference for some years and is now helping to set up a small charity in Ireland called Breadline Africa. She has had an interest in theology for many years, studying it with two different groups.

GARRET FITZGERALD is a former Taoiseach (Prime Minister) and Foreign Minister of Ireland, who is now a lecturer, writer, consultant and company director, as well as being a member of the Council of State and an active Chancellor of the National University of Ireland, which comprises four of the State's seven universities. He is the author of half-a-dozen books, the most recent being *Reflections on the Irish State*, Dublin: Irish Academic Press, 2003 and of several papers for the Royal Irish Academy.

SEAN FREYNE is recently retired from the Chair of Theology at Trinity College and is currently Director of the Joint Programme for Mediterranean and Near Eastern Studies there. He was a student and later a colleague of Enda's at Maynooth. He has studied in Jerusalem and Tübingen and is the author of several books on Judaism and Early Christianity, most recently *Texts, Contexts and Cultures, Studies on Biblical Topics*, Dublin: Veritas 2002.

JON FULLER is a family physician and Jesuit priest who has been providing clinical care to persons living with HIV/AIDS since 1983. He is on
the staff of the Adult Clinical AIDS Program at Boston Medical Center
and is an Associate Professor of Medicine at Boston University School
of Medicine. He is also an adjunct member of the faculties of Harvard
Divinity School and Weston Jesuit School of Theology. He was founding president of the National Catholic AIDS Network (USA), and from
1991-2003 was a member of the International Working Group on
HIV/AIDS of Caritas Internationalis. He co-edited *Catholic Ethicists on
HIV/AIDS Prevention*, New York and London: Continuum, 2000 which
was awarded the prize in ethics and philosophy by Alpha Sigma Nu,
the national Jesuit honour society.

PATRICK HANNON is Professor of Moral Theology at Maynooth. He
holds doctorates in Divinity (Maynooth) and Law (Cambridge) and is a
member of the Irish Bar. He is the author of *Church, State, Morality and
Law*, Dublin: Gill & Macmillan 1992/ Christian Classics 1993.

STANLEY HAUERWAS is Gilbert T. Rowe Professor of Theological Ethics at
the Divinity School, Duke University. His most recent book is *With the
Grain of the Universe The Church's Witness and Natural Theology*, London:
SCM, 2002.

SEAMUS HEANEY's first book, *Death of a Naturalist*, appeared in 1966.
Since then he has published poetry, criticism and translations for which
he was awarded the Nobel Prize for Literature in 1995. His most recent
writings include *The Spirit Level* (1996), *Electric Light* (2001) and *Finders
Keepers: Selected Prose 1971-2001*, (2002).

LINDA HOGAN lectures at the Irish School of Ecumenics, Trinity College,
Dublin. A former student of Enda's she is author of *From Women's
Experience to Feminist Theology*, Sheffield: Sheffield Academic Press,
1995 and *Confronting the Truth: Conscience in the Catholic Tradition*, New
York: Paulist Press, 2000.

JAMES F. KEENAN SJ, finished his STD at the Gregorian in 1992 having
studied with Josef Fuchs and Klaus Demmer. Among his books and articles are *Catholic Ethicists on HIV/AIDS Prevention*, New York and
London: Continuum, 2000, that he edited, assisted by Lisa Sowle Cahill,
Jon Fuller, and Kevin Kelly and more recently, *Jesus and Virtue Ethics*
(with Daniel Harrington) Sheed and Ward, 2002 and *Moral Wisdom:
Lessons and Texts from the Catholic Tradition*, Sheed and Ward, 2003. He is
presently finishing a book on the Works of Mercy and working on a
book on the need for ethics in church leadership.

KEVIN KELLY is Emeritus Research Fellow in moral theology at

Liverpool Hope University and parish priest of St Basil & All Saints, a shared Roman Catholic–Anglican church in Widnes, near Liverpool. A frequent contributor to *The Tablet, Priest and People* and *The Way*, his most recent books include *New Directions in Moral Theology: The Challenge of Being Human*, London: Geoffrey Chapman, 1992, *Divorce and Second Marriage: Facing the Challenge* (Revised & enlarged edition), London: Geoffrey Chapman, 1996, *New Directions in Sexual Ethics: Moral Theology and the Challenge of AIDS*, New York and London: Continuum, 1998 and *From a Parish Base: Essays in Moral and Pastoral Theology*, London: DLT, 1999. He serves on CAFOD's Expert Advisory Committee on HIV/AIDS.

NICHOLAS LASH is Norris-Hulse Professor Emeritus of Divinity at theUniversity of Cambridge, where he has lived since 1968. Amongst innumerable other acts of friendship over the years, Enda celebrated the Lashes' nuptial Mass in Fisher House, the university chaplaincy, in 1976, and (in the same chapel) their Silver Wedding Mass in 2001.

TERENCE MCCAUGHEY is retired from his post as Senior Lecturer in Irish at Trinity College Dublin, where he also lectured in the School of Biblical and Theological Studies. He is an ordained minister in the Presbyterian Church and a former President of the Irish Anti-Apartheid Movement. He is author of *Memory and Redemption: Church, Politics and Prophetic Theology in Ireland*, Dublin: Gill & Macmillan, 1993.

JAMES P. MACKEY has held university posts in philosophy and theology in Ireland, Britain and the USA, and is presently Emeritus Professor of Edinburgh University and Visiting Professor at Trinity College Dublin. His books have been published in six languages; amongst them *Life and Grace*, Dublin: Gill & Son, 1966, *Morals, Law and Authority*, Dublin: Gill & Macmillan, 1969, *Tradition and Change in the Church*, Dublin: Gill & Son, 1968 and *Jesus, the Man and the Myth*, London: SCM, 1979. His latest book is *The Critique of Theological Reason*, Cambridge: Cambridge University Press, 2000.

MARY ROBINSON is the Executive Director of the Ethical Globalization Initiative. She served as United Nations High Commissioner for Human Rights from 1997 to 2002 and as President of Ireland from 1990-1997. Before her election as President, Mrs Robinson served as Senator, holding that office for 20 years. In 1969 she became Reid Professor of Constitutional Law at Trinity College, Dublin and now serves as Chancellor of Dublin University. She was called to the bar in 1967, becoming a Senior Counsel in 1980, and a member of the English Bar (Middle Temple) in 1973. Educated at Trinity College, Mrs Robinson also holds law degrees from the King's Inns in Dublin and from Harvard University.

GERALDINE SMYTH OP is an ecumenical theologian. Her research interests reach into the field of political and religious identity; theology and ethics in civil society and public life; and the role of theology and religion in overcoming violence and peace-building in Ireland and beyond. She is a Senior Lecturer in the Irish School of Ecumenics, Trinity College Dublin.

IMOGEN STUART is a sculptor. Born in Berlin in 1927, she moved to Ireland in 1951 where her work is represented in churches and in public places throughout the country. Her infuences range from German expressionism to Early Irish Christian Art and she works in wood, stone, bronze, steel, clay, plaster and terracotta.